Sex and the Single Girl

Sex and the Single Girl

Helen Gurley Brown

**BARNES
&NOBLE
BOOKS**

NEW YORK

To David

ACKNOWLEDGMENTS

The author wishes to acknowledge with deep gratitude the generous contributions to this book made by: Cleo Bryan, Mary Alford, Alice Belding, John Clerc-Scott, Charles and Drisa Cooke, Saul David, Marilyn Hart, Pamela Hedley, William Hoy of the Pickwick Book Shop, Tom Jones, Charlotte Kelly, Mary Louise Lau, Arthur Pesterre, Noreen Sulmeyer, and Dr. George Watson.

CONTENTS

INTRODUCTION

Why republish *Sex and the Single Girl* at this stage of our lives? Because my friends Carole and Lyle Stuart of Barricade Books thought it was a good idea to reprint the little classic and I took the "why not" approach along *with* them! The book caused something of a commotion at the time of its original appearance in 1962. Through the years women have come up to me in restaurants, at airports, on the street, to tell me the book changed their lives (for the better) so why not republish?

We decided *not* to update in any way, though some of the original observations may sound a little quaint—Gregory Peck the quintessential desirable man? Rudi Gernreich the unqualified best creator of single-girl wardrobes in the world? Yet many of the basics do hold up.

I don't live totally in a single-girl milieu, as was the case when the original was written, but I do know lots of single women, work and live with them and will make a few comments about this group *now* if I may. I haven't conducted an official survey of single women nor did I do one for the original book—just dealt with what was happening to my girlfriends and me. This time I'm only dealing with *friends*. May I continue?

How is it with single girls these days? (Forgive my continuing to call women girls but I think in many ways we continue to *be* girls all our lives.) At around age 25 we often take on adult responsibilities—marry, have children, create homes for other people but I think the basic *girl* is still in there whooshing around—loving fun, being spontaneous, mainlining on enthusiasm, don't you? How it is with single girls/women these days I think is *good*. We surely *hope* so ... so many *out* there! The U.S. Census Bureau reports that single women over the age of 15 now represent 48 per cent of the female population—nearly *half*. Since I wrote *S & S G*, three things have improved for this category of female:

1. She isn't perceived to be a loser if, by age 30, she isn't married.
2. She doesn't have to feel guilty (sluttish) about participating in and enjoying sex—*au contraire*, she happily participates.
3. Career opportunities for all women have staggeringly improved. Not many female presidents of companies or countries yet, but nobody says you can't be one just because of gender. Indira Gandhi, Golda Meir, Margaret Thatcher did lead their countries and Secretary of State Madeleine Albright and Condoleeza Rice are major somebodies. Single or married, women are encouraged to have terrific jobs, helped by others to succeed in them, financially rewarded.

Something else kind of wonderful has happened to single women. You don't have to be so beautiful anymore to be cherished and adored. When I was growing up in Green Forest and Little Rock, Arkansas and later in Los Angeles as a single girl, pretty was what you were supposed to be if you had a brain in your head. I'm being funny—having a brain in your head *wasn't* what it was about, beauty *was* whether you had the attribute or not. Know what? Brains have become almost as treasured as beauty … *almost!* Oh, I know, the fabulous-faced one is still utterly desired. "His happiness blonde" is what a friend of mine calls the young gorgeous creature a substantial male friend of ours married recently.

If you had to or could choose one or the other, I would *almost* choose smart! People like to be *with* you, you "*get* it," and your brain can be a nifty asset for the company you work for. Not that everybody doesn't appreciate beauty as much as ever—we *worship* beautiful! Mercifully you can get *more* beautiful with incredible cosmetic and dermatological procedures these days and, of course, your body can be okay with the discipline of exercise and not cramming down chocolate-ripple cheesecake. I'm happy to celebrate this new development for single and not single women. Among my single friends I find virtually nobody desperate to marry just for status—the act must evolve from a long or short-term relationship. At some point both parties agree they want to make it "official." A relationship could have lasted for months or years, of course, both parties loving and respecting each other and still may sunder. She meets a great new person, he takes a job in the Belgian Congo making continuing intimacy difficult or it's just *over* … the good has been extracted.

Among single women I know, being with a man in a loving relationship is as natural as grape juice though they may not live together and the loving may not lead to marriages.

Is there lots of dating? Is the Mississippi a river? Is Elvis Presley a legend? A date can be anything from coffee and danish at Starbucks, *AIDA* on Broadway or checking out the Weimaraners at the Westminster Dog Show.

Sex, as we have said, is enjoyed by single women who participate not to please a man as might have been the case in olden times but to please *themselves.* A few—perhaps not few enough—young women perform fellatio as a way to endear themselves to a baby hunk, enjoy or *don't* enjoy the act all that much. Does a single woman worry that a new partner might be HIV positive? She asks but, after he declares he isn't, she may still request that he use a condom during the first few weeks of their sexual friendship until she can ascertain whether he tells truths or lies. If "truths" win out, birth control is probably then up to her, the pill being popular and reliable.

After a night of carried-away unprotected sex, if she's worried about having conceived, a trip to the doctor next morning may eradicate a possible pregnancy. The finally F.D.A.-approved abortion pill—RU 846—for eradicating pregnancy didn't become as popular as some of us thought it might, the procedure is actually more expensive and requiring more time than an abortion. Several visits to a doctor's office are needed as you take the pill.

Okay, that's the group that *doesn't* want to make babies. There's also the group that *does*. An attractive woman I know asked a friend—handsome, healthy, brainy—if he would consider impregnating her. If successful and a baby made, he would bear no responsibility whatever for parenting, wouldn't even have to see mother or baby if he didn't wish. He turned her down cold.

She next went the artificial insemination route—not as science-fiction as you might *think*. Sperm can be ordered on the internet—California and Virginia have the best banks. Cost varies—may be $200 a vial and you will need about 12 vials in order to keep trying for impregnation until the procedure "takes" (you wouldn't want to go back to the bank mid-procedure only to find daddy's sperm deposit had been depleted). You are supplied background information on the donor—age, race, background, measurements (height, circumference of neck, ankles, etc., = no, not penis size!) You are not shown a photograph but a CD of his voice is available.

Now you take your sperm vials to a fertility doctor for the impregnation, the procedure is successful only about 10 percent of the time. If baby-making doesn't "take," you could next go for in vitro fertilization, a procedure often used by married couples having trouble with conception. The price of in vitro is $10,000. The whole life-creating adventure can run between $25,000 and $30,000.

My friend—age 41—actually got pregnant with donor sperm (helped along, perhaps, with hormone shots at the doctor's office every day for three weeks and blood tests to make sure everything was going smoothly), then regrettably had a miscarriage. She's resting up a bit before adventuring again.

Motherhood plans worked out differently for another young woman I know. Her boyfriend, a substantial magazine editor, said yes when asked to father a baby. Now daddy, still unmarried to the child's mother nor living with her, is thrilled with his offspring. "My little princess," he coos as he cuddles. "Daddy's little angel!" Nice!

Do single women split the cost of dates? You don't divvy up at the restaurant table but, since women frequently make as much (or more) money than men, he is asked to the *next* restaurant dinner, the bill paid quietly and without a fuss, by her.

Are married men off limits? Not always. Same downside (and upside?), trials, and rewards as ever. Plusses: good sex, admiration, even adoration from him. We're not talking about outright being kept but delicious prezzies and trips are often in his portfolio.

The married man is rarely a good marriage prospect, of course, already *having* a wife he isn't eager to discard. I've always felt—and said—however that a married man is okay for occasional use, the word "use" not seen as a pejorative. I think useful is a good thing for *all* of us to be. No, I don't want adultery in my own marriage, and some people think I'm a lunatic and immoral to suggest a married man can, in his way, accommodate or enhance the life of a single woman, but it seems to me faithfulness is the responsibility of the married *woman*. If she wants him unshared and unstrayed, lots of things she can do—not what this book is about. A womanizer does-n't often change stripes or spots. A cheated-on-wife might just avoid marrying him in the first place.

Gay men? After all the studies and research, we *still* don't know why they are, do we—nature or nurture, and why didn't *we* become lesbians? Whatever, these men, while not for sleeping with, can be wonderful friends. Some of mine from single days are still in my life. Yes, some women marry gay men, knowing or *not* knowing they are, but can it be fun to have him pining for somebody across town or cross country in San Francisco as you are accommodated?

Where do you meet men? Same places they were always met. Work is a good supply depot—both coworkers and people dropping in—and, of course, you meet males outside the office in meetings, conferences, seminars. For many of us, work isn't nine to five but more like nine to nine sometimes. Good to have those precious hours to get acquainted—and sink into—a likely person. Casual pick-ups at the museum, a sports event, or restaurant can't be counted on to harvest much wheat. The airport lounge or an actual flight can be productive if you're lucky enough to sit next to a possible.

Friends are important. Some of my single girlfriends stay close to old college buddies, even high school friends and they introduce each other to "possibilities." The internet is a new meeting arena, possibly more interesting to women over 40 than younger women. A friend of David's and mine met his wife in a chat room—she 40 years younger than he. What do they give each other? She gets a famous, talented guy, a nice person, and the lifestyle that goes with an acclaimed worker in the film industry. He gets youth, pulchritude, affection and, yes, I think now love.

Blind dates? Certainly! There are the scruffy ones and the keepers. One of mine I have now kept for 43 years! After a year of dating, David didn't want to get married so I put the heat on. Either make the commitment or burn to death! (i.e. you will have to do without me if you choose to continue your silly singlehood!). Blind date finally committed—we were married before a judge in Beverly Hills. David says he isn't sorry. If he were, it would be very expensive to get rid of me. All our holdings are mutually owned—I could sell off stocks and bonds, our home, grab the cash without even a discussion.

Are there enough single men to go around these days in the U.S. or lots more single women than men? You might think more of *us* but technically that isn't the case (until a woman is over 40). Ages 25 to 29, the U.S. Census reports 4,509,000 unmarried women, 5,146,000 single men. Ages 35 to 39 still *more* men—3,860,000 of them to 3,656,000 of us. Nice going! Those figures don't report homosexuality, of course—men not available to females for sex or romance; such delineation could bring the available-men figures down a bit.

I should point out that female homosexuals are acknowledged and taken more than seriously these days, weddings reported in newspapers, chronicled on television. After age 40, women begin to outnumber men and over 60, don't ask! Ages 65 to 69, 2,031,000 women, 265,000 men. Yikes! It gets *worse*! Ages 70 to 74, 2,412,000 women to 814 men. If your widowed or divorced mommy is looking for somebody to wed, bed or just date, her chances would seem maybe a little stronger than winning the Publisher's Clearing House sweepstakes—you know, subscribe to *Reader's Digest*, *G.Q.* and *House Beautiful* and get ready to receive 10 million in your mailbox. These people never get near the word "possible" in their promotion, only the words "get ready to win!" I believe the government has cracked down a little on their promises. Whatever, the dating/mating possibilities for an older single women seem to be skinny as seaweed.

What do single women complain about in the behavior of their men these days? My industrial-strength charmer-friend Nancy says they don't know how to give compliments the way we do. Nancy says they could lie a little—"You have the most beautiful body," "Your lips are ripe raspberries—I could nibble all afternoon," even compliment on something that isn't wonderful. She would like to see them carry on in bed the way *we* do. After first exposure of his penis, "Oh, that's so *beautiful*—do you carry that around with you all day? Don't you need some kind of support?" Are they fearful of being taken advantage of if they flatter, Nancy wonders. Alas, some single men are already into the "pamper me" syndrome even before a ring circles your fourth digit. "I'll catch the opening stock prices, honey, okay? You scramble the eggs."

What about money and the single girl? Some young women seem to fantasize that riches ought to just float down from the treetops. They envy J.Lo and Britney Spears not so much their men and their fame as their moola ... *millions* coming in at such a tiny age. Well, in any era, glitzy ones wallow in their golden slush piles but they aren't us. Would it be maybe a good idea to try to *marry* rich? The idea always surfaces but can't swim! Our heroine knows rich bachelors are less plentiful than free cosmetic surgery and the small crop can be maddeningly choosy.

Can Tom Cruise and Donald Trump marry *anybody* or not? So let's skip celebrity bank-account envy or trying to acquire capital by acquiring his and get on with asking our boss to put the raise through before Christmas, socking a bit more into the I.R.A., the mutual fund, the savings account. As mentioned earlier, all categories of women find it easier hauling in money through their work these days if they want to pack the supplies in the knapsack, sharpen the picks, tie the rope around their middles and start climbing! Being a wildly successful career woman, single or married, isn't all roses and honey-suckle of course.

A successful climber I know (C.E.O. of a small electronics firm, written up in *Forbes* magazine), says she is so exhausted from being a dynamo, stretched tighter than a body stocking over a pitcher of martinis (okay, *you* come up with an analogy!) she is thinking of announcing a baby which she won't really have—an "escape baby" she calls it—so she can go home, care for two children already there, and resume being a regular human being.

Okay, your single years should surely be delicious at least *some* of the time and I'll repeat something I said in the original book, still true now: Married women are as often as not envying *you!* I'm grateful to my toesies for my 37 years of being single. David says isn't it a shame we didn't know each other earlier, could have married sooner, think of all the years we missed, years that were wasted. David, I tell him, they weren't wasted! You had two other wives ... are they to be considered something for the garbage disposal? One of them gave you a a son—not with us now, alas. I had romances. I've never gone into detail about them with David but they were frisky enough (if sometimes traumatic) so that I never have to be unfaithful *now* wondering what's out there in the romance/sex department.

I *know* what's out there—not as good as what I have. Some famous person—don't remember who—said "life is what happens while you're making other plans." There are soul-numbing, devastating days for single women *and* married ones, even some for the other sex. I'm counting on you to enjoy the good ones, make life special for people around you because you've got the love, compassion, the energy, the need inside of you to *do* that! Would you please get started!

Sex and the Single Girl

CHAPTER 1

WOMEN ALONE? OH COME NOW!

I MARRIED for the first time at thirty-seven. I got the man I wanted. It *could* be construed as something of a miracle considering how old *I* was and how eligible *he* was.

David is a motion picture producer, forty-four, brainy, charming and sexy. He was sought after by many a Hollywood starlet as well as some less flamboyant but more deadly types. And *I* got him! We have two Mercedes-Benzes, one hundred acres of virgin forest near San Francisco, a Mediterranean house overlooking the Pacific, a full-time maid and a good life.

I am not beautiful, or even pretty. I once had the world's worst case of acne. I am not bosomy or brilliant. I grew up in a small town. I didn't go to college. My family was, and is, desperately poor and I have always helped support them. I'm an introvert and I am sometimes mean and cranky.

But *I* don't think it's a miracle that I married my husband.

3

I think I deserved him! For seventeen years I worked hard to become the kind of woman who might interest him. And when he finally walked into my life I was just worldly enough, relaxed enough, financially secure enough (for I also worked hard at my job) and adorned with enough glitter to attract him. He wouldn't have looked at me when I was twenty, and I wouldn't have known what to do with *him*.

There is a tidal wave of misinformation these days about how many more marriageable women there are than men (that part is true enough) and how tough is the plight of the single woman—spinster, widow, divorcee.

I think a single woman's biggest problem is coping with the people who are trying to marry her off! She is so driven by herself and her well-meaning but addlepated friends to become married that her whole existence seems to be an apology for *not* being married. Finding *him* is all she can think about or talk about when (a) she may not be psychologically ready for marriage; (b) there is no available husband for every girl at the time she wants one; and (c) her years as a single woman can be too rewarding to rush out of.

Although many's the time I was sure I would die alone in my spinster's bed, I could never bring myself to marry just to get married. If I had, I would have missed a great deal of misery along the way, no doubt, but also a great deal of fun.

I think marriage is insurance for the *worst* years of your life. During your best years you don't need a husband. You do need a man of course every step of the way, and they are often cheaper emotionally and a lot more fun by the dozen.

I believe that as many women over thirty marry out of fear of being alone someday—not necessarily now but *some* day— as for love of or compatibility with a particular man. The plan seems to be to get someone while the getting's good and by the time you lose your looks he'll be too securely glued to you to get away.

Isn't it silly? A man can leave a woman at fifty (though it may cost him some dough) as surely as you can leave dishes in the sink. He can leave any time *before* then too, and so may you leave *him* when you find your football hero developing into the town drunk. Then you have it all to do over again as if you hadn't gobbled him up in girlish haste.

How much saner and sweeter to marry when you have both jelled. And how much safer to marry with part of the play out of his system *and yours*. It takes guts. It can be lonely out there out of step with the rest of the folks. And you may *not* find somebody later. But since you're not finding somebody *sooner* as things stand, wouldn't it be better to stop driving . . . to stop fretting . . . to start recognizing what you have *now*?

As for marrying to have children, you can have babies until you're forty or older. And if you happen to die before *they* are forty, at least you haven't lingered into their middle age to be a doddering old bore. You also avoid those tiresome years as an unpaid baby sitter.

Frankly, the magazines and their marriage statistics give me a royal pain.

There is a more important truth that magazines never deal with, that single women are too brainwashed to figure out, that married women know but won't admit, that married men *and* single men endorse in a body, and that is that the single woman, far from being a creature to be pitied and patronized, is emerging as the newest glamour girl of our times.

She is engaging because she lives by her wits. She supports herself. She has had to sharpen her personality and mental resources to a glitter in order to survive in a competitive world and the sharpening looks good. Economically she is a dream. She is not a parasite, a dependent, a scrounger, a sponger or a bum. She is a giver, not a taker, a winner and not a loser.

Why else is she attractive? Because she isn't married, that's why! She is free to be The Girl in a man's life or at least his vision of The Girl, whether he is married or single himself.

When a man thinks of a married woman, no matter how lovely she is, he must inevitably picture her greeting her husband at the door with a martini or warmer welcome, fixing little children's lunches or scrubbing them down because they've fallen into a mudhole. She is somebody else's wife and somebody else's mother.

When a man thinks of a single woman, he pictures her alone in her apartment, smooth legs sheathed in pink silk Capri pants, lying tantalizingly among dozens of satin cushions, trying to read but not very successfully, for *he* is in that room—filling her thoughts, her dreams, her life.

Why else is a single woman attractive? She has more time and often more money to spend on herself. She has the extra twenty minutes to exercise every day, an hour to make up her face for their date. She has all day Saturday to whip up a silly, wonderful cotton brocade tea coat to entertain him in next day or hours to find it at a bargain sale.

Besides making herself physically more inviting, she has the freedom to furnish her mind. She can read Proust, learn Spanish, study *Time, Newsweek* and *The Wall Street Journal.*

Most importantly, a single woman, even if she is a file clerk, moves in the world of men. She knows their language—the language of retailing, advertising, motion pictures, exporting, shipbuilding. Her world is a far more colorful world than the one of P.T.A., Dr. Spock and the jammed clothes dryer.

A single woman never has to drudge. She can get her housework over within one good hour Saturday morning plus one other hour to iron blouses and white collars. She need never break her fingernails or her spirit waxing a playroom or cleaning out the garage.

She has more money for clothes and for trips than any but a wealthily married few.

Sex—What of It?

Theoretically a "nice" single woman has no sex life. What nonsense! She has a better sex life than most of her married friends. She need never be bored with one man per lifetime. Her choice of partners is endless and they seek *her*. They never come to her bed duty-bound. Her married friends refer to her pursuers as wolves, but actually many of them turn out to be lambs—to be shorn and worn by her.

Sex of course is more than the act of coitus. It begins with the delicious feeling of attraction between two people. It may never go further, but sex it is. And a single woman may promote the attraction, bask in the sensation, drink it like wine and pour it over her like blossoms, with never a guilty twinge. She can promise with a look, a touch, a letter or a kiss—and she doesn't have to deliver. She can be maddeningly hypocritical and, after arousing desire, insist that it be shut off by stating she wants to be chaste for the man she marries. Her pursuer may strangle her with his necktie, but he can't *argue* with her. A flirtatious married woman is expected to Go Through With Things.

Since for a female getting there is at *least* half the fun, a single woman has reason to prize the luxury of taking long, gossamer, attenuated, pulsating trips before finally arriving in bed. A married woman and her husband have precious little time and energy for romance after they've put the house, animals and children to bed. A married woman with her lover is on an even tighter schedule.

During and after an affair, a single woman suffers emotional stress. Do you think a married woman can bring one off more blissfully free of strain? (One of my close friends, married, committed suicide over a feckless lover. Another is currently in a state of fingernail-biting hysteria.) And I would rather be the other woman than the woman who watches a man *stray* from her.

Yet, while indulging her libido, which she has plenty of if she is young and healthy, it is still possible for the single woman to be a lady, to be highly respected and even envied if she is successful in her work.

I did it. So have many of my friends.

Perhaps this all sounds like bragging. I do not mean to suggest for a moment that being single is not often hell. But I do mean to suggest that it can also be quite heavenly, whether you choose *it* or it chooses *you*.

There is a catch to achieving single bliss. You have to work like a son of a bitch.

But show me the married woman who can loll about and eat cherry bonbons! Hourly she is told by every magazine she reads what she must do to keep her marriage from bursting at the seams. There is no peace for anybody married *or* single unless you do your chores. Frankly, I wouldn't want to make the choice between a married hell or a single hell. They're both hell.

However, serving time as a single woman can give you the foundation for a better marriage if you finally go that route. Funnily enough it also gives you the choice.

What then does it take for a single woman to lead the rich, full life?

Here is what it *doesn't* take.

Great beauty. A man seems not so much attracted to overwhelming beauty as he is just overwhelmed by it—at first. Then he grows accustomed to the face, fabulous as it is, and starts to explore the personality. Now the hidden assets of an *attractive* girl can be as fascinating as the dark side of the moon. Plumbing the depths of a raving beauty may be like plumbing the depths of Saran Wrap.

What it also doesn't take to collect men is money. Have you ever noticed the birds who circle around rich girls? Strictly for the aviary.

You also don't have to be Auntie Mame and electrify everybody with your high-voltage personality. Do *you* like the girl who always grabs the floor to tell what happened to *her* in the elevator? Well neither does anybody else.

And you don't have to be the fireball who organizes bowling teams, gets out the chain letters and makes certain *somebody* gives a shower for the latest bride.

What you do have to do is work with the raw material you have, namely you, and never let up.

If you would like the good single life—since the married life is not just now forthcoming—you can't afford to leave any facet of you unpolished.

You don't have to do anything brassy or show-offy or against your nature. Your most prodigious work will be on *you*—at home. (When I got married, I moved in with six-pound dumbbells, slant board, an electronic device for erasing wrinkles, several pounds of soy lecithin, powdered calcium and yeast-liver concentrate for Serenity Cocktails and enough high-powered vitamins to generate life in a statue.)

Unlike Madame Bovary you don't chase the glittering life, you lay a trap for it. You tunnel up from the bottom.

You *do* need a quiet, private, personal aggression . . . a

refusal to take singleness lying down. A sweetly smiling drop-dead attitude for the marrying Sams, and that means *you too*.

You must develop style. Every girl has one . . . it's just a case of getting it out in the open, caring for it and feeding it like an orchid until it leafs out. (One girl is a long-legged, tennis-playing whiz by day, a serene pool at night for friends to drown their tensions in. Wholesomeness is her trademark. A petite brunette is gamine but serious-minded. A knockout in black jersey, she is forever promoting discussions on Stendhal or diminishing colonialism. An intellectual charmer.)

Brains are an asset but it doesn't take brainy brains like a nuclear physicist's. Whatever it is that keeps you from saying anything unkind and keeps you asking bright questions even when you don't quite understand the answers will do nicely. A lively interest in people and things (even if you aren't *that* interested) is why bosses trust you with new assignments, why men talk to you at parties . . . and sometimes ask you on to dinner.

Fashion is your powerful ally. Let the "secure" married girls eschew shortening their skirts (or lengthening them) and wear their classic cashmeres and tweeds until everybody could throw up. You be the girl other girls look at to see what America has copied from Paris.

Roommates are for sorority girls. You need an apartment alone even if it's over a garage.

Your figure can't harbor an ounce of baby fat. It never looked good on anybody but babies.

You must cook well. It will serve you faithfully.

You must have a job that interests you, at which you work hard.

I say "must" about all these things as though you were under orders. You don't have to do anything. I'm just telling you what worked for me.

I'm sure of this. You're not too fat, too thin, too tall, too small, too dumb, or too myopic to have married women gazing at you wistfully.

This then is not a study on how to get married but how to stay single—in superlative style.

CHAPTER 2

THE AVAILABLES:
THE MEN IN YOUR LIFE

Dᴜʀɪɴɢ ʏᴏᴜʀ ʏᴇᴀʀs as a single woman you will find, through no effort on your part, that you have become "The Girl" in a man's life, often a married man.

Being The Girl doesn't necessarily mean you are sleeping with him, although you may be. You could be the love of his life whom he didn't marry fifteen years ago or a girl he sees but barely knows. He can have other flesh-and-blood girls at the same time. You are simply the girl he dreams of when his mind takes flight from his real-life situation. You are his Girl.

Why doesn't he dream of Marilyn Monroe or Natalie Wood? Do *you* dream of Kirk Douglas or Rock Hudson?

12

Like you, he'd rather dream of someone Possible who might conceivably be, or perhaps already has been, his.

To be The Girl imposes very few obligations. You may not have to do anything but just exist. Flirting may start his imagination boiling. More often he makes his choice independently of you.

During the past seventeen years I believe I was The Girl of at least twelve eminently successful men. And as I mentioned earlier, I'm not beautiful or even pretty. No man, to my knowledge, has ever looked at me across a crowded room and said, "Her. Could you get me a date?" Yet I managed to sink into the consciousness and subconsciousness of an advertising tycoon, a motivational research wizard, two generals, a brewer, a publisher, a millionaire real estate developer and two extremely attractive men who were younger than I.

Being The Girl is a wonderful way to feel loved and appreciated when you are without a husband. Men who put you in that category, if they *do* decide to tell you about it, write lovely letters, say ego-building things and send gifts they cannot afford.

Marguerite Clarke (I'll use fictitious names from now on to protect the guilty) is pretty but naïve for a girl of thirty-one who has been married and divorced. One of the men in our office is so nuts about her he is simply beside himself. Contradictory as it sounds he is also happily married. Marguerite is a friend of his wife's and has never led him on. Yet he leaves love offerings of flowers on her desk, gets her raises before they are due and arranges for her to buy everything from electric blankets to hi-fi records wholesale. He also advises her on taxes, insurance and stocks. He even introduces attractive male visitors to her. A kook? Not at all. He is enjoying himself in a way that is harmless to his wife. He is making Marguerite feel beautiful, wanted, important and protected. That's what being The Girl is.

Another girl I know works for the telephone company. She has an older admirer in the same company. She is twenty-three. He is fifty-nine. Every Christmas, birthday and in-between holiday like Valentine's Day and Easter he presents her with a modest piece of jewelry or cash gift. His first offering came though they had hardly spoken. She, aghast, tried to give it back. He said, "Mary Jane, you are a beautiful young woman. I am not after your body though I might be if I were younger. As you may or may not know I am absolutely alone in this world. I don't make very much money, but I have no one to spend it on but me. It would give me the greatest pleasure to give you things. You need never tell anyone about it. I certainly never will. But please do me this favor."

Mary Jane decided she would. She has always been kind to him but their friendship never became carnal. Mary Jane is getting married next month and leaving the telephone company. One of the things she will miss is Mr. A.—her devoted and undemanding admirer.

An advertising agency art director calls up Betsy Alexander one Friday each month and has for six years . . . after his art directors' club dinner, his one night of stag freedom. If she's home, Betsy has a drink with him at a neighborhood bar. In six years he has kissed her twice, tried other times but seems not to have been too disappointed at being refused. Betsy feels if she had responded to his passes with cries of passion he would have fled like Rumpelstiltskin. He simply wanted A Girl to check in with. Betsy finds being considered divine by a nice man who calls every month for six years not too hard to take. So it doesn't get her anywhere—it keeps her ego burnished. Another case of being The Girl.

Enough To Go Around?

What if you aren't The Girl in anybody's life or what if you are? Where are the other men coming from . . . the out-in-the-open admirers? According to statistics there isn't even *one* man for every girl (over four million more single women than men at the last count). Actually, the statistics merely state there are not enough *marriageable* men to go around. Nobody said a word about a shortage of *men*.

You probably have quite a collection yourself right now if you will just count them.

Besides bona fide beaux, pals and lovers, whom we will come to in a minute, there are the men you work with whom you may never see away from the office but with whom you gossip, drink coffee and solve problems. It's fair to count everybody from the mailroom boy up to the chairman of the board as being among your men if your paths cross frequently.

There's your boss, surely among the most important men you'll ever know if you're lucky enough to have a nice one.

I think maybe a girl should never work for a stinker. Life is too short, and as long as we are in more or less of a boom economy, it's possible to change jobs easily. I'm thinking of secretaries who have a particularly personal relationship with a boss.

I worked for years in three Beverly Hills talent agencies which represent movie stars, writers and singers. Sounds glamorous, and maybe I was young and sensitive, but I always felt those places treated secretaries like three-toed sloths to be kept sequestered from the public. At one of these establishments, particularly posh, we girls had to use the back stairs while clients and executives were free to scamper up the elegant, antique-lined front stairway.

After I left there (it seems to me I was *asked* to leave) I got a job as secretary to an advertising agency head (not the ty-coon I mentioned a few pages back). Well I had no idea bosses could *be* like that . . . kind, warm, generous. Mr. B. was a civic and industrial leader as well, and through our offices strode some of the most important people in America. (That's how I met a number of the men to whom I became The Girl.) I worked for him five years and he was responsible for my getting a chance to write advertising copy. His wife is one of my best friends, and through the years they have introduced me to hundreds of exciting people.

It sounds as though I'm sidetracked, but this is just by way of saying you might as well work for a good guy. Count him a blessing and put him on your list.

So Make a List

Other men to tote up as yours are your father, uncles, broth-ers, cousins, family friends, clergyman, doctor and dentist. All perfectly good entries.

Add to the collection the shoe salesman who remembers your size, the milkman, the Fuller Brush man (they're usually darlings), the high school boy who collects for the paper, your landlord, the butcher who pounds veal thin for your scallop-pine, the freckled child who boxes your groceries, whoever services your car, plus your insurance man, tax man, broker (and anyone who buys a single share of anything can have one of them) and your hairdresser.

Oh yes, include the husbands of your friends. They smoke pipes, wear tweeds, watch football. No matter how platonic your relationship—and it probably better be—they're part of your world of men.

What about husbands of women who aren't your friends? Married men are a weighty subject and we'll discuss them at length in a moment. For the time being, yes, put your favorites on the list.

As I see it, about the only men you can't include are bus drivers (who seem singularly impervious to female charms, probably because they see us clawing each other to pieces getting to a seat) and bartenders. I consider bartenders untouchables though other girls tell me they can be warm and friendly.

There, you ought to have about thirty men to keep you from feeling that you live in a manless world.

Now let's classify the men with whom you actually go out. Though they all have a great deal of each other in them, I think they fall into the following categories.

The Eligibles

These are the men you *could* marry, maybe. They are single, reasonably attractive and introduceable to your friends. Among them is the dreamboat you meet on the ski train and would be happy to meet at City Hall the next day, but he isn't ready to take himself off the market. Or the serious chap who falls hard but you don't quite share his enthusiasm for the Civil War. (I know a girl who married one of these Civil War buffs and he insisted on taking his entire set of Lee's Generals on their honeymoon. And they went to *Gettysburg* yet!) Whether your chemistry is compatible or not, these men are Possible and their numbers are lean. I'd say you meet two in a good year.

The Eligibles-But-Who-Needs-Them

They aren't married, okay, but you couldn't care less. They are the weirdies, the creepies, the dullies, the snobs, the hopeless neurotics and mamas' darlings. They seem to have been hiding under logs most of their lives until some well-meaning friend uncovers one and says, "Pauline, I've got just the man for you!"

You usually meet them on blind dates or by taking a chance on a Charles Boyer voice that dialed your telephone number by mistake and persuaded you to rendezvous.

The numbers in this crowd are legion. You could meet three a week.

The Don Juans

We might include them with the creepies, but I think they deserve a category of their own and a special rundown.

No girl is really ready for marriage, I believe, until she has weathered the rigors of a romance with a Don Juan. It's part of her training. A married girl doesn't appeal to him—she has someone to run home to and that spoils his fun . . . reveling in the thought that she is alone, miserable and missing him after he has gone.

The two Don Juans I have known I would stack up against anybody's for pure D.J. talent. They had two things in common—the unrequited need to make girls fall in love with them and an all-consuming vanity which kept them chained to their haberdashers. Allen was a kind of sartorial genius who practically opened up Brooks Brothers on the West Coast. He wore their narrow shoulders and skinny pants when everybody else was padded to the gills. He even gave all his girls Brooks Brothers shirts for Christmas—a different color each year. Paul, whose fantastic looks could have popularized gunny sacks, if he had favored them, was the helpless prey of an expensive tailor in Beverly Hills.

Paul flashed his snow-white-chopper smile at me for all of

three weeks before deserting for a minor night club singer from San Francisco. Allen, who came along the same year (how could one girl be so lucky?), was far deadlier, smarter, and a more consummate operator. He lasted, or I lasted, incredibly for five years, off and on, though there were long periods when we didn't see each other.

One of the great sadnesses of a relationship with a Don Juan is that you lose so much self-respect. It's not only that he doesn't want to get married. It's that you know all the time he is unworthy of you—ruthless and sadistic in his boyish way —but you are too hooked to do anything about it.

You find yourself stooping to things like looking for alien lipstick on glasses in his apartment. I remember plowing through a bunch of love letters from one of Allen's Other Girls as unabashedly as I would have scanned my own bankbook. He had conveniently left the collection on top of his desk. I read every line and cried for three days . . . mission accomplished!

A Don Juan is the only man who doesn't squirm when you have hysterics. He considers it a vote of confidence.

A Don Juan may sleep with only one girl at a time but he has a dozen fringe associations that keep you in purgatory. And while making impassioned avowals of his fidelity, he manages never to let you forget how irresistible he is to other women.

When he's late for a date he explains it's because Daphne telephoned and he couldn't get her off the phone. Daphne was all upset because of a fight with her mother. Who is Daphne? One of his ex-girl-friends of course (so may Daphne's *mother* be for all you know) but somehow she doesn't sound very ex.

Allen was the vortex of a storm of girls who hovered about

him with their career and emotional problems. Models he would send to photographers. Secretaries he would get placed in friends' offices. Actresses he would introduce to agents. His own ex-wife was part of the job. Jocelyn would call from Portland, Miami or Spain to say she was having a problem with her teeth, her passport, her poodle, and Allen would comfort her. Her real problem was Allen.

To the girl Allen was going with he explained this sort of thing as lending a helping hand to those in trouble—just like the Community Chest. How could anyone be so uncharitable as to construe this as lust? Well, I'll tell you who could. I could and *did. Finally!*

I remember our last date . . . preceded by any number of "last dates." It was for lunch on a Tuesday, and that morning he called to see if we could make it Friday. It seems he was driving Janet Van der Hofstadt and a private nurse to Ensenada that afternoon. Janet was in a little trouble and the doctors in Ensenada were excellent and cooperative. He'd just get Janet settled in the house she'd rented, be right home and . . . fade out. End of romance.

The reason I think a Don Juan should be part of every girl's past (heaven help you if you are just beginning to go through one) is that it gives you a chance to get the romantic dream (white knight, white charger) out of your system. A Don Juan is unbelievably romantic.

His telephone conversation would make a movie scenario, though a bad one. It runs something like this:

SOUND: PHONE RINGS.   RECEIVER UP

YOU: Hello?

D.J.   (QUIETLY) Darling . . . how long has it been since I've held you in my arms?

YOU: (FLUSTERED BUT PLEASED) Oh, Mark, honestly.
         . . .

D.J.   Answer me . . . how long has it been?

YOU: Well, I'd say about one day, six hours, three minutes and forty-five seconds.

D.J.   That's too long. What are you wearing?

YOU: Oh, I have on a little green ribbon knit.

D.J.   I don't like you in that dress. Or any other dress. I'm going to come over there and tear it off your lovely body. (THEN JUST BEFORE YOU FAINT, CHANGE OF VOICE EFFICIENTLY) Darling, we're going to a cocktail party at Frank Baum's. Pick you up in fifteen minutes. Bye, darling. (KISS SOUND)

A Don Juan's drive and attention to detail are awe-inspiring. He will work with as much zeal to snare a mousy girl as to seduce a beauty queen. He doesn't stint on good restaurants, good wine or good theatre tickets. He is afraid to take a chance on inferior props for his act. And one of his major props is his status. He is single and *seems* available.

A Don Juan is patient. The average man with an urge will charge like a Pampas bull, smear your lipstick, scatter your bobby pins, crush your rib cage and scare the living daylights out of you. When you don't respond, he is baffled and hurt.

Don Juan would curl his lip at such tactics. He never makes passes without first establishing desire. He will devote several nights to the project if necessary, which it rarely is.

Many Don Juans write letters—in purple prose that enables them, by leaving a note in your mailbox, to snap you back like a rubber band just when you're beginning to pull away.

He sends gifts and flowers.

One Don Juan I heard about gave each of his girls a large

fake-fur dog about three feet high that would be named after him, lie on his mistress' bed, and be her live-in companion. Months after our hero had been sent packing, there would be his big furry namesake looking reproachfully at her out of his blue-bead eyes.

A Don Juan is sick in the head of course—as sick as any chap who thinks he is Napoleon or pads around in tennis shoes peeping in windows. But he is also the man, alas, who can temporarily make you feel like Audrey Hepburn sneaking past the palace guard to fall into the arms of Gregory Peck.

You can be forewarned about a Don Juan and walk right into his trap like a sleepwalker because one of his skills is making you feel you're *different* from all other girls. Advising a girl already in the clutches of a Don Juan is like talking to a zombie. She can't hear you. You might as well try to stop a launched missile as try to break up the affair. And it will end one of two ways: He will get tired and mosey on to his next prey, or his *prey* will tire of his subtle torture and flee. It may even require several fleeings but finally one of them will take.

The Married Man

I don't have to describe a married man. He is as available for observation as the common housefly and about as welcome to many single girls as the common cold.

I think he is much maligned. It isn't his wife who doesn't understand him. She understands him perfectly! It's his girl friend. And what she doesn't understand is how come he doesn't get a divorce.

It's simple. He doesn't want one. Because of the children, because of the community property and because in many cases he doesn't really dislike his wife. He may be tired of her and tired of her understanding him perfectly, but basically they are pretty good friends. And the stronger the pressure from his girl friend, the more angry and tearful she is, the longer he looks at his projected alimony payments, the more friendly he starts feeling toward his wife, who, by this time knowing she is in trouble, has started to behave like a living doll.

To be fair, probably every married man (and woman) has thought of divorce, and perhaps seriously enough to say "what if" to an attorney. But between the thought and the final decree lies an area as broad, stormy and unnavigable as the Straits of Magellan.

Now just where does that leave the single girl with a married man in her life? It leaves her with very poor marriage material on her hands, that's where.

But since we agreed not to talk about getting married, let's explore the pros and cons of having anything at all to do with a married man.

These I would say are the cons:

1. He almost never gets a divorce.
2. He is practically useless on Saturday nights, Sundays, holidays and nine times out of ten on your birthday.
3. You can't introduce him around as your beau.
4. He dives under tables in restaurants when friends of his wife walk in.
5. He never introduces you to his boss or other influential figures in his life.
6. While not free to make you an honest woman, he has a screaming fit if you *look* at another man.
7. He will say just about anything that pops into his head ("You're beautiful, you're sexy, you're the love of my life") except what you really want to hear, which is "Will you marry me?"

8. He tells lies.
9. You may fall in love with him and suffer.

This is what's in his favor:

1. He can be your devoted slave and remain "faithful" to you for years.
2. He will love you more passionately than the woman he married, and prefer your company to hers.
3. He will spoon-feed you the praise and appreciation you rarely get from the single fellow who thinks telling you that you have pretty eyes might be construed as a proposal of marriage.
4. He is often generous with gifts and money. If he isn't, you can explain the economic facts of life.
5. Any visiting married man on expense account is the greatest date since Diamond Jim Brady. He will take you to the best restaurants, the best night clubs, order the best champagne.
6. He will give you sound advice about your job, insurance, investments and even about getting along with your family and other men.
7. He is frequently marvelous in bed and careful not to get you pregnant.

It seems to me the solution is not to rule out married men but to keep them as pets. While they are "using" you to varnish their egos, you "use" *them* to add spice to your life. I say "them" advisedly. One married man is dangerous. A potpourri can be fun.

There's no gainsaying that to take a married man seriously and fall in love is like dope addiction—dangerous and degrading. And you have to watch both of you every second because his greatest pleasure seems to be in *getting* you to take him seriously and fall in love!

But by and large I think you hold the better cards. Even though he has someone at home to bind up his wounds when it's over, you are free to heal yours with a man younger than he, freer than he, and he suffers.

His Wife

What about the harm you may do his wife?

I'm afraid I have a rather cavalier attitude about wives. The reason is this:

A wife, if she is loving and smart, will get her husband back every time. He doesn't really want her *not* to. He's only playing. (She may have played herself on occasion.) If she *doesn't* get him back, it's probably because she's lazy, blind, or doesn't want him. If he's a hopeless chaser, like the Don Juan, he will chase regardless of who does or does not give him succor, so no need to feel guilty.

Many people have said this before me but no man or woman is attracted to just one person in a lifetime. If a man, married for years, wants to take a single girl to dinner, it can hardly break up his marriage. If the dinner is paid for by his expense account and he's a thousand miles from home, so much the better. He may arrive home a happier, more contented man.

Girls who live in New York, Chicago and Los Angeles seem to have greatest access to expense-account men because there is more dashing back and forth of executives between these places. However, large companies have branch offices in many other cities, so any number can play. These men are collectors' items. They give you a chance to put on your prettiest dress, your prettiest smile and to polish your charm, and they leave town before you can get serious about each other.

Case Histories

Jennifer McCone, a pretty girl of twenty-nine, works for a public relations firm. Her company president, fifty-two, met Jennifer at an office party he gave for all West Coast employees. (He lives in New York.) After the party he asked Jennifer to dinner at Scandia, one of Los Angeles' most glamorous restaurants. Many Aquavits and Danish beers later they were getting Jennifer's coat from the check room and noticed a gift shop. He suggested they look around. While Jennifer was browsing among the only gifts that cost $1.98 (back scratchers) her escort spotted a handsome chafing dish. He said, "I'd like to take one of these back to New York. Why don't we get one for you too?" Jennifer accepted graciously. A nice gesture from a man who could afford it.

The next time he came to the Coast, this charmer asked Jennifer if she would like to make him Crepes Strawberry like they'd had at Scandia. Jennifer said she'd love to. Smooth operator? Certainly. An archfiend? Certainly not! Any girl in the company would have jumped at the chance to make him Crepes Strawberry and Jennifer was flattered he picked her. After the crepes and whatever she fixed to go with them, they went to the Crescendo to hear Shelley Berman. Beddy-bye in between? Who knows? *I* don't. Who cares? Not *me*.

Here's another case history. The account supervisor on an advertising account that bills millions comes to the West Coast to make television commercials twice a year. His long-time companion during these junkets is a chic forty-one-year-old buyer at a department store. He loves the good life and is popular. During his visits (usually about two weeks) a movie star couldn't be seated at the front booth of Romanoff's any oftener or go to more glittering parties than our heroine. Are they having an affair? Probably. Would the lady like to slit her throat? Doubtful. She looks twenty-three while he's here.

I have found the most trying quality of some married men is their fetish about secrecy. They don't want you to tell a daisy, your diary or anybody you know that you know them. If the public relations man thought Jennifer had talked about the chafing dish he would have taken cyanide (after first having Jennifer fired). There isn't much you can do about this obsession except *pretend* not to tell anyone.

For example, an insurance executive, infatuated with an accountant in his office, casually takes the elevator from the twelfth to the main floor at the time of her coffee break. Watches synchronized, she uses the stairway from the twelfth floor to the eleventh, *then* takes the elevator to the main where they meet. (We hope he doesn't make her climb all twelve flights on the return trip to further avoid suspicion.) Nobody has ever seen them arrive or depart *à deux*, so he thinks nobody knows they meet. Just *everybody* knows, that's who. And they would respect him more if he weren't such a sneak.

In addition to dining with visitors, these are some of the things I think you can do successfully with a married man and never hurt you, him or his loved ones.

A. Meet for coffee.

B. Meet for lunch.

C. Have dinner with him (with others along) on the nights you all work late.

D. Have a wonderful working relationship. Help him make his company or his job a smashing success.

E. Flirt with him anytime, anywhere (except in a board meeting) including under his wife's nose. Flirting is as healthy as orange juice and just as sweet. His wife might pick up some good pointers.

F. Have *innocent* dates, such as a malt after the night school class you both attend. My friend, Laura Phillips, has been having a hamburger with the instructor of a writing class every Monday night for twelve weeks. Then he walks her to her car and she drives home. Alone. Harmless, but he's happier, and she has another man on her list.

It's a question of taking married men but not taking them seriously. And not taking them home—too often. Don't try to marry one. Use them in a perfectly nice way just as they use you. There are lots of them around.

The Homosexual

How do you tell when a man isn't a man? Anyone can spot the effeminate chap who floats instead of walks, but how do you identify someone who *looks* perfectly male? I've known girls who even married homosexuals and didn't know they were until their wedding night. (Which comes from not having slept with the man you're going to marry, which I consider complete lunacy.) However, many homosexual men like girls too, and in that case if you never know, you aren't wounded.

If you'd like a spot check just to make sure, I think you use your instinct. And add up his two and two to see if you get four. Or seven.

Suppose he's over thirty and lives with another man. The situation bears watching. If he has a male roommate and he's over *forty*, there's very little doubt about his sex. He's a girl.

How else can you tell? Homosexual men are usually tied in with their mothers. While despising the old girls for their smothering, possessive ways, they do them obeisance. One boy I know goes on trips with mother to Nassau, Japan, Buenos Aires—like Violet and Sebastian in *Suddenly Last Summer*.

If a man is more solicitous of another fellow than he is of you, it's entirely possible the other fellow is his lover.

I remember dating an attractive boy who worked for a broadcasting company. We were at his apartment playing Monopoly and I felt at any moment he would stop putting up hotels on Boardwalk, pass "Go" and make a pass at me. It was high time. About this point the phone rang and it was his roommate. This was their conversation: "Hello, Ralphy? Where *are* you? *Where?!* Oh, Ralphy, I don't *like* those people and you promised you wouldn't *see* them! Do you have your topcoat with you? Good. It's kind of chilly. I left some marinated herring in the icebox for you. Oh, nothing much. I'm playing Monopoly with a girl."

So I concentrated harder on getting up some hotels on Park Place.

It's not always easy to tell a homosexual even if you have a suspicious nature. One of my dearest friends had me fooled for years. Spencer, I shall call him, was a charmer, successful with a plastics business, more outgoing than Dinah Shore. When we met he lived with his "brother" who actually looked very much like him. One night the three of us were driving home from a party and "brother" tried to steer the car off a Laurel Canyon cliff. I attributed this whim to his drinking but discovered later they'd had a lovers' quarrel. "Brother" resented *me* and felt suicidally inclined.

When "brother" departed and another brother moved *in* (this time no family resemblance) I became mildly disillusioned.

Prior to that, Spencer had me convinced that while he and *I* were only friends and had kissed only once, chastely on

New Year's Eve, numerous girls all over town panted for him —airline stewardesses, a Sands Hotel dancer, some blonde from Fort Worth destined to inherit oil, and a rather permanent amorata in Hermosa Beach he only saw Friday nights. I later concluded that the stewardesses, the dancer, the Fort Worth dazzler and the beach girl were all boys.

A single girl who is slightly, although unconsciously afraid of marriage, will be attracted to homosexual men because she feels safe with them and they in turn with her. Nobody is clambering over anybody to get married. You're someone female he can take to parties, introduce to parents and with whom he can present a heterosexual façade to the world. But never kid yourself that the man who doesn't kiss you good night is restraining himself out of respect. He isn't for girls, that's all. Or if you date an enthusiastic kisser who never even *tries* to proceed south of the border, look to his maleness. If you check and find he isn't trying to go further with any other girl either, chances are his hormonal balance is a little out of kilter.

Before you rule homosexual men out of your life, however, let's consider. Are they really monsters? Some very famous and beautiful women are married to them.

Psychiatrists tell us homosexuals have a strong sex drive. They are little boys, or girls, in an arrested state of sexual development (except the ones who are so strongly developed that they like boys *and* girls). The former, like you and me, arrived at the age of puberty when girls like girls and boys like boys. Only they never left it. They have tremendous emotional problems, which presumably respond the least of any to psychoanalysis. (If you think *you* have trouble and are about to open your veins over a *man*, consider how much lonelier and sillier you'd feel if it were a *girl*.)

While you turn up your nose at homosexuals, a lot of other

homosexuals (undeclared), whom you don't criticize because they're married and baseball-oriented, are running around loose. I suspect a bunch in one of my former offices. They ate together every noon, told bawdy stories to each other, drank en masse at five o'clock and whistled at waitresses. They *seemed* to be as masculine as the Neanderthal man in the forest primeval, but how come you never saw them with a girl? If you ask me, they were less masculine than the slender reedy fellow who does a fantastic mambo and prefers *my* company to a man's. If you still ask me, they were making a tremendous show of their maleness because they had some creeping doubt about it themselves.

As for declared (overt, as they say) homosexuals, they make wonderful friends—loyal, sympathetic and entertaining. They will sit by your bed when you have a strep throat while your other beaux and girl friends are out watching the Santa Claus Lane parade or some damn nonsense. They are good confidants and will give you sound advice about men. They have the most exquisite taste, the most handsomely done apartments (often on green stamps) and give the best parties of anyone I know. They are frequently devastatingly attractive—and a girl can't surround herself with too many attractive men.

The Divorcing Man

This person is usually overrated as marriage material. He has his interlocutory decree (or whatever is the comparable document in your state), true, but still has time to serve before his divorce is final. If he has children, chances are he's still more married than single. Certainly during those first few months after leaving his troubled Shangri-La, he is in shock. You hold his hand, cook his food and reassure him that the kids won't forget who is Daddy. And what does he do? He goes over to *their* house on the least excuse. He mows their yard, mends their roof and has endless talks with *her* (described by him as "arguments") long after it's supposed to be *over*. While you figure to get a license the minute he's free, he figures it's time to look at some other girls. After all, you remind him of the awful transition period! Count the divorcing man a friend but don't consider all your problems solved just because you helped him solve *his*.

The Younger Man

This chap is better marriage material than you may think. I know of four happy marriages in which the groom is from two to eight years younger than his wife. In three instances the girls are treated like princesses, pampered, petted and adored. In the fourth the wife is no more taken for granted than in most marriages.

If you don't marry a junior he can still be a wonderful date, keep you on your toes and swinging.

CHAPTER 3

WHERE TO MEET THEM

We've discussed *who* the men are. Now let's see *where* the men are!

Actually, in trying to make the statistics a little more palatable for single girls, the compilers include entries in their "available single men figures" you can't touch (because they're locked up somewhere) or wouldn't want to (because they are drug addicts, perverts, or have I.Q.s under 40).

Here are the best places to find the men you *would* fall on with glad cries.

Your Job

Most of the men in the world leave home every morning and check into a job, give or take a few writers and painters who work at home and must be flushed out other ways, a few millionaires—too rare and exotic to bother about—and parasites who only check into tennis clubs. (Let's tell ourselves they'd be a bore anyway.) Unemployed men, of course, may not be checking in currently but will later. If they don't, add them to the untouchables.

The rest of the men are reporting daily to places we girls can report to too! (Garages, missile launchings and live-bait barges hire girl clerks.) Now . . . it seems obvious to me that if you aren't meeting any men through your job, you are in the wrong job.

From nine to five is actually a marvelous time to sink into a man. After five, many single men are already involved with somebody else so you can't get *to* them. (Never mind that this broad is holding your potential slave *her* slave with three-inch fillets and herb soufflés like his mother *never* made. Temporarily he's not completely get-atable.) If you are a feast for the eyes during the daylight hours, however, he may just turn to you when *she* has run out of recipes.

Many of the men in your company will be married, of course, or else they are soft-skinned, pink-cheeked little lambs barely out of high school. Face it. What covey of men outside of Trappist monks *hasn't* been decimated by matrimony? Even though hordes of your male co-workers are married, plenty of unattached or "detached" men from the outside should at least be *calling* on your firm, thus giving you access to them—salesmen, consultants, suppliers, clients, friends of executives, even naughty chaps from the Internal Revenue Service who are auditing the corporate books.

It really is important to surround yourself with men every day to keep up your morale. And what's to stop you? You're not a wife-at-home who is lucky if she sees two adult males all day long—the postman and a suspicious-looking "veteran" selling magazine subscriptions.

Sometimes a girl meets the wrong kind of man for *her* in

her job. That calls for a job shift. For example, if you're the cerebral type who enjoys lectures at the university, but your only playmates at work are the Neanderthal-type crew of your plumbing-contractor boss, consider a change. (Probably some plumbers attend lectures like mad. I just don't happen to know them.) Conversely, a sweet, mousy girl might be wasting her time in a music-publishing house. The males there are as slippery and glittery as eels, a type of wildlife that has no rapport at all with mousy girls.

So, it's not only a question of going where the men are but going where *your* men are. If you never even *see* somebody you could be happily ensconced in a bomb shelter with, it's probably time for a move.

Many companies do not allow dating among co-workers and clearly they are not with it! Why else do they suppose you are working except to cover a few items like food, rent, car payments, bank loans and other trivia? (Bona fide career girls to the contrary notwithstanding.) Managements who think romances lower the work output are right out of their skulls. A girl in love with her boss will knock herself out seven days a week and wish there were more days. Tough on her but fabulous for business! A girl with a crush on any co-worker jumps for joy at having to work overtime with him. There she is in the hushed, sexy atmosphere of after-five with dinner money *and* him on her hands.

If your company frowns on intramural dating but there is good material at hand, I would say date anyway. You will undoubtedly be fired, but imagine leaving under such a romantic cloud . . . a woman so attractive to and attracted by the opposite sex, she was willing to collect her unemployment insurance for them!

Veronica used to date one of the salesmen in this "hands off your co-workers" atmosphere. She finished work before he did and would wait in his car, lying down in the front seat to avoid the Gestapo gaze of management or its informants (like her girl friends!). Every time Ronnie opened his car door, he would suffer a momentary spasm of horror thinking he'd found a dead woman in the front seat! Veronica was subsequently asked to leave the firm, but by that time she had decided she could never be really happy with somebody who had a set of nerves like that!

Naturally you mustn't be flagrant about your dating. Besides being an affront to your less fortunate girl friends, holding hands with a conquest at lunch or favoring him at the water cooler with your Mount Everest look ("I could climb all over you") may send *him* off to the next county!

In companies that *do* allow dating, I have known unmarried twosomes who left the same bed in the morning, drove to work in the same car, shared the same elevator and were so cool to one another in the hall, you would have sworn they were in litigation.

That's how you have to play it.

The quality of men you meet at work is usually pretty satisfactory. At least they are not chaps who go to movies all day in hopes of sitting next to a nine-year-old girl.

Generally there's no great strain or embarrassment to getting better acquainted with a co-worker. You've been properly introduced. He can't suspect you're chasing him just because you both attend the same staff meetings. You're free to lower the boom as unobtrusively as Lucrezia Borgia mixed poison.

It's also less humiliating to be looked over as you file or clean test tubes than be displayed on spec at a cocktail party. That last bit has the feel of the Christians being looked over by the lions.

Another advantage of a job is that it offers you a chance to meet some of those pleasant traveling executives on expense accounts. And they're so meetable!

An executive secretary, for example, has one of the all-time great spots for meeting men. If you're a top secretary but working for a dullard, consider abandoning him for somebody shinier. The caliber of beaux you meet through him is in direct relation to the caliber of success *he* is. You may have to start as a "second girl" in his office and move up. Don't be afraid to.

If you adore your job, men or no men, stay. Getting lost in your work, getting raises, getting recognition—these are some of the all-time thrills. They are particularly available to single girls who haven't houses, meals on time and the business of dropping off nine pounds of weekly laundry to distract them.

But if it isn't a very interesting job *and* you're not meeting any men in it or through it, think once more about the ones pouring out of cars on parking lots, out of buses, streetcars, taxis and commuter trains. They're checking in somewhere. Shouldn't you be checking in there too?

Friends of Friends (Personal Sponsorship)

The best of all possible ways to meet men, I think, is through friends, on a planned basis. Somebody picks somebody out for you and picks you out for them.

Heaven knows they can make some hideous mistakes, and you wonder if they've taken leave of their senses or are trying to drive you into a nunnery. It isn't so surprising that they misjudge. How many gruesome twosomes have *you* seen flourish? Aren't you continually fascinated by who finds whom attractive? And who doesn't?

I know a man who is absolutely daffy about a girl twice his size. Nobody would have picked *them* for lovers. When she stands between him and the door, you can't see *him* at all and very little of the door. How are friends to know, really, who will "take" and who won't? The next time somebody sends you a "discovery" she could only have discovered under her kitchen sink among the Drano and empty beer bottles, forgive her. The next find she comes up with may be a jewel.

A true married-woman friend frequently shows the skill of a Broadway producer in lining up talent. We don't know for sure why she does it. She isn't always thanked. Possibly some primordial instinct drives her to try to get everything matched up for procreation. (She winces at scrambling eggs that might have hatched. She goes completely ape when her cat has kittens, even if they must be put to sleep the next week.) Maybe she likes you or maybe she hates you—and all single women—and wants you hustled into her own discontented group. Perhaps it's her intensive background as a shopper. She can't see an ocelot-covered piano bench marked down at a sale without trying to figure which one of her friends can use it. She can't see an unclaimed bachelor without trying to figure out which of her friends can use *him*.

At any rate, she's indispensable. For one thing, a married girl has access to different sets of men than yours—not necessarily better, just different. If it's on your behalf (not her own), she can be bolder. When she says to an attractive bachelor at a party, "There's a girl I'd love you to get to know. Why don't you come by the house Wednesday?" nobody will impugn her motives. You can say roughly the same thing to the same man (about yourself) and nobody will doubt *your* motives either. The trouble is that your motives are completely unacceptable in polite society (the same society that criticizes you for not being married, by the way) and it's better to keep them at home in a mason jar.

Do let your friend help rope. You tie!

The husbands of married girl friends could help too, if they would, but they're usually damned uncooperative. A wife can badger her mate for months to canvass the office for "somebody nice for Jeanne"; he can be sitting on top of a virtual Cary Grant and never mutter a word. Probably he doesn't have anything against his wife's girl friends. He just tends to consider bachelors a vanishing but admirable group —like the bison—and is determined to help preserve their dwindling numbers.

A married man whose wife you don't know is hardly more helpful. Even if he has no plans for you himself, he is loath to do anything that might take you off the market. At best he will introduce you to another married fellow and thus insure your still being in circulation a year hence.

Occasionally a kindly, lovable, philanthropic husband does cooperate with his wife in sponsoring romance for a single woman, and those couples deserve a place in Westminster Abbey—later.

Getting a shiny gift-wrapped male from a friend is a relatively painless way to meet him. It's super-respectable, even innocent. It was their idea you get together, wasn't it? You can even convince yourself that you are doing them a favor.

Also a friend-sponsored man spares you those painful mid-romance discoveries. If a find is represented as a single, practicing architect, he has usually put up a few buildings and files a separate tax return. Contrast him with the fascinating real estate magnate you meet on the plane who, it turns out, actually manages a six-unit motel with his wife. (It can take *weeks* to unscramble a pack of lies like his.)

Motherly sponsors will usually arrange a rendezvous in their home. For example, they might invite you and their find to come by for cocktails. Then, if you like each other, you can take off from there. If he presently remembers a boss he was supposed to pick up at the airport, or you recall an aunt you forgot you'd asked for dinner, *c'est la vie*. Your sponsors can try again.

A small dinner party is an equally satisfactory way for friends to introduce friends, providing, of course, that the hostess is not one of those predatory females who won't let you shine for trying to outdazzle the Kohinoor herself. Beware the married girl who only *thinks* she wants you to meet and marry a delicious find. She will arrange an evening for you, her husband, the find, and herself. Then she wears a gown that would bring a wooden Indian to life. She insists on having the find teach her how to cha-cha-cha that very night, and if the conversation ever *does* get around to you, which isn't likely, she will lapse into a kind of catatonic withdrawal until things liven up. Obviously this girl needs you as bait worse than you need her!

My husband was a find. (Which is probably why I like the system.) A dear friend plotted our meeting for three years. The first year was hopeless because David was in the middle of a divorce. The second year he was drowning himself in starlets, or so she reported, and not apt to appreciate the charms of a plain but sensible girl like me. "Is there really any hope?" I queried, as we went into our third fiscal year. "Yes," said Ruth. "Sit tight."

One day, when Ruth felt that David was possibly going down for the third time, she arranged a meeting—with no great expectations, I'm sure. If the meeting hadn't "taken," she would have produced other girls for David. (A matron can't afford to let a good bachelor get away when she has many needy friends.) The meeting took, however, and we were married . . . as I may have mentioned, with little more than a year's labor with the trident and cast net on my part.

Now suppose a friend of yours, either man or woman, knows somebody you would like to meet, only they haven't thought of it and you have. Be forthright. In as frank and charming a way as you can, ask them to introduce you.

For example, Alice panted to meet the thirty-year-old scion of one of the wealthiest men in the world . . . oil yet. (This is a true story, as all mine are, with names and sometimes occupations changed.) Her coveted was actively engaged in running his father's company, and Alice knew a man who knew him through business, an ex-boss of hers. One day she telephoned him and said, "Mr. Adams, I'm going to be very frank with you. I want you to do me a tremendous favor, and when I tell you what it is, please don't be afraid to turn me down. I'll simply understand it's something you can't do. I'd like to meet Frank Glazer (pause) and I think you know him. You probably also know he's one of the most eligible bachelors in the city and he's dated girls, girls, girls without finding anyone to marry. I'm not nearly as eligible as he is—who *is*, for heaven's sake?—but it's possible he'd like me. What do you think?"

Mr. Adams, probably not typical of ex-bosses, said, "Alice, I think it's a wonderful idea. Now let me think about this and see how we can fix it up." A week later he called to ask if she would join him and Mrs. Adams for dinner in a restaurant. Frank Glazer would be in tow. After dinner he and Mrs. Adams would bow out to visit relatives. Then she was on her own.

Like many true stories, this one has no happy ending—or unhappy ending either. Alice and Frank met, dated several times, so you might say their introduction "took." (She, incidentally, boned up on his work with books on oil refining and Saudi Arabia.) However, as she might have suspected if she had been truly honest with herself, this young man hadn't remained single for want of finding somebody. He could barely sort *through* his finds! He played the field because he loved it.

Not all the desirables turn out to be so difficult to land.

Think carefully now. Who do you know with information that could lead to the capture of a most-wanted fugitive? Act now. Other bloodhounds are on his trail.

Blind Dates (You're on Your Own)

When people ask you to their home to meet a man, that's a blind date of sorts, but the blind dates now under discussion are those more casually arranged. Instead of meeting in a friend's patio, protected and nurtured like a debutante, you identify each other under the clock at the Biltmore by carnations in your lapels.

Blind dates happen many ways. Somebody gives somebody your phone number; a girl friend rings up to say her date brought a pal. (He's probably standing at her elbow as she describes him on the phone, so don't quail when her knight of the evening turns out to be a slope-chested, liver-complexioned Lilliputian.)

Another kind of blind date is when you decide to take a chance on the "voice" who has dialed your phone number by mistake. He does, after all, sound a little like Laurence Olivier. (And will look more like Sir Laurence's Richard III, beak nose and all.) But let us not be cynical.

Blind dates are a perfectly good way to meet men. You may feel like Madame Curie going through pitchblende trying to find one usable gram of radium, but don't despair. All you need is one usable man.

In some ways it's good to start the duel without seconds.

It's often easier to talk with a blind date alone than under the beady gaze of a matchmaker—especially a "confused" one who can't remember which one of you she's selling.

Every girl's blind-date experiences would make a television series, save some which are completely unfilmable of course. Classic is the predator who tries to devour you like Little Red Riding Hood as the last course of his dinner. And the nature boy who wants to perform the rites of spring right in your living room when he picks you up. Everybody has propped up the chap who is tipsy by nine, tanked by ten and passed out cold on the parking lot by midnight. Then there's the stingy sadist who not only wrecks stomach linings but *budgets* by drinking *your* liquor and eating your salted nuts, hours after you were supposed to keep a restaurant reservation.

Some blind dates are strong on talk but light on listening. You might as well try to get through to somebody singing in the shower behind a closed door. Others there wouldn't be any talking at all with if you didn't speak up. You feel like Scheherazade trying to keep your head from being severed by telling fascinating stories.

Some blind dates are oily, some are mossy, some are creaky and some are . . . just right!

The more blind dates notched in your gun, the more wary you become of accepting really *blind* blind dates . . . those not arranged by someone you trust.

It's okay to be a little choosy. Barbara told me of a recent blind date who turned out to be a bellboy at night, a bookie by day. Sometimes he made book by night but said it wasn't too safe using the hotel house phones.

To avoid wasting too much of your precious time on the Totally Hopeless, it's a good idea to make your first meeting at lunch instead of dinner, cocktails instead of an evening.

You can always make a second date. Finishing a good book or polishing the silver may enrich your life more in the long run than a free dinner with a drag.

Active Sports

Never mind you were voted the kid most likely to drown when all the kids on your block took off for the old swimming hole. Never mind that a baseball flying at you kindles the kind of panic that routed the Carthaginians before Scipio. Never mind when they handed out the muscular coordination you were in the powder room redoing your mascara.

Men like sports; can you afford *not* to?

If you play anything yourself, you're bound to be where the men are! You don't actually have to be very good or play championship anything. You may play *at* it with girl friends as amateurish as you, but *doing* it allows you to be down at the courts, out on the links, up on the ski trails . . . like we said, where the men are!

Take skiing for example. The slopes are littered with men and not all of them are married. Even the ones on litters will be back again as soon as the broken bones have knitted.

I'd almost guarantee it. On a ski weekend you'll talk to at least a dozen nice strangers. A double chair lift finds you paired off with a new man every time you go topside. Likewise the T-bar lift. Nobody will pick you up when you fall. That would be patronizing you. But even if you ski by yourself (I know several girls who do) you're apt to have a pretty decent time. Incidentally, those who ski even a little bit say it's so exhilarating you tend to shelve all your weighty problems. The first time you stay upright all the way down a slope with trees flying past like telephone poles on the highway, you feel a thrill like the sweet part of danger.

Ice skating is a dandy way to rub shoulders with boys even if you occasionally rub derrières with ice! If you skate alone, boys will come by to skate with you—innocent as being tagged at a dance! And if they don't, there's that compensatory thrill again . . . skimming over the ice like a snowbird . . . grrreat!

Tennis is terrific fun and a man mecca too. Even if you're on the courts with your fifteen-year-old cousin, there's a chance you'll meet the boys playing in the next court.

The watering places are laced with men. If you water-ski or surf, you're sure to be caught in a male-strom.

Sailing is male. Very male. But you can't just draw a bead on a seventy-foot ketch with lots of promising crew members spilling out of the fo'c'sle and climb aboard. You've got to be invited. The way to be invited is to know who owns the boat, of course. But there aren't enough boat owners to go around . . . not of the kind of boat we're talking about. There are even fewer of them than single men on cruises.

A friend of mine crewed with the late Humphrey Bogart for several years, but he never brought a girl along . . . figured *he* was lucky to be there.

I suppose by kind of hanging around in the general area of boats you might eventually be tapped for a sail. I heard of a girl who got herself asked to the barnacle scraping of small craft, it being understood barnacle scrapers are eventually rewarded by being allowed to crew on the scraped craft. It seems like an awfully fingernail-corroding way to get an invitation.

You could get a small boat of your own, of course, and put-put around. A secondhand dinghy with an outboard motor costs roughly $99.50, and a canoe with a couple of paddles is even cheaper. Or you can rent something. But all this presupposes you know how to handle a boat. *Do* you? The men in boat yards look just marvelous but you can see I'm little or no help in suggesting how to meet them.

Anyway, archery, ping-pong, badminton, roller skating, bowling, golf (hunting and shooting are expensive so we'll skip them) are all sports men dig. If you do too, a man who might not otherwise may dig you.

There's another plus to athletics. After a workout, your muscles feel so taut and singing (once past the painful beginning) you get to liking your body with that feel and won't tolerate it any other way. Don't forget, too, how smashing girls look in ski clothes, skating skirts and tennis whites.

If you're a real hothouse flower, you can still participate in sports. (I know you hoped you couldn't, but you *can!*)

A thin-ankled fashion plate I know plays touch football with her husband and some friends occasionally on a vacant lot. Her specialty is halfbacking the Statue of Liberty play. Margaret usually lasts about three minutes but claims it's been a marvelous help in getting the feel of the game so she can understand her husband's passion for it.

To be actively sporty, sometimes all you need to do is lie down. Your red-blood count may be thirty, but you can still take your grass mat, your suntan oil and a good book to the beach, and park where the men are. Don't always move in a safe, sane little band of girls.

One girl alone on a beach towel is a man attractor. (And if no one comes near, she hasn't done anything to cry into her pillow about.) Four girls together are a stop signal to flirtation. Eight girls together murder it unless a roving volleyball team comes along looking for a game.

A working knowledge of sports can serve you well. If you know who's batting what in which league and a few famous plays of the Baltimore Colts, you're considered a brilliant conversationalist. If you don't know a double-header from a yacht with two johns (and can't *learn*), I've found that it helps hypo your interest to have a small bet on one of the teams. Or to know somebody's brother or cousin you can root for. One football season I "adopted" Jon Arnett of the U.S.C. Trojans. I pretended I was his mother and felt how she would feel watching the game. (Actually she probably had cold compresses on her head with somebody staked out at the TV set to tell her when it was over.) Then because of some N.C.A.A. ruling (I never understood *that* either) Jon was benched for a semester and I lost heart. Now on Rose Bowl day and during the World Series I simply chloroform myself.

One more thought on man-jammed sports arenas. Race tracks are. Save your lunch money, bet the favorites to show and you'll be fraternizing with fellows at the cashier windows after every race. Well, it *could* happen.

I think you could skip boxing arenas. Nobody will pay any attention to you anyway.

As for indoor brain games like chess and bridge, I know of no places where men gather officially to play them except at tournaments—where you will be flogged if you so much as snap open your purse to look for a bobby pin. If you know these games, though, bully for you. Another of your special pluses with men.

Bars

Even men who don't hunt, golf, ski, skate, swim, shoot or sail *do* lift a glass now and then, and they often lift it in bars. On gazing the length of an average bar, a girl would think this must be the place! There they are—men in flocks . . . just ready to be swept from their bar stools and made off with!

Isn't it a shame there's a catch to the men you meet in bars?

Ginger says they're like the steaks you get in Mexico. They *seem* like regular steaks and have regular steak names on the menu, but when you order a Chateaubriand for only $2.95, it tastes more like château plaster. It wasn't cured properly or something.

Men in bars look like men all right, but maybe *they* weren't cured properly or something. Anyway, they act funny! If you're in a bar alone or with another girl, they treat you as though you were somebody you're not. They figure you're a little bit lonely (now isn't that silly of them!) and possibly an itsy witsy bit frantic or else why would you be here? Therefore you must be distress merchandise which can be had more cheaply than regular goods. These bar belters don't seem to realize it's little old fun-loving but moral-fibered *you* underneath.

Now certain bars have been adopted by companies in the neighborhood and have a "safe," home-folksy atmosphere. No question of mistaken identity there. Your cohorts know it's you all right . . . the real you. But if you're in that bar too often, even drinking with pals who love you, it means you ain't got no place else to go, and you're still distress merchandise.

I have a feeling many girls will not buy my prissy attitude about bars for one moment. It's true that I get drunk easily and may be asleep in a chair before the real fun starts. Some of my best girl friends spend a minimum of six hours a week in their company bar, and, since they are pretty and popular, are always surrounded by fellows who fight to buy their drinks. But I must stick by my stand. Working out at the bar isn't getting them any good take-home men. Better they should be home doing their double-chin exercises!

Some bars in big cities are famous get-acquainted meccas.

When the bar closes at 2 A.M., everybody goes home with *somebody,* and very warm friendships are undoubtedly formed—at least from 2 A.M. to 9. Can you afford to pass *them* up? I'd say yes! If that's such a great way to meet men, how come those same girls are back the next night forming new friendships?

If you are a shy violet like me, if you're not a raving beauty like I'm not, you feel more shy and less beautiful on the prowl in a bar than almost any other place on earth.

Going to a bar with a date is different. Respectable as being in church. You may even do a little flirting with the man on the next bar stool while your date goes to check the dinner reservations. Then you aren't distress merchandise. Men you meet with another man are *cured!*

Also, at vacation spots I would say it's okay to let down the bar to bars. I don't know why it's different there but it is!

Parties

Like bars, parties are touted as classically good sources of men. Men *go* to them and in a convivial, girl-meeting mood. Ought to be a simple trick to pick off a large enough collection to last up to and maybe through the crucial Christmas season.

This is possibly a true appraisal for the pretty, busty girl who has only to stand still, draw in her breath to draw a crowd. But if you're like me (leave bust measurements out of this) and you have to sink *in* before love blossoms, you may find the men have come and gone from the fray without you *or* your phone number.

A few years ago I met a yummy chap at a bon-voyage party. (My boss's wife was going to China.) We chatted long enough for me to learn that he managed the basement section

of a large department store and was working his way upstairs. A few weeks later I just happened to be shopping in his
store (like Japanese planes just *happened* to be over Pearl
Harbor) and stopped to ask him if he had had lunch. That
was a pretty brassy move for me because I die when turned
down. He hadn't. We went up to the tearoom, had a very nice
talk, and made a date. He kept saying, rather overingenu-
ously I thought, that he had no idea I was so pleasant and
hadn't thought me attractive at all at the party. Hmmmmm!

I'd better back down right now and admit that some relatively plain girls do just fine at parties. I'm just not one of
them.

There are parties and parties of course. Cocktail parties are
the ones I hate most but I can't ever remember missing one!
You owe it to yourself to go to everything from company
picnics to embassy balls on the chance that *he'll* be there.

Parties are also a reason to look your prettiest, to wear a
new dress and your most razzle-dazzle smile and kind of
generally hone your personality against new and old friends.
The best parties I know for sinking into men are small dinner
parties.

Get-Acquainted Clubs

I imagine the risks of blind dates are paltry compared to
what you might encounter at a lonely hearts club (one
advertised in the paper). They're probably on the level or
the police would pounce, but they do seem like a last—or
even later than that—resort.

A well-sponsored Los Angeles group gives cocktail parties
for "singles" at the Interlude on the Sunset Strip about once
a month. Admission is usually three dollars for girls, five
dollars for men. The one I went to was pleasant enough, very

chic and respectable but sterile. I tell you, a party without a single married man in it is kind of spooky . . . and dull!

Political Clubs

Pretty swinging usually. The fellows are there to get a candidate elected and you're there to pick one out for *you!* These partisan groups can be a lot of fun—even if they are over-distaffed—especially in a big election year. Don't wait for that, however. Call the Republican or Democratic head-quarters (both if you have no scruples) in your city and ask what organized group you might join.

Alcoholics Anonymous

I don't know her personally but a friend tells me a friend of *hers* plucked herself a steady beau and subsequent husband from A.A. She was about forty-three, had no drinking problem of her own, but since outsiders are permitted to attend A.A. meetings (presumably to do research or because they have a problem person at home), she wandered into the Beverly Hills Chapter meeting, sat next to a famous writer, and bagged him within the year. Seems almost ghoulish, doesn't it? I suppose a man *would* be very susceptible to a woman he met under these circumstances . . . one who understood and accepted his most serious problem.

If you are going to try this approach to men, I suggest you pick a wealthy chapter of A.A. Might as well start with a *solvent* problem child, like say someone with liquid assets.

Vacations

Vacations can produce marvelous men or be as fruitless as mud. The best rule seems to be not to plan to meet men, and then you may.

Louise and Paula gathered up their sultriest clothes and flew to Las Vegas not long ago, having heard that's where half the men in the world were. They were there all right, but the only ones who engaged them in conversation were the Western Airlines ticket agent and Dunes Hotel clerk. The others had brought their own girl or wife or something and showed more interest in how the poker chips were stacked than anything else.

Angie went to a dude ranch in Arizona the same weekend with no expectations whatever. She never even got to peek at her new Harpo Marx autobiography. The place was swarming with men.

Carol considers her trip to Europe something of a classic success in meeting men. With no more money than most people take trout fishing, Carol spent six glamorous, man-packed weeks in Europe.

She didn't know anyone there when she left home, but she had a system: she went armed with names and addresses of friends of friends of cousins of friends—all she could lay hands on and not necessarily men. (People are wonderful about sharing their European contacts; so will your friends be.)

Arriving in each city, Carol would drop a note to the "names" in that area (the postal system is marvelous—letters arrive almost as quickly as telegrams) saying whom she was a friend of, where she was staying, and that she'd love to say hello to them in person. Then she would go sightseeing, return to the hotel later to learn who'd called up. If respondents (nearly all respond because Europeans are polite) were tepid, she let them off the hook. But usually they invited her for tea, to an art exhibit, down to the country, to a christening or said they'd be by in fifteen minutes to buy her an apéritif. This all sounds like too much luck to be true, but this is a true story . . . because Carol *made* it come true.

One day she was sitting on the stone steps of a mansion in Grasse, France (the perfume belt), teeth chattering, stomach growling, wondering just what in hell she was doing there. She knew *what* she was doing. She was waiting for the divorced sister of a friend of a man in Paris, who was a friend of a girl in Detroit Carol had gone to college with, to come and take her off the doorstep and give her some sherry. But *why* was she doing it? Actually she knew *why* too. Because it was part of her credo . . . leave no stone step unsat upon in Grasse or anyplace else that might produce delightful memories.

This meeting turned out not to be memorable . . . it didn't produce any men . . . the sherry was only fair. But the same system produced half a dozen "true" romances . . . one with the manager of a cosmetics firm in London with whom she not only *could* have danced all night but *did* . . . another with a first-rate painter in Paris, an embassy member in Brussels, an importer in Rome and an American rancher in Naples. No action in Capri or Sorrento. Carol used the time for postcard writing, diet and sleep.

She is sure much of her luck came from traveling alone. It takes guts, though. Undoubtedly it can sometimes be risky. But it seems to work in Europe. People are charmed by a lone attractive girl and are inclined to take her to their bosom. Two or more girls, they figure, have each other and need no mothering.

According to Carol, all smart girls go to Florence . . . or any other Italian city. When an American girl steps out her hotel door, she is set upon by those gentle Florentine wolves. They are not ravening so much as they are genuinely crazy about American girls. Many of them are dreadfully poor. Men who look like sculptures are selling souvenir catalogues *outside* the galleries . . . or else selling that stuff they pour over ice that tastes like Lavoris would if you *drank* it. But they are charming and courtly and you can store up enough flirtatious looks and florid compliments to last into your dotage.

I don't have the exact odds for meeting men in all vacation lands. Friends tell me they have had fabulous luck in Honolulu and Mexico City (traveling alone or with friends), also Nassau and the Canadian Rockies.

Others say they never met a man.

The situation probably changes hourly.

In the United States it's best to take a playmate unless you're stopping with friends who can entertain you. You can check into Dallas, Miami or Palm Springs in your prettiest gown, and those cities, like all the others, have a way of not even looking up.

Planned vacation tours exclusively for bachelor girls and men sound intriguing. I don't know anyone who's been on one yet. Maybe they all got married and never came back!

Traveling on Business

This is terrific fun. Someone else pays. You usually travel first class. You have a mission in the city even if a man never casts his shadow on your Val-a-Pak. It's the old cry. Girls with something to do and places to go are better game than placid creatures who are kind of underfoot with their "Here I am, would you like to do something about me?" attitude.

Carol, alone in Europe, for example, used business as an excuse to meet and talk to people not otherwise approachable. Her business was the next thing to monkey business, of course. She made it up! In Paris, for example, she visited a reducing salon, also famous for bust development, and chatted with the hep manager about exporting the same techniques to the States. In Rome, she called on the American Consulate to ask if there were any Italian knitwear companies who wanted representation in the United States. (She knew how well the Marchesa di Grésy and others had done.)

You may think Carol sounds like a kook. Or one of those shot-out-of-a-cannon aggressive types. Actually she is a sensitive scaredy-cat but she does have a nimble brain and quiet, personal guts. In contacting Europeans on business she did nothing show-offy or that could really backfire. She just wanted to fill her trip with all kinds of people. Once home, she realized she was in no position to import bust development *or* Italian sweaters. She was much too busy managing the office of a C.P.A.

Louise, on legitimate business as a traveling fashion consultant for a bra and girdle company, spotted an elegant, steely man on the train down from New York. He was seated across the aisle with a beautiful older woman, slathered in mink from chin to hem (not the wet-rat kind but opulent, pulsating mink).

Louise listened to their conversation (finding it a damn sight better than her thoughts) while pretending to sleep. During the miles of eavesdropping she gleaned that the man was an attorney, probably single, as he never talked about his wife, and that he was a family friend of the woman's—she had five children. They had met on the train accidentally and she called him Marcus. As Louise feigned sleep, she even heard them talking about *her*. They thought she looked tired and seemed rather young and alone, and surmised she might be traveling on business. Louise, feeling a bit warped and woofed from days on the road, thought this couple as shimmery as Prince Ranier and his Grace—or at least Grace's mother.

At 30th Street Station in Philadelphia when she couldn't get a cab, the dapper attorney came to her rescue. His lady friend had departed. He said strangers in their city often hadn't the knack of hailing taxis and he offered to share his with her. Bliss, thought Louise. Pure bliss! To her consternation, however, as they sped along the cool Philadelphia streets that night, he didn't try to get better acquainted. He barely talked. The shared taxi was strictly an act of kindness. They reached his hotel first, he paid his fare, bid her good night and a pleasant stay in the city, and disappeared like Rumpelstiltskin.

Louise brooded about him for two days. He hadn't asked her name or where she was staying so he couldn't call *her*. And since he had evinced no red-hot interest, she couldn't call *him*. Besides, she didn't know his name . . . not *all* of it. Her fingernails down to the half-moon, she finally picked up the phone, dialed the Warwick, asked for the name of the attorney who lived there—Marcus somebody. The switchboard girl who could have been a pill but wasn't, supplied the name quickly. Apparently he was a favorite. Louise, still a pussyfooter, didn't ask to speak to him even then. On leaving the city, she sent him a little note saying she appreciated his kindness at the terminal, that she was traveling in the East on business, that if he were going to be in New York City—her next stop—during the next two weeks, she would adore to have a drink with him. She mentioned her hotel.

How much did she have to lose? If she never heard from him again, there was no person-to-person embarrassing rebuff. He did call her in New York, however, suggested that she hop on a train and come down to Philadelphia for dinner with him at his club, the Brookline.

Knowing she ought not to do anything of the kind and should insist on his coming up to see her, she got right on the train!

They had a marvelous evening. They danced. She met some of his friends, and discovered that he was extremely rich, played golf with Eisenhower and was about as good a marriage bet as Cardinal Spellman. This was the most bachelor bachelor she had ever met . . . a good gray bachelor with a permanent hotel suite for a home, his golf cronies, an occasional girl, and that was that. But it was a lovely petite adventure. Carol got back on the train at midnight to look for her next Philadelphia lawyer.

Sometimes you can embark on petite adventures on trips—business and pleasure—that you wouldn't quite have the nerve or impetus to embark on at home.

Planes, Trains, Boats

Planes can be great providers of men, for temporary use at least. It's blind luck when you sit next to a Possible, but remember . . . airline stewardesses have full date books and marry young. (Too bad we civilian girls can't prowl up and down the aisles and pop down next to the Most Likely too. Oh well!)

Whether the man is date material or not, he can make the trip go faster; and if your four-leaf clover is fresh, you may sit next to a downright fascinator. There's something sexy anyway about being sequestered 20,000 feet above the earth almost as close to a strange man as a banana to its skin, motors humming (yours and the plane's) and nothing to do but get to know each other. (Faster jets than ever are going to come along and louse up everything, of course. You won't even get to unfasten your seat belt, much less delve into your respective childhoods.)

I don't have to tell you to be sure you *sit* next to a man. If you see a lady bearing down and there are still empty seats in the plane, be ruthless. Pile your hatbox, coat and newspapers in the seat next to you and go to sleep immediately. Remove everything and wake up smiling when a man appears. Incidentally, if you should draw a real bore, male or female, simulated sleep may be the only defense. If they keep poking you in the ribs so you'll wake up and talk, which any self-respecting bore will do, yawn and say you think your infectious hepatitis might be coming back. That may send them to the lounge for the rest of the trip!

Trains were once almost as gay and romantic as *The Hucksters* said they were. The last one I rode still had vestigial traces of glory . . . the snowy-white napery, the marble washbowls, but no vestigial exciting men like Vic Norman in *The Hucksters*.

Travel on boats is strictly B.Y.O.M. (Bring Your Own Man). For every unattached male over nineteen, there are thirty-nine females to track him. Vivian managed to snare the purser on a recent cruise and was enormously pleased. They smooched in deck chairs, stole kisses by the lifeboats, shared midnight brandies and cigarettes in the bar . . . all very romantic. She made the mistake of dating him ashore a year later, at which time he showed her his color-slide collection. There she was . . . Kodachrome No. 73 in a brilliant collection of 104 Kodachromed ladies. (He had made thirty-one voyages since hers.) Talk about somebody with a good thing going!

On cross-country buses it's probably better if you don't talk to *anybody*. Just take Nembutal.

Driving in heavy traffic offers possibilities. Leave the window rolled down on your side and always look interestedly into the next car. It might be a Possible. If the snarl is severe enough, you may become acquainted after several shared stops at red lights.

Sales Conventions

The lid's off! Most manufacturers hold conventions. So do professional groups. If you can get assigned to work at one, you're apt to have fun galore.

Polly has attended four for her sweater company and reports it's like being the only sorority girl on fraternity row on a Saturday night. I think she has become the unofficial convention sweetheart. This is a serious sort of convention— her company's sixty salesmen, from all parts of the country, some without their wives, some single or *permanently* free of wives, are there to work, but they also have time for fun and games and visits to the city's best night spots. Polly has heard Mort Sahl fourteen times.

See if you can track down a convention!

Business Banquets, Luncheons

There they are again . . . men! . . . Row upon row. It would seem that all you need to do to corner a year's supply is sweep into the hotel dining room and scoop them up.

Not so! A man at a business luncheon is in one of his male moods and can make you feel as *de trop* as a dowager in the men's locker room.

"Okay," they challenge you across their parsleyed potatoes and wilted lettuce, "you're here in your crazy hat, but leave us not forget we men run things and this is a business meeting." Your feminine wiles will have all the potency of salted garden snails.

If the luncheon concerns you as a business woman—perhaps someone from your company is speaking—go anyway, and to banquets too. It's a good way to permeate a man's consciousness so that when he meets you under more convivial circumstances you won't have to start from scratch.

The Man Next Door

Excellent! Talk about being in the right spot to wait out his other romances! If he doesn't get sick and tired of your watchful eye at the front-door aperture or your listening ears against his walls, or move from the neighborhood *prematurely*, he's sure to succumb to your blandishments finally . . . hot fudge brownies on a plate when he's starving but too dumb to fix breakfast . . . martinis in a pitcher to celebrate the management's painting his kitchen. Don't go *too* far with the culinary bit. I know one young lady who is virtually running a free cafeteria for a building crew. It started when they came over, pitifully, to borrow a peanut-butter sandwich, and the situation worsened steadily. Remember, you deserve spoiling too.

Neighbors make good extra men at parties—and competent bartenders too.

Shopping in Men's Departments

Rarely will you meet your love, or even a date for Sunday brunch, among the briar pipes and Harris tweeds. Another place, true, where the men *are* but alas, not adventurous ones. Those who spend their lives shuttling between inventory and stock control are usually married and security-minded.

Shopping for tie racks and other male accessories, however, is a good way to *practice your femininity*. Donna says a sort of gracious-lady attitude sweeps over her in men's departments as she trustingly asks whether Oxford is as nice to be next to as broadcloth. I wouldn't want it back but this must be how it was in the Edwardian era when men were all-wise and women were all wiles. I must say the staff at Brooks Brothers, Los Angeles, can make you feel like a grand duchess pondering some sartorial tidbit for the duke. They're the *most,* and adorable.

Brief Interludes

Waiting for the bus, buying a magazine, guiding your groceries through the checkout line, borrowing books from the library, rounding a corner with your arms full of packages and crashing into a divine overcoated thing are all ways that movie heroines meet princes traveling incognito. But no ordinary girl can devastate a prince or anybody else that fast, or even have him asking where she works. If he *should* ask, she ought to be suspicious because he'll probably try to sell her insurance.

There are of course even more dramatic crash programs. Magda Lupescu bagged King Carol of Rumania by throwing herself in front of his Rolls-Royce as he was returning from a party. Cars were slower in those days. You and I would run the risk of being halved. If we weren't, who wants to be treated like rare old Napoleon brandy just to keep us from suing?

Strangers Across a Crowded Room

You've got to be a beauty contest winner before anybody is going to fall flat on his face over you across a theatre lobby

or an intersection. However, if you keep seeing the same attractive stranger in more or less the same place every day—
say, where you eat lunch—you may eventually start chatting
and a nice friendship will develop.

Riding up or down the elevator with a man you don't know
but would like to, may work out eventually. This can happen
in your apartment or office building. Elevators have the same
coziness of airplanes, but you don't have as long to work. Be
sure you smell nice on these occasions and are charm itself
to the elevator operator. And in the new automatic express
elevators your chances are even better.

Church

Friends tell me it offers spiritual benefits, but few men.

Man Bait

Let's assume you're in one of the places where the men
are. You're sweet and scrubbed, groomed and coifed, per-
fumed and palpitating . . . but when it comes to making an
overt move, you have all the aplomb of Molly Cottontail
gazing into the eyes of a bloodhound.

This book is written on the premise that you, like me, are
warm and friendly on the inside but outwardly a pitiful,
cowering coward. You may even cling wantonly to the dream
of the days when men did the chasing!

It's okay. You don't have to open a single conversation if
you don't want to. You'll flunk anyway if the act renders you
such a shambles you can't get your breath for five minutes.

There are perfectly good ways of making it easy for a man
to talk to *you* which he's probably dying to do but is merely
shy. (Isn't it embarrassing? That men are shy too!) The thing
to do is give him something to start a conversation *about*.

Wear a lapel pin with a message printed on it. I'm serious about this. I have three. One says, "I have gray hair, brown eyes and a black heart," and has always been a smash hit. Another carries the *Ladies' Home Journal* slogan, "Never underestimate the power of a woman." Another, which I thought very clever at the time though nobody gets it, and I'm not sure I do either, says, "Fight that will power."

Once people see writing on you, they won't rest until they've read it. Total strangers will put on glasses to make the grade, and after that, they almost have to say *something* to you not to be rude.

Any silversmith in town can make up your favorite slogans, or you can write to Allan Adler, 8626 Sunset Boulevard, Los Angeles, who made my pins. They are of heavy wrought silver, cost about $18 apiece (well worth it) and are about the size of a silver dollar. You make up your own messages.

A loaded charm bracelet is a conversation piece. By the time you've explained what all the charms represent, you're on friendly enough terms to exchange Christmas cards.

Any unusual jewelry is a come-on, but it should be beautiful or you'll look too Ubangi. A huge but delicate cameo is a crowd-pleaser. So are garnets like a grape cluster—if you have garnet money.

Carry a controversial book at all times—like Karl Marx' *Das Kapital* or *Lady Chatterley's Lover*. It's a perfectly simple way of saying, "I'm open to conversation," without having to start one.

Gloria has been tugging around Rupert Brooke poetry for years. It started because she genuinely liked Rupert Brooke. We *know* what her motives are now. Apparently girls who read poetry are considered very romantic and approachable.

When you beach, pool or lakeside it, have the maddest beach towel you can lay hands on. One with a checkerboard background, for example, actually invites a game. (Never mind that you've never mastered the jump play—just bring the checkers!) Other towel charmers I remember are Catalina's giant Model T Ford in red, gold and black; a gingerbread man; a friendly, whiskered lion; and dozens of others. The towels cost three to six dollars and have a practical dry-off side too.

Play solitaire on your towel. Someone may come over to make it gin.

Have a memorable beach hat or two. Ditto a crazy ski cap if you ski.

Drive a funny car . . . though not so funny it won't *run!* A really crazy old car is more interesting than a shiny new one. Donna piloted a 1940 Buick station wagon around as late as 1956 with the name "Ferny Briar" painted on its side. There was no Ferny Briar, nor ever had been, nor was there another car like that one in North America. Its real wood sides had long since become as wormy as driftwood and the roof leaked so badly that Donna used to drive about town with an umbrella open inside the car. (How about *that* for starting conversations . . . if not with you, *about* you.) But everybody knew Ferny Briar and accorded it special attention . . . Donna too!

Paint your car hot orange . . . or shocking pink.

Ride a bicycle to work. Or a Vespa. Be the only girl who walks while everybody else rides.

If you must, though I wouldn't recommend it, you can bump into the man who is bringing a sherry flip from the bar to his girl. She will leave while you are mopping him off, and the least you can do is buy him a get-acquainted drink!

CHAPTER 4

HOW TO BE SEXY

Now we know who the men are and where they are, and we've planted ourselves squarely in their paths. Scented and smiling, with charm bracelets dangling, we've even invited them to start a conversation. But now with a longing like red blood cells for oxygen, we yearn to exude that old black magic which will have them on the ropes.

Have you got it? Can you get it? Are you sexy? Let's see. What *is* a sexy woman?

Very simple. She is a woman who enjoys sex.

Being sexy means that you accept yourself as a woman . . . with all the functions of a woman. You like to make love, have babies, nurse them and mother them (or think you would). Being sexy means that you accept all the parts of your body as worthy and lovable . . . your reproductive organs, your breasts, your alimentary tract. You even welcome menstruation as the abiding proof of your fertility.

A woman who feels all this is sexy. She wears it like perfume. It doesn't matter how remote she is from the salons of Fifth Avenue and Wilshire Boulevard or whether she knows what *Playboy* magazine is all about. She's got smell No. 5, which is even better than Chanel of the same denomination.

The Australian sheepherder's wife in the movie *The Sundowners* (played stunningly by Deborah Kerr) had it.

"Older women" often have it.

So if you think only the *jeunes filles,* the voluptuous or sleek-cat creatures are the sexy ones, you have been living in the rumble seat of an Essex roadster the past twenty-five years.

Gorgeousness has little to do with sexuality either. (And mark this as one of my rare, unbiased appraisals of the advantages of beautiful women over plain ones!) The physiologically sexy woman, be she droop-shouldered, flat-chested, horse-faced or bone-headed, will find somebody to be sexy with. She's got it. He'll find it.

Once Upon a Time

Why are some women sexier than others?

Well, the truth is everybody starts out sexy . . . or with terrific potential. A sixteen-month-old baby girl is the prototype of sexiness. Watch her play peekaboo, wiggle her lovely fanny or turn to give you a last melting look before wriggling off to bed. Furthermore, she likes her body. It feels good when she's dried off with a terry towel. At night she may fall asleep across her doll because that feels good too.

She will be sexy all her life if nobody interferes.

Unfortunately, in our society somebody nearly always interferes!

When she touches herself with pleasure and curiosity, her

mother will take her hand away and say, "Naughty!" When she expels squashy brown cones not unlike the modeling clay she likes to play with, her mother will put over the idea they are icky, dirty . . . to be flushed away quickly. If the child isn't dim-witted, she figures out that where the cones came from is dirty too.

At six, when the little girl asks a few perfectly reasonable questions like how did she get here, and how come her little brother has more interesting things on his front than she, her mother will give her the halibut-eye and a phony answer or worse, pretend she didn't hear the questions and hustle her out to play. The little girl concludes there is something mighty funny about baby production and little brothers' anatomies too.

Even if enlightened parents answer this little girl's questions in a direct, factual way (I know one fortunate little boy whose parents told him the facts of life so satisfactorily, he said in the next breath, "Now tell me how they make peanut butter."), she will still learn to equate sex with dirtiness from her playmates, her playmates' parents, her teachers and other benighted adults.

All her growing-up years she will be exhorted to keep her dress down, her knees crossed, her thoughts pure, never to let anybody touch her *there;* never, never to touch herself, and to protect that part of her body as though it were precious jade . . . or is it more like guarding a Mongolian idiot— the kind relatives used to hide in the attic when company came?

One fine day—maybe on her wedding night but probably sooner—she will want to unlock her chastity belt and she won't be able to find the key. People have been hiding the key from her since she was a tiny baby.

A few girls, mercifully, manage to survive this cultural

blight and come through with most of their sexuality intact. Certainly parental education along these lines is growing more enlightened.

How About You?

How many "naturally" sexy women are there? Are you one?

Kinsey says one-third of American women achieve orgasm most of the time. They're sexy (in the context we're talking about). One-third rarely achieve it. They aren't (again in this context). And one-third achieve orgasm about half the time. Are they sexy? Perhaps.

A single woman in many instances doesn't have a regular sex life (again according to Kinsey; she may be perfectly capable of enjoying one, but long lapses occur between involvements). Therefore she can't measure her sexuality as a married woman can.

If you feel you aren't "naturally" sexy—sexy on the *inside* —it's possibly because you haven't had a real opportunity to find out. You may still be a virgin. Or you may have been paired with the wrong man. Kinsey (and I really did read another book once) says nearly everybody in our culture is paired incorrectly. Ideally, seventeen-year-old boys and thirty-five-year-old women would be teamed, and thirty-five-year-old men and seventeen-year-old girls. Thus people at the peak of their sexual powers would be together and so would those in the beginning stage and decline of theirs.

If you can't match the quantitative enjoyment of a man, that doesn't mean you're a second-class participant. Men usually arrive at maturity less deadened sexually than girls and so may achieve more climaxes. They weren't as often admonished to keep their dresses down and their knees together! Also, men's sex equipment being more in the open, they were apt to experience a perfectly happy sexual climax just by rubbing against bed sheets in their sleep. Not much scolding parents can do about *that*. And having found out how wonderful an experience it was, they were freer to seek it again consciously than a totally unawakened girl.

In determining sexuality we must remember too that women differ in their capacities and it has nothing to do with how much quashing their sexual curiosity got in girlhood. Some appetites crave three hot fudge sundaes at one serving. Others are happy and sated with one.

A woman who even occasionally enjoys an orgasm from the roots of her hair to the tips of her toes is sexy. And remember we're talking about sexy only in this one sense—in terms of being sexy within yourself . . . able to enjoy sex.

Why Be Sexy If You're Single?

Are you totally, horribly, hideously, irrevocably offended by this whole discussion of sex? Do you feel it is a subject better left for married girls to probe? If so, by all means skip this chapter! Or skip the whole book! It is written for girls who may not marry but who are not necessarily planning to join a nunnery. It is also for girls nearing thirty or beyond. If you are as virginal as a Sunkist orange and plan to stay so, good for you! That's your affair (oh dear, what have I said *now?*). You can still tell whether you're sexy by how tough a struggle it is to control your desire, or whether you gratefully use "singleness" as an excuse not to give in.

Most of the single women I've known well in the last twenty years have experienced sex gratification with someone at some time, if only with the man they later married. And they were concerned with their own enjoyment or lack of it for two reasons: They instinctively knew that a girl with a "natural" predilection toward sex is sexy. They also figured as long as they were involved in an affair, they deserved some of the joys as well as most of the headaches.

But—I must point out again—this is a one-woman survey. I don't know whether my friends are typical (or whether we're still friends after the way I'm using them!). They were all working girls. They all live in a big city. They are above average in brain power.

My thought would be that no matter how unassailable your virginity or unattainable your charms, most girls want to *appear* to be sexy. Sex is a powerful weapon for a single woman in getting what she wants from life, i.e., a husband or steady male companionship. Sex is a more important weapon to her than to a married woman who has other things going for her—like the law! And other fields in which to prove herself . . . housework, bookkeeping, nursing, mending dishwashers, motherhood. A smart single woman doesn't prove herself in *any* of these fields before marriage. She doesn't have to prove herself in sex either. But she should act as though she *could* if she wanted to.

A married woman who uses sex as a weapon is being a kind of rat. By the traditional convenants of marriage she is supposed to sleep with her husband in return for his giving her his name, a home, an income, and a father for her children. If she blackmails him for dining-room chairs by withholding her body, he has every justification for losing the rent money at poker. A single woman who doesn't deny her body regularly and often to get what she wants, i.e., married or more equitable treatment from her boy friend, is an idiot.

We have been discussing one kind of sexiness . . . the most authentic kind . . . the kind which is self-generated.

If you are pretty certain you aren't sexy by this particular definition, what can you do?

You can wait until you are married and work it out then. That is a popular solution and has efficacy. Why solve your problems with somebody you won't have around permanently? On the other hand, why jeopardize the pleasure of your early married years by letting your fears deepen and set? And what if you don't marry?

No one is suggesting that you go on the prowl for a perfect bed mate. That is the nymphomaniac's unfortunate way. Far from being the sexpot many people think she is, having fun fun fun, she is frigid, technically. Instead of eschewing sex entirely like many psychosexually impaired people, and hiding in the basement, she is on a frantic search for the one penis that can unlock her sexuality. From man to man to man she goes with her burning but unspoken question, "Can *you* help me feel something?" And all the time the key to her sexuality is within herself. Only *she* can unlock it ⋮ . . . with *qualified* help.

The "right" man does sometimes help a "cold" girl realize her sexual potential, but this compassionate assist comes more often in marriage than outside. If a husband doesn't get to a mutually enjoyable level with his wife, she may cut him off without any sex at all. He'd better help her like it. If a single woman isn't having a good time in bed, her partner would just as soon not know about it! And he really isn't suited to help with her emotional problems anyway, since he is maybe her worst one!

It might be supposed there is more frigidity in single women because of their perpetual anxiety about public—and divine—disapproval of their so-called promiscuity. Actually a single girl can have enough anxiety to fill Grand Canyon, and it won't diminish her sexuality if she has it. A happy marriage may give her the confidence to be sexy without guilt. No. I won't even go that far! A guilt-ridden participator is guilt-ridden, wed or not.

If your problem is deep-rooted; if you find sex absolutely abhorrent, or even if you don't really "mind" it but nothing nice ever happens to you, the most practical "cures" are effected through psychiatry. It's a presumptuous thing to tell anyone to go get a psychiatrist—like go get religion! And it's expensive. I only suggest it because getting people turned on who were turned off is one area in which psychiatrists have a long record of achievement. Remember, frigidity isn't a physical disability. It's a curable state of mind. Unfortunately, however, you can read about your problem and gain great intellectual insight like mad and still not be able to slay your fear-dragon without professional help.

Is She or Isn't She?

Now we come to a paradox. A woman can be sexy and *not* be sexy. She can have a patina of sexiness and be as cold as ice! Some of the coldest girls in history have been the most fatally fascinating. George Sand (Aurore Dupin), the mistress of more than one famous man, said her body felt like a "marble envelope." One of the great movie-star courtesans of our time, who has had prime ministers deserting their posts and oil tycoons drowning themselves in their own oil, is virtually "sexless" by her own admission to friends. Prostitutes rarely enjoy their work. According to medical surveys, they are nearly all frigid, at least with "clients."

How can it be that a totally unfeeling woman can attract so madly, almost as inexorably as a genuinely feeling one? Because she can put on a sexy act, and if her zeal is great enough and her act polished enough, no one will ever know she isn't a genuine, 102 per cent, dyed-in-the-wool sexpot.

After all, most of the men a girl attracts she never sleeps with, and if she does, her "authenticity" is seldom doubted anyway. (This act is harder to maintain in marriage where she may get bored playing Tondelayo the jungle princess every night and finally confess her perjury.)

Until then, what a playmate the pseudo-wildcat is! She doesn't worry one moment whether or not *she's* having fun because she *never* has any anyway, but she never lets on. She will spend the entire evening in selfless concentration doing what makes a man happy. She either doesn't know what she is missing or is too shy, yes shy—too unsure of herself and anxious to please, to demand equal rights. What man wouldn't like this except the most perceptive and emotionally mature man?

As for being genuinely oversexed, I don't think there is such a thing. Although in our society it's considered slightly immoral to enjoy oneself too often or too much in bed, calling someone oversexed would be to describe her as overendowed with the life force—to say that she was overliving. I imagine the few people actually fortunate enough to be "oversexed" (not nymphomaniacs or Don Juans because their interest is compulsive) simply make love in quiet and peace and never tell anybody. Those who brag are in doubt about their own powers.

To sum up. One way to be sexy is to be sexy inside yourself. You will attract like a magnet. We are not talking about men to marry you but *men* . . . as many as you want in this capacity.

More Black Magic

Another way to be "genuinely" sexy, though not recommended, is to be an actress.

And still another method by which women attract men is that phenomenon called "chemistry" . . . the inexplicable affinity of one person for another. Only is it really so inexplicable? The fascination might better be defined as subconscious preselection. (I wish Havelock Ellis or somebody were here to help!) One man is unerringly drawn to plump, buxom girls because his mother was one and for years she was the sex sun of his galaxy. Another man likes skinny, caved-in girls because that's how *his* mother was. Just as often the guy with the plump mama likes skinnies and the other guy likes fatties because that's how their mothers *weren't*. A man may gravitate to icy angels because his first love was the five-year-old cool-as-ice angel next door. I know a man who traces his predilection for pale, thin girls back to a science teacher who haunted his dreams with her skimpy wrists and paper-white skin.

A girl can preselect too. You may like men who are like your father, or not *anything* like your father, like the hero of a "good" book or a "bad" book. You may unconsciously search for a man who treats you rough because he coincides with your early indoctrination into sex, i.e., sex is dirty, therefore you can only enjoy it with a man who isn't nice. (Havelock, for God's sake, where *are* you?)

I know a girl who was seduced by her uncle at age ten (he was only fourteen); though it was a shocking experience and he was packed off to military school, she now goes only for men who look and act like him.

When you meet the man who fulfills your preselected needs and you his, it's no wonder a giant staple remover couldn't get the two of you apart!

All cultures have a kind of composite girl, or girls, whom they consider sexy. Ours currently are Brigitte Bardot, Elizabeth Taylor and Marilyn Monroe. In your father's time they were Clara Bow, Gloria Swanson and Theda Bara. In his father's time she was Lillian Russell.

These "ideal" girls vary not only from era to era but country to country, just as with other tastes. The British and Germans abhor cars with chrome. For Americans, the chromier the better. In the Middle East in our time a king seeking a new queen picked a girl our guys considered thirty pounds overweight. In French Equatorial Africa where bulbous bosoms earn few green stamps, the really desirable chicks have plates in their lips. This, like the ancient custom of foot-binding in China, makes the girl feminine and helpless, and she can't run away. In the case of the dish-lipped lady, she can't even feed herself.

Although there is much wailing at the wall among us who do not fit the current masculine ideal of female pulchritude (Joan wishes she'd lived in Pericles' time when big bulking girls were the rage), fortunately a man's individual pre-selection will generally supersede the national favorite. Also, the girl he enjoys in his fantasies may not be the one he woos and weds or even beds. He prefers somebody he can be comfortable with and maybe even feel superior to. Men!

The Better To Please Him

Besides a more or less general agreement on the current national best-sellers in female form, certain trappings are often agreed on as girl-enhancing for a particular period. These too differ madly from place to place and time to time, but a smart woman in any culture packages herself to please her particular clientele. This is something you *can* do, sexy on the inside or not.

Many of these personal adornments and attitudes are dictates of the *haute couture*. And oh, how men do scream about fashion! At this writing they're in a snit over the relaxed waist and low-heeled squared-off shoes. I'm sure they were just as teed-off about powdered wigs, hobble skirts, bee-stung lips and padded shoulders. Or were they? It's a funny thing. The guy who says, "Honey, I'm sure glad *you* don't paint your fingernails or wear all that goo on your mouth or go around in those crazy-looking dresses," is the guy who, at a party, deposits his wife at the first potted palm to chase the girl with the reddest lips, the shimmeriest fingertips and a crazy dress with no waist at *all*.

Obviously these accessories haven't anything to do with our intrinsic worth as women or our intrinsic sexiness. If I've said it once, I've said it a dozen times I guess. A sexy woman is sexy regardless of her last year's permanent wave and round-toed shoes. A good woman, a dear woman, is that to the core.

Maybe we can compare sex to food. Dover sole is Dover sole and just as nourishing fried in corn oil and served on cracked china. But how much more enticing slathered with toasted almonds and beckoning from Wedgwood.

The sheer stocking, the twenty-four-inch waist, the smoldering look have nothing to do with successful mating or procreating, but they say to a man, "I'm with it. I have tried to make myself beautiful for you. I've gone to a lot of trouble because I think you're worth it and I like myself. I want you to notice me and want me."

What if certain insecure men and women make almost too much of an effort toward sartorial splendor? Is that less attractive than if they said the hell with it and never brushed their teeth or combed their hair?

Does all this attention to "sexy detail" pay off? I'll say it does! Here is a true story:

An ex-roommate of mine was nutty about an executive in

her firm. She went absolutely ape the day he started to work there and she launched a campaign to get him. (We never knew why exactly. He had tiny little hands and a tiny little head, and many people thought a tiny little brain. But he was Madge's sunshine and she wanted him to shine on *her* alone.) In four weeks she had husked seventeen pounds from her five-foot-two frame to make her large bust really amount to something. She made up her face—never a pretty face— with the infinite care of a Geisha. She plowed every sou into the silkiest, witchiest dresses. And from someplace she got the guts simply to "put on" all the sexy airs she had ever seen a sexy girl wear. She worked like a Trojan to learn and perfect her art. When some guy called her on the phone, her other roommate and I used to shut ourselves up in the kitchen where the syrup at least had passed the Pure Food and Drug Act. You wouldn't *believe* a man could absorb so much sugar!

It was the most amazing metamorphosis I have ever seen. And her other roommate, now living in New York, would swear to this too. She went sexy to the last detail. When we sent her off to work in the morning, cleavage cleaving, perfume wafting therefrom, we feared for the sanity of the men in the office, to say nothing of the work load.

And did Madge get her man? No. Not ever. She just wasn't for him, I guess. But she had other guys dropping like yellow-fever victims. Perhaps because she thought she was only interested in one particular man, to others her sexiness had a kind of maddening insouciance about it. Anyhow it felled them.

Madge married within the year. It was inevitable. And I'm sure she forgot old pinhead. But this was a case of a mouse (big bosoms to the contrary notwithstanding) wanting to be sexy . . . willing it. She never had it but she got it . . . by adopting sexy attitudes and trappings.

How To Be Sexy

Outside of some mildly eccentric fellows who are sexually aroused only by girls who wear hobnail boots and paperclip necklaces (old pinhead may have been one of them), or union suits plastered with chicken feathers, I think we can nearly all agree on what attitudes and accessories are sexy—and what aren't—in our time. Bear in mind you are sure to know a girl who does all the don'ts and none of the do's and has more beaux than a Greyhound bus can load, as well as other girls who do the do's and don't the don'ts and whose loneliness is heart-rending!

Clean hair is sexy. Lots of hair is sexy too.

Skimpy little hair styles and hair under your arms, on your legs and around your nipples, isn't.

Lovely lingerie is sexy. Carol's beautiful half slips (she has them in ten colors) always peek-a-boo a bit beneath her short sheath skirts when she sits down. Paula wears creamy beige silk shirts, not thin enough to see her bra straps or elastic through, but thin enough to show the tracery of lace bra cups. Both girls are perfect ladies with a sexth sense about clothes!

Girdles are not sexy. I know they are a necessary retaining wall against wavy buttocks but they are *not* magnetic.

Not sexy either are: food particles between your teeth, baggy stockings, bitten fingernails, borrowing money (very unsexy), flesh not secured firmly to the bone, and jitters (the dart-around, jerk-about kind that makes people feel *sand-papered!*).

Being able to sit very still is sexy.

Smiles are sexy.

It is unsexy to talk about members of your family and how

cute or how awful they are. Or about your boss a lot—he's another man . . . a rival.

Talking all the time about *anything* is unsexy. Sphinxes and Mona Lisas knew what they were doing!

Gossip—surprise, surprise—is not unsexy! How can you not discuss your friends when they are the most fascinating creatures on earth? Try not to say anything you promised you wouldn't; and gossip, don't lampoon. Be just a teensy bit careful too about saying anything derogatory of a girl your guy has been dating.

Being seen without your make-up by somebody who always sees you in it can be sexy provided it isn't in public and your hair is shiny bright. A friend of mine who visited Marlene Dietrich in her Hollywood Château Marmont apartment on business said he couldn't remember what he was there for. Marlene was the absolute end in a black hostess thing and schoolgirl-scrubbed face.

Being seen in bed is sexy—I mean times when you have no intention of letting anybody get in with you. A man once told me his secretary, a rather nondescript little creature, had stayed overnight at his house after they worked late. His wife was present all evening. The next morning when he went to her room to wake her (his wife slept late), he also awakened an almost uncontrollable urge to pile into bed with her. The sight of this little waif, hair streaming out across the pillow, asleep in one of *his* beds was enough to convince him they'd better work at the office hereafter.

Clothes that fit are sexy. Shoulder seams at the shoulder. Waistlines at the waist (unless it's against the law that year). I think more people buy things too sloppy than too small, on the theory they're going to grow another foot or that a size 16 gives you a lot for your money.

Skin-tight skirts and sweaters are sexy, but wearing them is like trying to meet men in a bar. If the sweater and skirt are *that* tight, a man figures you must want action badly and you are distress—you know—merchandise.

A black dress is sexy. *The* black dress. The dress you paid more for than you should but every time you wear it you feel bitchy and beautiful. Incidentally, if you have bony shoulders and a small bust and decolleté styles are not for you (or even if your shoulders and bust are fine), a cocktail dress with a solid bodice but long chiffon sleeves and throat part is infinitely alluring. The crepe part comes up to the top of your bosom and the chiffon fits like skin above that and forms the sleeves.

Perfume is sexy and, unfortunately, the costlier the perfume, usually the sexier! Any good French perfume wafting from a pretty girl's bosom is about the nicest thing that can happen to air! Three inexpensive perfumes I've found that smell nice are Max Factor's Hypnotique, Revlon's Intimate and Fabergé's Aphrodisia. (Of course there are many more.) Douse the perfume on cotton, put another piece of dry cotton in front of it and tuck it inside your bra. Use the same cotton again and again to build up a residue of scent. Remember, if *you* can't smell it, probably *he* can't smell it either so you're being wastefully stingy.

Good health is sexy. Tired girls are tiring! Enough energy to dance till dawn when other girl-blossoms are losing their petals is a great plus. I know a man who says he married his wife because she had so much vitality and enthusiasm. He never says enthusiasm for *what,* but apparently for *everything.*

Being delighted to be called on the telephone is sexy (unless it's four o'clock in the morning, in which case hang up, put the phone in the icebox and toddle back to bed).

Some girls find it easier to be sexy and oomphy on the telephone than in person. They don't have to worry about how they look and can depend altogether on how they sound.

Light up when a guy calls. It isn't going to establish you as overeager Edith. I'm not even for being cool to a man who has recently been a swine in the way he has treated you (if it's somebody you adore!). You'll have the grand showdown later. Meanwhile don't dissipate its impact with petty carping.

About your telephone voice . . . or any-other-time voice, it's a tough assignment to change its timbre, but movie stars have sometimes lowered theirs a whole register. Lauren Bacall has, I believe. Listen to voices in movies. Most of them were willed into being by practice, practice, practice. If you squeak or squawk, are thin or reedy (and only dogs can hear you in your upper register) or are decidedly nasal, consider a voice revise. (A high school dramatics teacher in your town with a great deal of savvy about these things could help you.) If you don't *know* how you sound—and most people don't, record your voice on tape. Ask someone you trust to tell you honestly. Not your family—they probably sound just like you do. A dictaphone machine will give you the good or bad news. If a test proves nothing really annoying about your voice, leave it alone (but get right to work on your fanny-paring exercises!). But if you have one of those voices that make people wish they or *you* were in the next county, *do* something. You would about bad breath, wouldn't you?

A girl I know did something. A switchboard operator changed her squeaky soprano into such a sexy contralto that her trunk lines were busy all day long with people calling up just to hear her say hello. (This is a true story; she was a kind of legend in Beverly Hills.) The callers, irresistibly drawn, would come in to see her too. Pauline was just a fraction as sexy-looking as her voice sounded, but she had beautiful skin and great legs to go with that voice! Fellows figured, anybody who cared enough to sound that seductive must have some other good points as well.

Liking men is sexy. It is by and large just about the sexiest thing you can do. But I mean really liking, not just pretending. And there is quite a lot more to it than simply wagging your tail every time a man pats you on the head. You must wag your tail, of course—his collie dog does *that* much—but there are about five thousand more aggressive ways to demonstrate liking, none of which is dashing along to the nearest motel. You must spend time plotting how to make him happier. Not just him . . . *them!*

Agnes, one of the most successful man-likers I know, holds open house in her minuscule office for any male co-worker's (or female co-worker's, for that matter) birthday. She serves jelly doughnuts and hot-plate coffee. When she hears some guy is interested in ophthalmology, she brings in a book for him. She's even been known to sew a button on a coat and remove a splinter. Sounds like good old Agnes, doesn't she? —den mother to the office. You should see good old Agnes— if you can get past the men blocking the doorway!

If you can be friendly and helpful without asking anything in return, you are well on the way to surrounding yourself with men. But suppose you're nice to a guy, lighting up and sewing on buttons and all that and one day you say to yourself, enough is enough, and you pop the question. Will he be your date for a cocktail party Saturday night? No, he says. Just plain no. Hate, hate! Kill. Kill. Kill! A pox on him and everybody under his zodiac sign! Do you know what that means? It means you didn't really like him for himself in the first place but were just being friendly because you *wanted* something. How do you feel when he's nice to you only because he wants to sleep with you—or needs a cosigner at the bank?

Not all men see you as date material. The most voluptuous chorus girl may be anathema to the chap who is only *en rapport* with Vassar girls.

Granted, it *is* harder to like men generously and selflessly when you're single. They are, after all, the enemy! One kindly smile from you, they think you're sweet on them. It's true, there has to be quite a lot of unrequited liking on your part for a while, but then men stop being suspicious and allow you to collect them as sons and lovers.

The Lively Art of Flirting

A sexy girl knows how to flirt. The deep-down sexy one may not flirt as much as the pseudo-sexy one, but it's handy knowledge.

Maybe you think you can't flirt. You think it means dropping your hanky or giving a long, slow wink, followed by a sideward jerk of the head to indicate "Meetcha out in the hall, honey."

Flirting is mostly just looking. Ready for a quick flirting lesson?

Select a man at a nearby restaurant table. (Somebody in the dentist's anteroom will do just as well. Place isn't important.) Spotted him? Look straight into his eyes, deep and searchingly, then lower your gaze. Go back to your companions or magazine. Now look at him again the same way . . . steadfastly, questioningly. Then drop your eyes. Do it three times and you're a flirt! (P.S.—you will have made him very happy.)

Want to flirt some more?

A man is talking to you, nothing very personal. Look into his eyes as though tomorrow's daily double winners were there. Never let your eyes leave his. Concentrate on his left eye . . . then the right . . . now deep into both. Smooth operators never take their eyes off a man even when a waiter spills a tray of drinks. This look has been referred to rather disdainfully as "hanging on his every word." It was good in your grandmother's day and it's still a powerhouse! (Is there any comparison between *this* and gazing all around the room to see if anybody good just came in?) Laura says a man she knows finds this look absolutely aphrodisiac. Looked at so, a man usually stops whatever he is saying and kisses the girl!

Never interrupt a man when he is telling you a story. Not for all the rugs in Persia. This is a terrible habit of girls, even with other girls. For example: Your date is recalling the day a woman fell out of the bleachers at a ball game. "It was last September at the Forty-Niners–Bears game," he says. "John Stromberger and Sam Hanks were with me and we noticed this woman. . . ." You barge in, "Oh, Sam Hanks, isn't he a madman? I went to grammar school with him. His sister married my cousin and their kids all look just like cret—" Your storyteller doesn't want to discuss Sam Hanks *or* your cousin's kids. He was telling you a *story*. You've interrupted him and spoiled his image of himself as a raconteur. It only took a second and you meant no harm, but save your comments till the finish.

The flirt reacts. She laughs at the jokes, clucks at the sad parts, applauds bravery. I really think it gets easier to flirt as you get older because you learn to listen to any man, employing the same charm and rapt attention you once reserved for seven-year-olds.

The Charmer

Being sexy is being charming, and if you can sum up what charm is, I think it's *total awareness*. A charmer has her antenna up and valves open at all times. With sensitive radar she detects what the other person wants to hear and says it. And she senses what he doesn't want to hear and refrains from saying *it*. Charming people, either men or women, are usually warm-blooded, affectionate and compassionate, but they are also *thinking ahead all the time*.

I had lunch the other day with a charmer, accompanied by her mother. Two of the girls in the party had babbled ten minutes or so about their new office manager whom the mother didn't know. Presently the charmer said, "You know, Mother, he's kind of like Joe Winslow at the bank . . . sort of Prussian." Mother was back in the conversation.

This particular charmer, so accomplished she should package it, puts everything in terms of *you*. "You would have loved it." "You would have fainted." In describing a gown she saw at the opera she says it was a little deeper than your red velvet coat. She remembers what you told her last time and asks questions *this* time. It's appalling the things people can forget you told them (like your left fender had just been bashed in and your insurance has expired) and never ask you about it in subsequent conversations.

The charmer, like the flirt (she's the same person), reacts to what you say. And will give you all afternoon to say it. She laughs. She gasps. She's vexed for you, glad for you, and she isn't a phony. If you ask her advice she will try to answer honestly.

Second only to that of the President of the United States, the state of your health is important to her. "Did your fingernails ever stop breaking off to the quick?" she asks. Or, "You were coming down with the flu. Are you better today?" Mother care like that. What adult can't stand some babying still?

A charmer tells you when people have said something nice about you, and never tells you when they haven't. She is reliably friendly, doesn't blow hot or cold. Most charmers are as popular with women as with men because from this person you get love—not trouble.

The Female Female

As for lessons in how to be more feminine, femininity is a matter of accepting yourself as a woman. We're back to that again! You can look like a Dresden doll and still hate men. That isn't being feminine. You can have halfback shoulders and *adore* men. That's feminine!

Some girls "hate" men because they secretly envy their "superior advantages," their jobs, their ability to exploit. (Haven't they ever seen some poor drone paying $1,000 a month alimony to a girl he was married to only a year?) Man-haters may secretly envy men's penises.

If you sustain any of these hates, you need help, probably professional, to find out how much nicer it is to be a woman.

However, if you really like men but would just like to seem a little softer and less self-sufficient, go on a "helpless campaign." Let a man push open every door. Stand pat. He'll do it and love it. Sit on your side of the car until he comes around to open the door. He may be halfway down the block before he realizes you aren't with him, but he'll be back— complaining but content.

Have difficulty with packages. He'll help carry.

Expect to have your cigarette lighted.

Now we're coming down the home stretch on how to be sexy.

Get it straight in your head that anyone who wants to kiss you or sleep with you isn't handing you a mortal insult but paying you a compliment. Oh, I know some men proffer their kisses and propositions with all the finesse of an invading army. It's hard to keep your temper. But cold heroines went out with cold showers. A girl who draws herself up to her full height to say, "Really, Bob Applegate, are you insane or something . . . *me* sleep with *you* . . . *I* never heard anything so funny in my whole life . . . ho ho ho ho ho," is a little gauche, to say the least. What if somebody ho-ho-hoed *her?*

Carol told me an interesting experience she'd had in group therapy (where men and women meet to discuss problems of personal relationship, usually under the guidance of a psychiatrist). She had described to them a "horrifying" encounter with the janitor of her building. He had greeted her at the elevator and said, "My, but you're a pretty little woman." Carol had fled down the stairwell. The group made her act out the scene with various members playing the part of the janitor until she finally got to where she could give the correct answer comfortably, which was "Thank you!"

A kiss is most successfully turned away (if that's what you really want) by remaining frappé cool. It's fun to kiss a wildcat. Who wants to buss a tray of sherbet? The affair itself is better refused wistfully, regretfully if you want to preserve your reputation as a responsive woman. You'd love to but you can't! You're attracted but you won't! This gentle withdrawal will take a little longer than a good swift kick (and if you're pinned by a hammer lock or half nelson, by all means deliver the kick). When you *can,* that is. However, if a man is only intellectually persistent to the point of becoming tiresome, you can demur with womanly but honest charm. As he points out that refusal will ruin your health and bar you from paradise, to say nothing of your next date with *him*, answer his "Why *not?*" with a gentle but feminine belt below the belt. Say, "You're *most* attractive. You're really lovely, but do you honestly suppose I can sleep with every man who asks me? The answer for now is no."

You're saying in effect, "I'm not pretending to be a virgin, so don't worry about *my* health! But since most men want to sleep with an attractive woman, don't imply that you are making me a present of the Davis Cup. I am very choosy. You have to be good to make the grade. Don't force it. If you want me, you might stick around awhile. I'm not promising . . . but at some future time . . . we'll see." (Paula has a Saint Christopher medal and bracelet charm, both engraved with "We'll see," from a man who I believe is still waiting.)

Sometimes a man will relinquish you with less fight if he thinks you sincerely want him but are taking your time, than if you've left no trace of doubt that you consider him a toad. (Then he has to keep on trying to prove that very night he isn't!)

When it comes to not turning things off and not sending him away, I'd love to go into detail about the efficacy of murmuring sweet nothings *while* being kissed on the mouth as against going on a you-initiated light-kiss binge across his nose, cheeks, forehead, ears, etc., etc., but I'd like to get this book finished and on the display counters, not banned in Boston. Besides, if you like kissing as much as I think you do, you don't need a guide.

CHAPTER 5

NINE TO FIVE

Now we're going to turn off men for a while and talk about your job. (Don't worry, we'll get back to them!) What you do from nine to five has everything to do with men anyhow. A job is one way of getting *to* them. It also provides the money with which to dress for them and dress up your apartment for them. (More on these later.) Most importantly, a job gives a single woman something to *be*.

A married woman already *is* something. She is the banker's wife, the gangster's wife, the wrangler's wife, the strangler's wife, the conductor's wife (streetcar or symphony). Whatever hardships she endures in marriage, one of them is *not* that she doesn't have a place in life.

A single woman is known by what she does rather than by whom she belongs to.

Gaining and keeping identity through a husband is easier in one important respect than through a job. You can't be summarily fired! A wife can be a lousy housekeeper, indifferent cook, lackluster bedmate, self-centered mother, dull-as-grime companion, and the law protects her! When she finally *is* dismissed, the man who served her papers often has to pay her half his salary. *Quelle* severance pay!

Nevertheless, while you're waiting to marry, or if you never marry, a job can be your love, your happy pill, your means of finding out who you are and what you can do, your play pen, your family, your entree to a good social life, men and money, the most reliable escape from loneliness (when one more romance goes pfft), and your means of participating, not having your nose pressed to the glass.

A job also gives you respectability. A single woman is still regarded in some suburban living rooms as not quite decent. Just try that charge on a lady broker at the New York Stock Exchange.

The better your job the better your standing as a single woman.

I have been thinking for several days now about how to tell someone to have a career. There is probably more phony literature on how to get ahead on the job than on how any girl can be beautiful! (Receding chins and squinty eyes are as ravishing as Grecian noses and saucer orbs if dredged in make-up. And girls making $57.50 a week are just a few positive thoughts away from five-figure incomes. I don't know whether these myth-makers brew it over a Bunsen burner and pour it in their coffee or grow it in the back yard and sprinkle it on cornflakes. They are at the very *least* on pep pills.)

The truth is not all girls can be beautiful and not all girls can have careers. They *can* actually but they don't. The careers are *there*, or a beefed-up job, which is the same thing. Yet in looking around my own office of about twenty-five girls, I *know* 85 per cent are never going to be career women. The question is why aren't they. Why aren't *you?*

There are several reasons.

1. You are under twenty-five and plan to marry and have children as soon as you can. Why start a career?

2. You are forty. Your good but uninspiring job gives you profit-sharing, retirement benefits, a pleasant, comfortable life. You're in solid. Why risk this setup for something flashier?

3. You are a beachcomberess at heart and nurture no dreams of glory. You'd rather be more relaxed and less income-taxed!

4. You have only moderately good mental equipment.

5. No employer to date has indicated you are anything but a menace to the company. They have kept you on out of compassion. How can *you* have the gall to hope for a great future?

6. Between your present job and the one you covet as Mink-Trailing Magazine Editor, Serious Actress, Buyer Who Goes to Europe Twice a Year yawn such chasms that you can't think how to begin to bridge them.

7. You are not going to risk one whit of your femininity by being a driving career woman.

I consider the first four reasons for not trying for the gold ring valid, sincere and reasonable. (The girl who is hell-bent for motherhood is missing another great creative experience which is to get paid for producing things in her head; *then* she could have babies, but I guess if you've gotta foal, you've gotta foal.)

The last three reasons for shunning a career are, in my opinion, worthless.

How Does It Work?

The biographies of large numbers of successful women reveal that they have arrived at their careers by three methods: (1) Vision; (2) Gravitation; and (3) Accident.

Many successful women heard Joan of Arc voices early in life. Never deviating from what the voices told them to do, they nurtured, babied, watered, fed and hatched their dream into an adult career. Most of them became architects, doctors, lawyers, astronomers, actresses, writers, bacteriologists, paleontologists, ballerinas—in short, the "I've got a vision" group were attracted to the demanding arts and professions.

Madelyn Martin, co-author of the "I Love Lucy" television show, is a good example. From age ten, when her prize-winning poem "Sunset" was read aloud to the sixth-grade, Madelyn was determined to become a writer. She never faltered in the pursuit of her goal and she reached it.

The gravitators are equally ambitious but not so inner-directed to a specific goal. From pigtail time these determined lasses work hard. They make A's, become student-body wheels, class valedictorians and the instant darlings of management. There is never much question they will arrive. It's just a matter of their gravitating to the work they were meant to do. Thousands of top-flight women business executives arrived through gravitation.

Motion picture and TV producer Joan Harrison is one. A graduate of St. Hughes College of Oxford University, she was brought from London to Hollywood by Alfred Hitchcock to be his secretary. Though an eager beaver, Joan never dreamed she would one day produce the chills that run up America's back every Tuesday when Alfred Hitchcock Presents.

Half the country's male tycoons didn't know as office boys

exactly what course *their* careers would take either. They did not so much plot their way to the summit as just arrange to their advantage whatever happened to them!

The third group—accidental successes—are no less impressive than the visionaries and gravitators. These are the girls on whom a career just sort of fell.

Swimsuit wizardess Rose Marie Reid made it somewhat by "accident." As a young girl in love with a lifeguard, Rose Marie spent every possible moment at the beach. She hated the shapeless shifts that passed for swimsuits, wouldn't wear them, designed and made her own suits instead. These svelte, form-fitting sheaths raised eyebrows as well as female spirits and male hopes. One day the owner of a department store asked Rose Marie if she would whip up a few of her designs for him. She was off and running at the success steeplechase.

Like Elizabeth Barrett Browning, who might never have had a chance to be a grande amoureuse if Robert Browning hadn't happened to her, the nonplanning career whizzes never realized *they* had it either until some wise, wonderful or libidinous employer got it out of them. Then they seem to have one thing in common with the planners and gravitators . . . drive. Their drive is latent, but once liberated, it makes them the greatest stretch runners of all time.

We are not so concerned here with career women who planned ahead. Chances are they are already nearing the launching pad. We are more interested in making you accident-prone in the right way and getting you into orbit if you aren't already.

These accidents are not quite so accidental as they seem. Rose Marie Reid did have the initiative to make swimsuits at home—and the imagination to make them beautiful.

The "accidental successes" usually help luck along by creating a favorable atmosphere around themselves. They are charming, pretty, fresh, alert, obedient and possessors of other Girl Scout virtues that attract opportunity.

I believe thousands more girls could be "accident-prone" and have careers if they were to give fate ever so small a boost. And I mean girls who started late and may not have any idea they have talent.

To spur you to action I ask you to project next Memorial Day. Could that be you at the washbasin with the Lux flakes doing your undies one more year because no one asked you to a picnic? Does the possibility lurk that next New Year's Eve will find you sipping eggnogs with your landlady? The bottom has been known to drop out for perfectly charming and popular single women on these grisliest days of the year. Think how much easier to bear if you have a really intriguing job to return to next morning and enough money to buy yourself a Ferrari to race around in and forget.

I hereby set down Mother Brown's Twelve Rules for Squirming, Worming, Inching, and Pinching Your Way to the Top. They apply specifically to girls who work in offices (the only places I've ever worked) and presuppose you have a boss. Hopefully you might adapt some of them to retailing, door-to-door selling or whatever you do for a living.

1. DON'T DEMAND INSTANT GLAMOUR

Just what are you putting up in return for the fascinating stream of callers, the luncheons at Twenty-One, your name on the masthead, trips to faraway places and tubs of money which you require in your first assignment after graduation?

Young hopefuls aren't the only opium addicts. A friend told me of a thirty-four-year-old divorcee who was "willing to accept employment" with his company if the job were challenging and interesting and she didn't have to work

Saturdays or after four-thirty because of the children. This girl couldn't even type!

Keep your shirt on! Give yourself time to get useful before you get difficult.

2. IN SWITCHING FIELDS PLAN FOR A TEMPORARY LOSS IN SALARY AND PRESTIGE

The important thing is to get *into* the coveted new firm.

An aircraft factory bookkeeper who wants a career in fashion may have to start as a department store salesgirl for *no* money, move into the gown shop, then to assistant buyer's job, to buyer, and finally fashion coordinator for several departments. A legal secretary on the same mission may plummet from her $600-a-month salary to $325 to start as secretary to the fashion coordinator. (Secretaries have a wonderful entree into almost any business. Jumping from girl Friday to girl executive is the hurdle. Read rules 3 through 12.)

Most companies get nervous when you come to them with vast experience in one field, but you're twitching to switch! Make it easy for them to take you. When being interviewed for totally unfamiliar work, don't chat too much about your ultimate ambitions. You've obviously talked them over with advisers who think you can make good. Just get *in*. Insist you won't be a malcontent in the menial job that's open. Save up money like mad beforehand, so you can subsidize yourself for a year or two.

3. GIVE YOURSELF FIVE YEARS TO DRY BEHIND THE EARS

Don't hari-kari if you're a slow starter. I held seventeen jobs (that's all I can count up now, but I think there were more) before "falling" into the secretarial job that led to copywriting that led to the fun and the money. (Three years ago I became Los Angeles' highest-paid advertising woman, though some other people have probably caught up by now.)

Child labor deserves a chance to mature! You need a few years to put boys first, to goof (My specialty was poison ivy. I would "come down" with it on Sunday and be unable to report to work until Wednesday, plastered with Mercurochrome and milk of magnesia to "hide the infected areas.") and try on different jobs. A lot of just plain luck is involved in getting into scoring position with *the* boss in *the* company. Of course if you keep spelling better and typing faster in some of your less exalted positions, your chance to score may come sooner.

4. TRY TO WORK FOR A BENEVOLENT MANAGEMENT

Some companies are still so narrow, mean and stuffy, particularly regarding women, that Elizabeth Cady Stanton couldn't have cracked them. A personnel manager I know gives un-pep talks to all girl job applicants to discourage them from ever trying to hold even minor executive posts. A chat with Old Ironsides and you're ready to will your corneas to the eye bank.

You'll never do all you're capable of doing until somebody fans you and loves you and appreciates you into it!

My husband, for example, has advanced his secretary, Pamela, to production assistant. She goes to story conferences, screenings, casting meetings and seems to keep her head when all others are carrying theirs in a basket. If anything ever happened to her, I think David would just get on the next boat to Mazatlan. He picked Pamela out of the studio steno pool five years ago because she was beautiful and had an English accent! He didn't know she had a brain, and *she* didn't know she had a brain. Encouraged to speak up by a boss who liked the sound of her voice, she spoke up so often and so well she now has a secretary of her own. (Pamela's four-year-old son is one of the sunniest, most secure moppets I have ever met, and a housekeeper has looked after him since birth. Pam's husband, an electronics wizard, is proud of his smart successful wife. They are having another baby that will also be cared for by a nurse when Pamela goes back to work.)

If you are working for toads, drain all the experience you can from the pond and move to a new one. It's still a boom economy. Don't be a scaredy-cat. Be sure *you* aren't the toad who's holding you back, however.

5. WORK FOR SOMEBODY RUNGS ABOVE YOU

The more brilliant the boss, the more you will have to reach and stretch and use all your faculties to keep up with him or her. Elizabeth Ornduff, vice president of I. Magnin Stores, credits her success with "always having had the luck to work for brilliant bosses."

You don't usually start with one. If you did, you might not be ready for him. Usually you have to work your way through some toads. Shiny bright junior executives are the worst. They're afraid to send you to the accounting department to cash their expense check for fear you'll pick flowers on the way. Poor things have to have secretaries, but try to work them off during *your* junior years too.

A "big" boss is usually delighted when you show promise and may even spot it before you do. The ad tycoon who sent me home with fresh-lemon radio commercials to write did so on the strength of funny letters I used to send him when he was out of town. It never occurred to me that I might do something creative (if you put radio commercials in that category!). I was already thirty-one and had been Mr. B's secretary for five years. And I would never have left him, dreamboat of all bosses, even then, if he and his wife hadn't goaded me to a copywriter's cubbyhole, mercifully in the same company.

6. DRESS BETTER THAN YOU CAN AFFORD

Rumpsprung gabardine skirts with nondescript paisley blouses do not *guarantee* failure, but it's a fact bosses love to have chic, sleek cats around to show off to company.

Do put everything on your back (or almost) for a promising job. Time enough to trade down to $12.95 shirtwaists when you're married and laundromatting or living on social security. I know one forty-five-year-old woman who landed a job as wardrobe selector for a network television show on the strength of her beautiful personal wardrobe.

7. BE A WOMAN

We owe the "battle-axes" of another era more than we can ever pay. They *had* to be hard as nails and drive themselves *in* like nails too to compete with men. Not you, magnolia blossom! The charm that brings him to your side after five will enlist him in your behalf at the six-months' salary review.

A famous magazine editor I know gazes deep into a man's eyes when he talks (like a flirt!), dimples when he compliments her, says, "George, or Frank, or J. P., what do *you* think?" ninety times a day. Not for an instant, not for a trice, does she try to outsmart men. Her work does it for her.

Publishing and advertising are both wonderful fields for women because you are paid handsomely *not* to think like a man. However, a company that deals in Geiger counters or paper-milling equipment can reap the benefits of women's business acumen as well as those selling products with purely woman-appeal.

8. DON'T BE A PILL

Was it you who told the switchboard where Iris really was the afternoon she was supposed to be at the dentist's? Was the last time you worked overtime without pay when you put up prom decorations in the high school gym? Do you manage to be frantically busy (writing a letter to your cousin) when a co-worker is stuck with a mimeograph assembly job? So don't be a girl scout, but I have never ever seen a genuine 102 per cent whiner-shirker-pill get anywhere.

9. LEARN THE FACTS ABOUT RAISES

It is up to a company to pay you as little as it can and still get you to stay (any company that makes a profit, that is). It is not in business to keep you contented like Elsie the Cow! You'd play it the same way if you were boss. Do you raise your faithful cleaning woman to fourteen dollars a day when you can still get a dozen other competent workers for ten?

The only way I know to get a raise is to be so good they can't get anybody like you for the same money, or even slightly more, so they may as well give it to *you*. It may take six months while they check the vaults to be *certain* that extra twenty-five bucks isn't going to bankrupt the company. Stay on their tail!

Incidentally, when you discover (by sneaking a look at the payroll figures in an unlocked desk) that the company cretin is making more money than you are, be philosophical. Nobody knows why, but every company has things completely screwed up in matching the rewards to the workers.

When you ask for a raise, be sure to adopt a martyred attitude and explain that you are doing the work of seven—providing that you plan to leave the company if the raise doesn't come through. You'll almost *have* to, to save face. Otherwise, take your Miltown and smile through the interview. You *love* the company, you *love* your job, you are just quietly starving to death. It doesn't hurt to point out *why* you need the money: your rent is so much, you send your folks so much, you're *already* bringing your lunch. This approach coupled with an unrecriminatory review of the work you've done may unlock hearts . . . and the cash box.

10. IF YOU'RE AFRAID YOU'RE REALLY A SLUG, START THINGS

Plan a picnic with a friend, write a fan letter to an architect who's completed a great new house, enroll for contract bridge lessons, visit a bakery to see how pastries are made, take your aunt to lunch, make a batch of fudge brownies for the kids in the mailroom. No frontal attacks on your job or yourself at this point (we'll *get* to them!). Just start minor creative gambits that will establish you in your own eyes as a woman of action.

11. FINISH THE PROJECTS

If you don't finish them, it doesn't count! These are relatively painless projects, however, and take only low-grade will power. If you've promised your pal at the service station to bring him the picture from *Life* that looks like him, bring it. If you've promised yourself an entire Sunday in bed reading movie magazines and drinking hot chocolate, flake out! Make your personal life a history of started and completed projects if you want to be the kind of person a career can happen to. There *is* a connection.

12. WHEN YOU GET IN SCORING POSITION, DO EVERYTHING YOU CAN

This takes straight high-grade will power. When you get with the right boss in the right company and figure this must be the place, pull out all the stops. *Do* take your shirt off. If there's work you could finish at home and impress the hell out of somebody at 9 A.M. next morning, take it home! If your fat little tummy should have been lopped off two years ago, lop it off.

Read, read, read. People have parlayed an ability to quote statistics at meetings into general managerships. (And I think some of them fitted the statistics to the need; they were never the same twice!) If your boss owns stock, check the market quotations, so you can chart *his* highs and lows. If he's for Beethoven, you're for Beethoven, Brahms and Mahler. Report your evenings at the concert.

If he likes his wife, *you* like his wife. If he hates his wife, you *like* his wife. (This will establish you as a saint.) Learn to run the projector so that when the hired projectionist has his coronary at the switches, you can be rushed in. Empty ash trays. Sharpen pencils. (Or the equivalent, if you aren't an office employee. Remember, you must translate these instructions to your own environment.) At this crucial stage you must do *everything you can.*

When I got the job as secretary to the ad man who later let me write copy, it was the first good job I'd ever had. I was so over my head I had to pump water out of my ears at five-thirty. Ordinary run-of-the-mill fluffs I couldn't seem to avoid —leaving two pages out of his speech to a high school graduation class, sending him to a luncheon at the Beverly Hills Hotel that was really downtown at the Statler. Somebody even stole $100 from petty cash the first week I had charge of it. Not *me*, but it might as well have been for all the raised eyebrows. But sensing that this was the man and here was the place (he really was pretty impressive with his autographed pictures of U. S. Presidents and Cabinet members brocaded along the walls with his best campaigns for Purex Bleach and Breast O' Chicken Tuna), I just did the best I could. He was a madman about punctuality. When he walked into the office every morning twenty minutes before everybody else, I was at my desk ten minutes before *him*—uncombed, unbreakfasted and unconscious but *there*. (During the change-over from Daylight Saving Time at the end of October, the moon was still up when I left home.) No coffee breaks. No typing errors. I did everything over until it was perfect. I figure I used about two reams of paper a week the first year. All this saved me until I had time to become a good secretary.

A friend preparing for an interview with David Selznick (who dictates like the runaway choo-choo in *The Great Train Robbery*) shut herself in her apartment for three days while her mother gave her dictation. She also scanned every book or play he had made a picture from, including the 954 pages of *Gone With the Wind*. She got the job!

After you get used to being introduced as the mayor's secretary or the girl with the highest sales book in her department or the only woman who eats in the executive dining room, you'll wear it like mink and wonder what took you so long.

I needn't remind you, career girls are sexy. A man likes to sleep with a brainy girl. She's a challenge. If he makes good with her, he figures he must be good himself.

Some men are supposed to prefer weak-headed women. I never met one who did. Not ever in my life! If they do, it must be because they have so little on the ball themselves they need a moron around to make them feel superior.

A career is the greatest preparation for marriage. You are better organized, better able to cope with checkbooks, investments, insurance premiums, tradesmen, dinner parties and the mixing of a really dry manhattan. You know how to please men. If a few more rushing brides stopped rushing and worked for a few years, they might not find themselves so thoroughly bored at thirty.

As for sleeping with the boss to get ahead, you will undoubtedly make certain initial advances in your career if a particular boss has promised them to you. However, these gains are precarious. If anything happens to *him*, the next boss may not be so susceptible to your charms and you'll be right back in the file room. As for going from company to company in search of susceptible bosses . . . *quelle* bore! You would probably do yourself more real good by staying right where you are and learning to read a statistical report. After all, girls to go to bed with he can always find. No real training is required, but where is a boss going to get a girl who can read statistical reports?

CHAPTER 6

MONEY MONEY MONEY

Nobody likes a poor girl. She is just a drag. It does take money to be successfully single—for clothes, an apartment, vacations, entertainment . . . to create an aura of seductive elegance about you, so no one will ever be able to feel sorry for you.

You probably think you haven't enough money to create this kind of illusion. As a matter of fact, nobody ever has enough money to do what he is doing! Many seemingly wealthy families are hopelessly in hock. Staying solvent doesn't seem to have so much to do with how much you earn as how you handle it. I have known girls making $100 a week who have bailed out their idiot boy friends who had $25,000-a-year salaries.

As a single, self-supporting woman you have one great financial advantage. People will *let* you live within your means. When you make cute little economies like riding a bicycle to work, everybody stands at the curb and cheers. Just try serving hot dogs and Kool-Aid at your barbecue if you're wealthy!

Being smart about money is sexy. It is part of the attractive American career-girl image—being able to reconcile a checkbook, having something to *reconcile*, being able to pay your own way (only don't you dare!).

Your opposite—the cashaholic who spends wildly to impress and is usually dodging creditors like hailstones—is one unattractive female. The man who tangles with *her* financial problems soon finds she's one of *his*, and boy, does he hate it!

No matter how little money you make, you can live on it . . . attractively. I *know*.

I was poor nearly always.

My father died when I was ten. A few years later my sister Mary got polio, and her subsequent hospital care and operations just about finished our insurance money. This was before the days of largess of the March of Dimes.

During the forties, Mary telephoned from her wheel chair for a radio survey company. Mother pinned little tickets on merchandise at Sears Roebuck's marking room for fifty cents an hour. I answered fan mail at a radio station for six dollars a week while learning shorthand. We lived in a tiny house hard by the right of way of the Santa Fe. The *Super Chief* or *something* went by twice a night. Talk about suspended conversations! Underneath Mary's and my bedroom, gophers were tunneling their way up. When the train wasn't going by, you could hear them *scrutch, scrutch, scrutching!* We never knew what night they might make it on through. To put it mildly, we lived frugally.

When Mother and Mary went back to my mother's family in Arkansas to live, I stayed in Los Angeles, first sharing an apartment with roommates and then living in a small apartment of my own.

While continuing to work my way through those seventeen jobs and sending money home, I became a really ruthless pennypincher. Buffalo nickels were not only squeezed; they yowled in pain.

Some people, especially the poor, seem to think it is unattractive and miserly to watch pennies. Did they pay $5,000 cash from savings for a Mercedes-Benz 190 S. L. when their yearly income was $9,600? *I* did. (And I wasn't kept!) But I drove a vintage Chevy and rode the streetcar for years.

Some of my save-money rules are too penurious (I know you're going to draw the line at making your own candles!) for any but really lean years. They are compiled for people who may also be under more than ordinary financial pressure but are determined to live in style. When the heat is off, you can discard the really stingy rules. The guiding principles, however, can be adapted profitably to any income.

Here they are:

1. Scrimp on what isn't sexy or beautiful or really any fun, so you can afford what is.

2. Don't spend a sou on anything you don't need. (You *need* iridescent gold eye shadow, but what about that essence-of-pine air purifier somebody was selling door-to-door?)

3. Never pay more when you can pay less. Marvelon shelf paper is Marvelon shelf paper whether you buy it in a department store or the outlet house, where it is ten cents a roll cheaper.

4. Economize on things that would bring you no extra happiness units if you spent twice as much. Are the guests really going to love you that much more and enjoy themselves double when you serve cracked Alaskan crab and jumbo

prawns with cocktails instead of raw carrots and cauliflower with a good cheese dip?

These are the general Save Rules. Now for specifics.

LIVING

Don't subscribe to a newspaper if you see one at the office or can borrow your landlord's.

Ditto magazines. Ask a friend to pass hers on after she's read them.

Type your letters on company paper.

If *you* pay the utility bills, turn off the lights when you leave home.

Have a party line. If people are talking when you lift the receiver, hang up gently and wait five minutes. This etiquette, plus your being gone all day, should keep you two *off* speaking terms.

Don't call the home folks—write letters. A dear friend of mine has a $45-a-month phone bill regularly and hasn't had a new suit in three years.

Be sure the long-form income tax return isn't for you. Twenty dollars invested with a tax man may save you $100, but let him be recommended by a friend.

Take extra jobs. Pressure-ridden executives work nights and weekends. Who are you to be too tired? If you type, someone can use you.

Don't baby-sit for money. That's beneath your dignity.

Give up smoking.

Carry some kind of hospital insurance, but modest. (I never carried *any!*) Because an appendectomy could ruin you.

Negotiate with doctors' offices about bills (or get healthy—see Chapters 8 and 9). Wear your oldest clothes and emphasize your modest circumstances.

Negotiate with *everybody*. When my rent was $75, I wrote the management, a large corporation, and asked them to reduce it to $72.50. I pointed out I'd been a model tenant, my tiny income had many places to go; and, if their apartment should be vacant just *six weeks*, they would lose more than my $2.50 reduction would amount to in *three years!* The reduction came through! I saved $240 in eight years.

Write fan letters to big companies. Sometimes they send samples. I wrote the president of Woolite (for woolens) to say I'd successfully washed my hair in it, very much like wool at the time. He sent a dozen cartons.

Rodgers and Hammerstein sounds good all over the auditorium. Move out of the gallery when a date takes you.

Brush your teeth with baking soda. Nine cents a box, and there's no finer dentifrice.

Men are to buy you cocktails. That's no way for you to spend *your* money.

Don't undertip. This little economy is unworthy of you.

Work for a rich man.

Get adopted by a wealthy couple.

BORROWING

What are you borrowing money for? I can't think of anything that would justify it except major surgery, long unemployment, family members in trouble or your being sued.

I never borrowed money for anything in my life during my single years except $400 from my boss' wife to augment a go-to-Europe fund. I didn't spend it and brought it back. I never bought anything on time payments either. Nothing! And, as I have mentioned, nobody started out any poorer than I or with more financial obligations.

Under my system you start funds for the things you want—

car, vacation, hi-fi, television, fur coat, furniture. You sneak up on these luxuries. When your fund is over the top, you buy! Or just have a general savings account, deplete it for the major purchase and pay back your bank account, sans interest.

However, not everybody is such a clever manager or thrifty shopper as I (i.e., everybody isn't as stingy). If you need to borrow money, try to get it at the lowest possible rate of interest.

Most people have no idea what installment buying really costs. Sellers are careful to keep the actual rate of interest as secret as a numbered account in Switzerland. They only tell you what your monthly payments are. If you multiply monthly payments by the number of months you pay, subtract the original purchase price of your goodie from this total, the amount left is interest. Divide the original purchase price into this interest, and you will get the interest *rate*. Don't be surprised if it's 18 to 25 per cent.

It is usually better to borrow the money for your major purchase and pay cash, thereby getting a better purchase price to begin with.

Try to borrow the money from a bank for their minimum interest rate. This is done by having collateral to put up—a paid-for car, furniture, jewelry. In some states your salary will suffice, but the interest will be higher.

If you have no collateral, a solvent cosigner on your note may do the trick. This can be a benevolent boss or a dependable steady beau.

If you have no collateral to put up and no cosigner, bank interest rates can be as usurious as those of installment-plan sellers. It is not uncommon, at least in my home state of California, to pay 1¼ per cent per month on the unpaid balance. Sounds little-bitty, doesn't it? It figures up to 15 per cent per year. If your payments extend over two years, the total interest is 30 per cent!

LENDING

If you love him and he's desperate . . . well, that's your business. People dear to you *are* sometimes caught short. Be sure it wasn't his or her own foolishness which will be repeated as soon as he or she gets his hands on a new source of revenue—*yours!*

In asking for the money back (if you have to ask), wait a decent time but not an *indecent* time. To a forgetful borrower, old debts tend to grow as faint as the sound of butterfly wings in flight.

DRIVING

Don't drive a too ambitious car too soon. It's hardly even a decent status symbol anymore! My Chevy, Catherine Howard, drank $2 worth of gas a week, a quart of oil a month and was hardly sick a day in her life.

Carry minimum insurance and drive like a police prowl car.
Wash the car yourself.
Don't re-tire; retread.
Walk.

EATING

Give up chewing gum, candy bars, starchy snacks, bread, jelly, preserves and soft drinks—all terrible for you anyhow.

Keep an almost bare cupboard. *You* don't eat much. Who are those other people you're feeding?

Cook with margarine.

Drink skim milk. It's cheaper and keeps you skinnier!

Cook with *powdered* skim milk. One-third cup plus three-fourths cup of water makes one cup of milk loaded with minerals and vitamins and it tastes fine.

Whipping cream from a packaged mix is cheaper, less caloric per tablespoon and has more food value than real whipped cream. (Cooking with cream and butter does pile calories on you and the guests you presumably love—so watch it!)

Try to like kidneys, hearts, liver, brains. Every nutritionist says they give you more health returns than filet mignon. Oh yes . . . they cost one-sixth as much. (P. S. *I* never learned.)

Ask the waiter to put the meat from your plate in a Bowser bag. It's for *your* breakfast, and you don't care who knows it.

Posh lunches with girl friends are to celebrate raises. Any girl who doesn't take her lunch to work three days a week is a spendthrift. Brown bag fare is healthier. Yogurt, carrot sticks and fruit are glamour-girl fodder. It's cheaper. And who wants to spend noon hours in a noisy, second-rate restaurant when you can shop, stroll with a friend or sit in the sun?

Anyone can take you to lunch. How bored can you be for one hour?

DATING

My eighteen-year-old stepson tells me girl friends pay for movies, gas and hamburgers when his allowance has run out, which is usually three weeks before it's due. This kind of talk sends chills to the very marrow of his stepmother's spine. When we got equal rights, that's one *I* left gift-wrapped. Here's *my* rule. *Never* go Dutch treat with a date unless he can't even pay his rent (and are you *sure* you want him?), or it's a project *you* promoted that *he* hates, like the ballet.

If you vacation with a man you aren't engaged to (I assume you're having an affair), *he* pays. You might, in a fit of generosity, kick in your plane fare; but, if the whole excursion is going to cost as much as if he weren't along, why take him? You might meet someone who isn't so stingy.

ENTERTAINING

Give big parties with one or two friends but don't B.Y.O.L. anybody. Who needs a party that isn't free?

Buy half-gallon jugs of red table wine or rosé (chill this) and serve in a shimmering Blenko glass decanter. Drugged by your charm, aficionados will swear it's Richebourg '53.

Martinis of reasonably priced gin or vodka are the specialité de la maison. Those who drink aged Scotch or bourbon will have to bring flasks.

Don't entertain deadbeats.

SHOPPING

More money has been squandered at sales in the name of thrift than has been loaned to underprivileged countries. Sales are okay for *some* furniture, Christmas gifts, lingerie between assignations, and linens (but how many towels do you wear *out* in a year?).

Buying staples at outlet houses is fine, but they are there all year long, so hysteria needn't prevail.

As for clothes, markdowns are usually things people didn't like well enough to buy at the original price. Are they prettier now that they cost ten dollars less? I know girls who have closets full of bargains and not one thing that makes them feel fabulous when they walk into a room. Last month Anne succumbed to some glorious brown alligator pumps marked down from $70 to $32.50. *Quelle* bargain! The only trouble is, Anne hasn't anything brown in her entire wardrobe and has been wearing them with royal blue and purple costumes. Another thing, Anne doesn't have decently heeled, un-scuffed *any* kind of shoes except the alligators. A little less time at the sale and a little more time at the boot . . . oh, well!

I know just two legitimate ways to buy clothes on sale. One is to keep your eye on a gown you've adored since its arrival but couldn't afford because it wasn't basic. If by some miracle it isn't sold in several months, ask the salesgirl when it will be marked down. Attend the sale and grab it!

The other legitimate sale purchase is when there's a big gap in your wardrobe. You've been wearing your raincoat for an evening wrap. What you really need is a black silk Balenciaga greatcoat for about $285—fat chance of having *that* in your piggy bank. Case every sale in the exclusive shops or expensive floors of department stores that carry this kind of merchandise. When you find *your* coat, but only *your* coat, reduced to $135, pounce!

If you only need a sweater or a purse—I suppose it's okay to prowl the sales. But so much sale merchandise doesn't quite have it. Or rather it has too much—one bow, one braid too many. For another five dollars you could have what you'd be really thrilled with.

The costlier the merchandise, the better the sale. No junk is hauled in for the occasion. The mark-up was greater to begin with, so they can afford to take more off. The styles are apt to be classic, so you can wear them longer. The fabric and workmanship are superb. You may enjoy these even in a boo boo!

As for picking up odd little dresses for $13, that is a luxury *you* can't afford, at least in my opinion. You need to look glamorous every minute.

Buy wholesale (if you're lucky enough to have a contact) but only things you've picked out at retail and somebody has arranged to order for you. I know a girl (me) who used to gobble up dresses in showrooms as though they didn't cost *money*. They didn't fit, were the wrong color, and I wouldn't have looked at them twice in a store.

Don't tie up your funds in cases of facial tissue and soap. Quantity buying of that sort is for large families.

Hand lotion and shampoos are pretty much alike. Buy big cheap bottles.

Watch for the invisible "pickpockets" in hardware and drug stores. Those innocent twenty-nine-cent items can murder twenty dollars.

GIVING

Buy certain-to-be-needed Christmas gifts through the year at sales.

Make your own presents. Pink-and-white checked cotton cocktail aprons with yards of pink grosgrain ribbon for a waistband and streamer sash are lovely. Total investment: one dollar and one hour each. Four red-and-white checked linen place mats with fringed napkins are charming. Just cut them straight and fringe!

Cook presents! A young Canadian friend has people drooling by autumn for her annual Christmas shortbread.

Gift the people who don't expect a return present (the rich, the men, executives repaying a business favor) with some tiny item—a pillbox, a bottle opener—wrapped like a precious jewel. *McCall's* Christmas issue usually shows how to cover eggshells in velvet and rickrack—that sort of thing.

Make your own Christmas cards. Rough cerulean blue art paper from the art supply store cut in squares, messaged in green India ink, sprayed with stickum, dusted with gold sparkles, then folded into a plain envelope, makes a lovely card. Mimeograph your own Christmas poem on a three-penny postcard.

Go in with other girls on shower gifts—four, six, eight of you. A bride is in no position to whine.

Don't give expensive presents to men. Madness!

TAKING

Are you really going to keep the fifteen-dollar bath salts when you need a purse? Exchange anything that isn't *you* unless it came from a dear friend.

Expect and encourage gifts from men. They are part of the spoils of being single.

DRESSING

We'll discuss wardrobe planning in another chapter. These are a few random thoughts on economy.

Never buy anything in a hurry. Your insecurity is showing! Impulse purchases you *may* make for a sudden date are a new wide, black velvet hairbow, fresh white gloves, one shampoo and set. If you do succumb to a dress—and who doesn't?—try to make it one you'll cherish when the big anxiety has ebbed.

Don't try to have too many clothes. Buy important things. A girl can have enough blouses and skirts to outfit the WAC and never have anything to wear.

Welcome hand-me-downs. If the fabrics are good, cut them into something new and chic.

The larger your collection of junk jewelry, probably the worse dressed you are! Take the pledge. Your saving the first three months should net you an important piece of costume jewelry.

Brush your woolens, sponge the spots, air them. Don't snuff out their life at the cleaners.

Wash your own sweaters—in Woolite. Press them with a barely warm iron.

Wear old clothes or *no* clothes at home alone.

Get a tan and go without stockings.

Do your own hair. I can't imagine why any girl under thirty-five except an entertainer would need weekly professional hairdressing.

Keep your nails virginally clean and omit polish.

"Forget" some of your lingerie. Anything you're not wearing out thread by thread is money in your piggie bank. An actress in her fifties now living in Europe wears only pants . . . no bra, no slip, no girdle. She has one of the world's great figures. Another actress, according to interviews, *doesn't* wear pants—so far she has landed the lushest parts, the handsomest husbands and hasn't had pneumonia. Why not *try* not wearing pants if you wear a slip. If you're small but firm-busted, you don't need a bra. (Carol uses Band-Aids across her nipples under fabrics too sheer to wear bra-less.) I personally am anti-girdle, not only because they're costly, but they drive me *nuts*. Leave them off too if you have a trim backside.

Wear everything you buy. No hoarding.

SAVING

Suppose with all this austerity you have not only managed to afford mink on a mouse budget, you have managed to save a little money. How do you make that money *make* money?

While it is accumulating, keep it in a savings and loan company rather than a regular bank, where interest rates are lower. Loan company accounts are insured to $10,000 just as regular bank accounts are.

Buying insurance that will pay you later is safe but extravagant saving. If you banked the same money that your premiums cost in a loan company and let the interest compound itself, you'd have far more capital at the end of fifteen years than the insurance will bring.

After you have put aside a small cash fund for emergencies, your straightest road to dollar-doubling is stock. It not only collects interest (dividends), your capital also grows as the company prospers. Please note:

A small portfolio of stocks is very sexy.

Any brokerage firm will be delighted to advise you no matter how small your investment. And it's fun to have a broker! Mine's a woman. Far from being high-pressure folks, they will probably keep you from plunging suicidally into speculative stock. No matter how attractive the tip, if the stock can go up four points in one day, it can go down! The only people to take hot market tips from are your boss or a wealthy beau. If the stock goes down, these two may be so ashamed of themselves they will personally make up your losses.

If you'd like to try your *own* hand at selecting stocks, here are twelve rules that have made a fortune in the market for advertising tycoon Don Belding since his retirement from Foote, Cone & Belding four years ago. Mr. Belding admits that few stocks meet this rigid check list, and when you find some that only miss on a point or two, you can use your own judgment. All the information needed to evaluate the stocks is in Standard & Poor's *Stock Guide*, available at any brokerage firm. Mr. Belding says the best stocks of all are chewing tobacco! Here are his rules:

Buy stocks in companies that:

1. Pay a 6 per cent dividend or more.
2. Have a long record of dividend payments.
3. Have a twenty-year low (market quotation) not less than 25 per cent of twenty-year high.
4. Have current assets to current liabilities at least four to one.
5. Have cash and equivalent more than current liabilities.
6. Have no burdensome long-term debt.
7. Have very little if any preferred stock.
8. Have modest capitalization of common stock.
9. Have a five-year record of advancing sales or evidence of progress.
10. Have a last report of earnings up.
11. Are impervious to bombing (away from congested centers or have several plants).
12. Are listed on American or New York or local stock exchange.

Now on to some other places to put your money sexily.

CHAPTER 7

THE APARTMENT

IF YOU ARE to be a glamorous, sophisticated woman that exciting things happen to, you need an apartment and you need to live in it alone! After your thirtieth birthday, a great Dane would do more for your image than two roommates, and dogs don't borrow sweaters!

Being Mama's or Daddy's girl and living at home is rarely justifiable either.

Parents who are ill and need you are one thing. A solution takes faith, patience and saving money until you can afford to hire semiprofessional care that will free you. If you are locked in an emotional death grip, that is something else and may require psychiatry.

If you are a widow or divorcee with children, living with an older family member may be a blessing. For others, the financial savings and fringe benefits of having roommates or

119

living at home can't possibly compensate for the sacrifice of freedom and prestige.

A beautiful apartment is a sure man-magnet, and not only because he expects to corner you in it and gobble you up like Little Red Riding Hood. A wolf can wolf any place! Besides, you're a big girl now. If a wolf is running around loose in your apartment, you probably want him there.

A man is pleased and soothed by a beautiful apartment (I'm ruling out houses as too expensive) just as he is by beautiful clothes (and don't think he isn't), a beautiful face or beautiful music. Few men really *prefer* the honest simplicity of log-cabin trappings. A man would rather put his feet up on a genuine Moroccan leather hassock. (Not that he's going to find a big masculine thing like that in *your* apartment!)

A man also makes a mental note of your ability to afford a posh pad and your cleverness at fixing it up.

A chic apartment can tell the world that you, for one, are not one of those miserable, pitiful single creatures. When your name comes up in the conversation, people will say with far more glowing admiration, "That girl has the most divine apartment!" than they will ever say, "That girl has the most divine husband!" One is something *she* created. You must value yourself in order to be successfully single, however, and you must sincerely believe you *deserve* beautiful surroundings, otherwise you're apt to put up with something dreary.

Think of yourself as a star sapphire. Your apartment is your setting.

To Furnish or Not To Furnish

Furnish by all means. Find a blank space in which you can create black, blue, green and pink magic! All but the most costly furnished apartments are stuffed at best with cheap modern stuff. At worst, which is most of the time, they are filled with sleazy junk.

If you haven't already discovered it, acquiring your own household possessions is a joy. It's creative. You'll see.

What Part of Town Should You Be In?

Don't live too far from your work. Driving or bus riding twenty miles each way to a job eats up precious time, money and energy. Wouldn't you rather be home making a chocolate soufflé or reading a novel?

If you are being courted by a man, try to live near *him*.

Roosting on a beautiful tree-lined street in a fashionable neighborhood would be lovely, but who can afford it? Don't pine. Some of the most amusing, chic and elegant apartments in any city, particularly New York, gleam like pearls in crazy old neighborhoods. I lived for eight years in downtown Los Angeles, possibly one of the most un-chic areas this side of the Ganges.

How Much To Pay

Not too much! If you try to show off in a building or neighborhood you can't afford, you must dress, drive, entertain and *live* poshly; and that way lies debtor's prison! A more impressive way to impress is with what's *inside*—you and the furniture! Dazzled by you both, nobody will remember they came through a slum to get to you.

In Japan many homes are drab, unprepossessing shacks on the outside. Rare beauty dwells within.

I learned how unimportant exteriors were by watching the transformation of an apartment in a rabbit-hutchy old building in Beverly Hills. Two friends paid $62.50 a month for a 20 x 50 cubicle and turned it into a corner of Versailles! Getting asked to dinner there was an occasion to wear your chinchilla.

Search a long time for a cheap, satisfactory apartment. Moving is trouble, expensive, and nothing ever fits in the new place. Leave your name and phone number with the owners of buildings you like and keep checking back for vacancies.

What To Look For in a Building

Views, fireplaces, patios are nice, but they jack the rent. You can live without them.

I personally like old buildings better than spanky new ones because they are better built, better soundproofed, have higher ceilings and more charm. They fix up more elegantly. But who am I to deprive you of garbage disposals and large sweeps of plate-glass windows? You'll have to decide.

Stove, refrigerator and carpeting are now provided in many unfurnished apartments. These also up the rent. If they don't come *with*, you can easily get the kitchen fixings second-hand, and carpets are no great problem.

Don't try for too many rooms or even too *big* rooms. It takes too much money to black-magic them. My friend Agnes lives over a garage in one enormous room with a tiny crumbling bath. A hot plate and icebox behind a screen make the kitchen, but you can see wonderful old sycamores through the windows. Agnes has gone chintz, ruffles and pewter, and the place has tremendous charm.

Check the soundproofing. Most modern buildings have paper-thin walls. Your conversations may be fascinating, but you can be bored to distraction by the neighbors'!

If traffic noise bothers you, don't forget to "listen" as you "interview" apartments. If the place is a fabulous buy *except* for street noises, you can learn to adjust, however. After five sleepless nights, nothing can keep you awake on the sixth, and then you're adjusted!

The outside of the building needn't be fancy; but if it has a greasy look, look further; the owner is probably mean and stingy and not a good landlord.

Pass up places that have playpens and children's toys around the front door. You want sophisticated, adult surroundings.

Before you move in, have a firm understanding with the management about painting. If the place has just *been* painted but in nauseous colors, insist they paint over—don't be shy. A good tenant is worth her weight in paint. To encourage the painting, tell the owner you plan to stay forever. You will also be doing extensive decorating which wouldn't be worth your while if the walls give you migraine.

If they agree to supply the paint providing *you* do the painting, don't! Painting is miserable work! I have never had a beau or boy friend who was willing to help, and I decided long ago all the slave labor was the lot of the married women! Fortunately men have other qualities to enjoy.

If for any reason you *are* forced to paint, try to hire a high school boy or other nonprofessional who'll paint up a storm for ten dollars.

Don't sign a lease for more than a year. You might want to go to live in Portofino for a year.

What Color Walls

It's a matter of personal taste, but why should I stop imposing my personal taste on you *now?*

I like oyster white or off-white walls. Everything, including *you*, looks divine in them. White walls are very vogue-ish now, and I think their beauty will survive the trend.

My next choice would be something in the beige family—possibly soft taupe or honey. Gray beige is beautiful. Plain gray is also neutral but a little cold.

Forest green and chocolate walls were the rage a few years ago and probably lost out because they made people feel hemmed in. You need something soft and lovely you can live with.

Apple green, powder blue or pink walls are too froufrou for my taste. These colors in a living room remind me of cheap dresses and cheap candy. In a bedroom they're fine.

Painting every room in your apartment in the same color isn't a bad idea.

Some people like crazy orange bathrooms or a chartreuse kitchen. These bathrooms and kitchens seem to be *trying* too hard! Anyway, that's one paint job you'll have to do yourself. Managements go apoplectic over deep colors.

Wallpaper can be beautiful, but don't worry—you'll never find it coupled with modest rent. See if you can get the management to scrape off the faded jungle vines you *will* find, and if not paint over them.

Inside the Castle

Now for the real challenge. Your walls are freshly painted and you're ready to move in. Or the walls are freshly painted in the place you've *been* in for a while. You have some furniture or you haven't.

How do you turn this pristine area into the poshest little arena in town . . . with no money?

It's very simple.

You can't.

There is *one* thing you can do without money. You can throw out, give away or sell everything that is junky and impossible of the stuff you already own. Out with it! If you give it to the Salvation Army or other charity, which isn't a bad idea, get a receipt. It's tax deductible.

There is one approach to decorating that costs very *little* money—the Greenwich Village approach. Make everything gay and colorful and warm and cozy, and no single item of furniture or refurbishing costs more than ten dollars.

This is a fine approach for the very poor or very young . . . college girls and young working girls.

Why isn't a crazy, colorful, cozy apartment good enough for *you?* Because you can't be a star sapphire among early Sears overstuffed and late-painted orange crates.

If nothing in your entire wardrobe, including coats, cost more than twenty dollars, it wouldn't be much of a wardrobe, would it? Neither can an apartment furnished completely on the thrift plan pack much of a wallop.

If you are into your thirties marching straight toward forty or forty gaining on fifty, you need a place with enough elegance to say successfully "up your backside" to society. You can *say* it living in a dormitory room at the Y.W.C.A., but nobody is going to believe you.

It's possible you've never even seen the kind of apartment I have in mind! There aren't very many of them around. I had only seen one when I did my single-girl place—the jewel in the rabbit-hutch building we just mentioned. Your apartment doesn't need to be a corner of Versailles—you'd probably hate it—but I think the kind of taste and bezazz and verve and elegance those boys poured into that apartment *is* what an exciting single woman needs in hers. When you see one of those places, you'll understand instantly the social and emotional good it can do you.

How can I be more specific about the elegance I think you can't live without? It doesn't involve Lorenzo de' Medici gilt commodes with gargoyles around the legs, though I think those would be divine! Elegance can be a couple of dog-eared volumes of Dostoevsky on a table (dog-eared because you *read* them). It can be a crystal bowl of real apples and oranges catching the sun—or a Ming vase worth $5,000. I can only explain by saying that an elegant apartment has unmistakable traces of grandeur about it . . . like a lady shopping in a supermarket in Bermuda shorts and a striped silk shirt just like everybody else, but the hand that pushes the shopping cart rests under a four-carat diamond!

Many of the so-called "elegant" effects are achieved for pennies . . . just exactly as they are in the Greenwich Village apartment. *But you must be prepared to sink money into some of the pieces.*

You can't afford to do this at twenty. You don't *need* to at twenty. And maybe you think you can't afford to at thirty. But unless you are under analysis five times a week or putting a little brother through college, *I* think you *can*. Follow the saving rules in Chapter 6 for everything *but* your apartment. You may also have to go into hock for a year or two while you acquire the major items for your *ménage*. Then you can retrench and live in quiet glory among them. No investment will bring you more daily pleasure.

How Much Will It Cost?

Depending on whether you have furniture that can be re-covered and refurbished, depending on how many resources you can scare up for buying things wholesale or at a discount, depending on how much sleuthing you are willing to do to track down treasures at a price, depending on whether you can sew and refinish things yourself—the investment I am talking about will run between $500 and $3,000. But you can take ten years to complete it. The important thing is to begin.

How To Get the Work Done

There are three methods of furnishing this elegant little fun-bin:

1. Hire a decorator.
2. Get advice from friends who know a lot about furniture and decorating and could do most of the job themselves.
3. Acquire the essential knowledge and do it yourself.

You think I'm going to recommend doing it yourself, don't you, but I'm not! Decorating is an art you may not have the wish, the time, the energy, the ability to learn. I never did. I can't even hang a picture without making a big hole in the plaster.

My single-girl apartment was decorated for me by the friends with the Versailles corner. They finally just couldn't stomach one more overcooked hamburger in my overstuffed mud hut. One windy night they removed two red and chartreuse flowered pull-up chairs that had originally cost nine dollars and gave them to a needy friend. I was allowed to bequeath a large faded red davenport to *my* needy friends as well as two dwarf lamps with bases carved like pineapples. Mark and Schuyler (I shall call them) threw out some other stuff which they said nobody was needy enough to need. They then took $400 away from me. I had recently won a contest conducted by *Glamour* magazine, and my prize was a trip to Honolulu. *Glamour* had generously given me $500 spending money, of which—you know me—I had used about

$35. They also sent money for a first-class round-trip ticket to New York for the finals of the contest. Naturally I had gone coach and pocketed the difference. God bless *Glamour!*

My friends invested this fortune in two enormous white rococo lamps, a low travertine marble table that went the length of one wall, having my one good print, a Dufy, reframed in something knock-your-eye-out, and several satin pillows.

I asked what they were going to buy with the rest of my money. They said there wasn't any rest, and there was a brief period during which we didn't speak. I moseyed around decorator shops pricing pillows to confirm that between them Mark and Schuyler had enough of my money to spend Christmas in Acapulco. All I found out was that pillows cost only slightly less than a good used Cadillac.

We made up. Gradually over the year, a few dollars and a few deeds at a time, the boys stole, cajoled, borrowed, coaxed, begged, painted and polished my apartment into something pretty terrific. It was moss green, hot pink and white. Since the rent was only $72.50 a month, I poured everything I could inside. People talked about that apartment. It brought me great pleasure.

My second apartment (which I took for the sole purpose of living near David and wearing him down to a frazzle, so he would marry me—and he did) was done by a decorator. "Done by a decorator" isn't as fancy as it sounds. She recovered a couch, put up draperies and bought a few new things.

By now I think you get the gist. Dumbbells—but smart enough to know they're dumb—get a decorator or smart friends to help them with their apartment.

My husband and I fight the decorator fight to this day, and I'm sure many people agree with *him*. He thinks decorators impose their own elaborate taste on you so that a place looks like the inside of a candy box but not *your* house . . . that they scavenge up a junky old chair worth $2 and sell it to you for $200 . . . that anybody with good taste can do things just as well as a decorator. Well, my husband is crazy! You can wear beautiful clothes and not have the foggiest notion how to sew them together yourself. You can adore crepes suzette but not be able to make up your own recipe.

It's an art to know what furniture to buy big and what to buy small, what to pay a lot for and what to cheat on. It isn't larceny, it's genius to recognize beauty in a broken-down cane-backed Jacobean chair, have it restored, then put it in just the right corner. Maybe it's worth $200 by then. A first-rate decorator has learned a million tricks to give your rooms that ooh-la-la which sets them apart from the do-it-yourself, loving-hand-at-home, didn't-quite-make-it look!

Decorator Fees

As for prices, a decorator usually buys wholesale—40 to 50 per cent off your retail price—then adds a fee on top of that (20, 30, 40 per cent) which brings the price back up! Decorators are usually more expensive than buying retail, however, because the stuff they come up with is more fabulous. They have very little truck with mass-produced furniture. Also the labor charges for making draperies, refinishing furniture, wiring old fixtures, is anything but cheap; and decorators charge a commission on those too. Occasionally they will do a room for a flat fee. Sometimes they work by the hour. Whatever their system, no doubt about it, they *cost!*

If you can't afford that professional polish for a whole apartment, you might at least call in a decorator for consultation. Some work for as little as $10 or $25 an hour, and in that time they may be able to whip up a plan you can follow yourself.

If you do work with a decorator, put yourself in his or her hands and don't interfere too much. All major purchases will be checked with you first, and you'll have lots of choices. It's possible that a sympathetic decorator will take an interest in you even with your small budget if you are lavish with appreciation.

Many stores supply a decorator with purchase, and that's better than no professional advice at all, I guess, but I'm not *sure!* Those stores are pushing their own merchandise, and I can't recommend buying too deeply from them. The dream apartment—even one room of a dream apartment—is never assembled from one store even if it's the best store in town. Objects that contribute that "memories could be made here" look to an apartment are lovingly assembled from all over!

I'm Decorating Myself

Suppose you can't or won't afford a decorator and have no friends who know more about the subject than you do.

I'm willing to concede you can furnish an attractive apartment with your own good taste, imagination and money. But if you want one that really goes into orbit—a yummy but not *gaudy* place that is totally sexy—you must do some of the things a decorator does. You *can* do them—and have a ball —but you'll have to work hard and get educated.

Although I regretfully admit I can't decorate the inside of a linen closet without help, I've assembled some decorating rules from professional and gifted friends that should help you.

General Rules

LEARNING

1. Creep up on decorating as you would any new skill. Remember how long it took to learn shorthand? Immerse yourself deeply in the world of cherry wood and Chippendale. Don't be in a rush to buy anything.

2. Take basic courses in decorating in night school. You can learn textiles, woods, traffic patterns, scale of furniture, etc.

3. Borrow library books until you can tell Duncan Phyfe from Duncan Hines.

4. Make your second home in furniture stores, furniture departments, junkshops, secondhand stores, antique shops, and thrift shops of the Salvation Army, Junior League, etc. (These contain discards people have given to charity as a tax write-off rather than sell for a pittance. They are sometimes terrific.) Just look a lot and get the feel of furniture.

5. Attend decorator shows, home shows, auctions, and get the look and feel some more.

6. Visit museums containing rooms of period furniture. Talk to the curator or attendant on the floor. They are gold mines of information and often like to chat.

7. Get acquainted with the owners of antique and secondhand stores. Tell them you're planning to furnish an apartment without much money but are determined to put beautiful things in it. You are just getting your bearings, and visiting their store is helpful and inspiring to you. Most antique dealers would have opened a liquor store if they wanted to make money. They deal in treasures for love and a modest livelihood. If you show genuine interest, they will probably

become expansive and give you a valuable education. They can't sell to you wholesale unless you have a decorator's license, but a dealer who "adopts" you may eventually tell you *his* source of supply. And you can slither over there and buy for a pittance.

8. See the inside of as many beautiful homes and apartments as you can. Soak up décor like a sponge. If there's a showplace you're longing to see but don't know the owner, try writing a charming note. Ask if you might drop by at an appointed hour for ten minutes. Say you are decorating an apartment and have in mind to see, first, as many beautiful and inspiriting houses as you can. Tell where you work and what you do, so nobody will think you're coming over to case the place for a burglary. Write on office letterhead. Enclose a self-addressed stamped envelope for reply or say you'll telephone in a few days. Some wealthy home-owners will be flattered and like to show off a bit.

BUYING

1. In some cities certain decorators will "lend" you their license (resale number) to buy wholesale, then charge you only 10 per cent of the purchase price as their fee. Actually they aren't decorators. They are just people with a license. This is a good deal. Look into it.

2. Investigate getting a decorator's license yourself from the State Board of Equalization or whatever agency supplies them in your state. This will allow you to buy wholesale. In order to qualify, you must lie your head off and say you are going into business. I have a license. It cost $150, but I've never bought anything with it. I get hopelessly confused in showrooms and run right back home to my decorator.

3. Plow the major part of your money into a few important pieces. If a woman has jewels, everything else looks expensive! In a small apartment these might be lamps that cost $80 to $100 apiece; a marvelous coffee table; and, my friends say, cushions!

They believe custom-made, satin cushions allow you to get away with just average couches and chairs. Opulent cushions say, "This girl is chic. This girl has expensive taste. This is an apartment wonderful things happen in." Mark and Schuyler believe in other expensive accessories too—a glass-topped Louis XIV gilt glove box to keep cigarettes in . . . ash trays that are *objets d'art*.

4. Keep to simple lines in big pieces of furniture. The bigger the piece the more basic it should be. Periods come and go; but, if furniture lines are basic, you can change the period oftentimes by reupholstering or changing the grain of wood (stripping and refinishing). Don't buy big antiques with a lot of gingerbread either. Fifteen gilt mounts on a Louis XVI chest will run the price up. Pay for ornamentation in one glorious gilt candelabrum that burns fifteen candles!

5. The *shape* is the thing! Don't worry about disreputable wood in buying secondhand pieces. Refinishing has become such a fine art you can sleek up the most careworn objects.

6. Don't try to have all woods in one room the same color.

7. Haunt your favorite junkshops, secondhand and antique stores and be ready to snap up bargains the minute they come in. Other predators will pounce if you don't. You'll be able to spot the real "buys" with a little experience. Most decorators have their own houses littered with finds too good to pass up which they know they'll use *sometime*.

8. Try to pick pieces that could go a number of different places. A pirate chest might do in the living room, bedroom, hallway or to serve buffet on!

9. Learn to see the dual possibilities of furniture. You could sell the works of a grandfather clock and probably get back its purchase price; then take off the door and have ground glass shelves put inside to display china or copper mugs. (See how smart *decorators* have to be!)

10. In a small apartment don't make everything little-bitty. Men are *not* happy in doll houses! For a really dazzling effect make some of the furniture oversized. Enormous lamps, a giant coffee table are the ticket.

11. Place expensive and inexpensive side by side. Mix periods. Mix old and new pieces. This is particularly important with modern furniture which is abundant, reasonably priced, easy to care for, but so masculine and stereotyped. A modern couch covered in thick creamy linen would be handsome with a fragile old Chinese screen or Spanish wrought-iron end tables.

12. Assemble a list of experts to do your upholstering, rewiring, refinishing, remodeling, hauling and installing. Naturally you will charm them into doing exquisite work at rock-bottom prices. (P.S. Some people learn to do their own upholstering, but we won't open that can of tacks here.)

13. Be prepared to chase your legs off. Take home and take back and take home again. Everything must be tried out in its actual setting.

To Please a Man

Now . . . a few notes on how to make your apartment sexy. One man I discussed this subject with suggested leaving black lingerie hanging on the bathroom door or across a chair in the bedroom. Typical male thinking! Poor darling doesn't understand girl-think! She wants her apartment to be sexy, not necessarily to encourage *rape*. The fact is, if the apartment is beautiful and tasteful, it *will* be sexy . . . no strewn lingerie, black satin sheets or mirrors on the ceiling needed.

The following are known man-pleasers!

Gobs of Pictures

Have a wall of pictures. Men are usually much taken by them. In the living room these should be fairly expensively framed—one of your major investments. If the picture wall is in the bedroom, the frames can be less costly. My wall of pictures was in the bathroom and proved so popular, I used to wonder sometimes if people who went in to wash their hands were ever coming *out*.

Ready-framed department-store stuff usually has that "I didn't know what I was doing so I left it up to somebody else and they didn't know either" look! It's better to select your own prints and frame them.

Travel Posters

Coax these from United, American, TWA, Pan-American or any of the foreign airlines who have exciting travel posters. They are a trifle masculine but look great in hallways or kitchens. I have a TWA matador over my kitchen stove that's really goose-bumpy.

Television

Have a TV set for quiet little evenings at home and shows of major importance but not too *great* a TV set or you'll never get out of your apartment. One of the impressive-income girls

I mentioned earlier is still viewing on a 9-inch set for this reason.

Books

Books say nice things about you and men adore them. The more the better. Augment the new ones you buy with paperbacks and secondhand editions.

Hi-Fi

Of course you'll want music both to tame him and inflame him but don't go overboard on equipment. You're no symphony conductor and there are many other places to put your apartment dollar.

My secondhand Girard turntable, Scott amplifier and speaker cost $150 total and always sound fine.

Don't have too many records. If a man gets tired enough of Fred Waring's Glee Club and *Gaîté Parisienne,* he may just bring over some new platters.

A Sexy Kitchen

Have an extravagant spice shelf with possibly thirty spices. They say you're a good cook. A man who is possibly a bit of a cooking buff himself will be enchanted with them.

Put all your cookbooks out on a shelf.

If you have beautiful Descoware pots and skillets, hang them up for show.

Ice-crushers, lemon-peel peelers, heavy stainless steel bottle openers, corks with carved heads on them—anything gadgety usually pleasures a male.

Towel Girl

Give the man who showers at your apartment a luscious toga-size terry bath sheet. Sometimes you can buy "seconds" at a sale.

If a man comes over direct from his office and just wants to freshen up before your date, supply him with a fluffy fresh face towel and his own small bar of soap. An extra razor costs only a dollar including blades if you'd like to keep one on hand.

Have an ash tray with two fresh cigarettes and matches handy in the john. Magazines and books are nice too.

Little Jewel

An enormous brandy snifter or large translucent bowl filled with dozens of loose cigarettes, opened whole packages of many brands and "name" book matches from good restaurants is a man attractor (or *anybody* attractor) if you can afford it.

Something in the Air

Pot-au-feu wafting from the stove or the perfume you usually wear clinging to the couches . . . both are among the nicest scents a savage beast ever encounters. One's for soothing, one's for rousing.

CHAPTER **8**

THE CARE AND FEEDING
OF EVERYBODY

As a single woman you don't have to entertain nearly as much as other people if you don't want to. You are a glamorous acquisition for anybody's party—a breath of oxygen at the married board. Feel free to be America's guest!

The time does come, however, when you can't avoid totting up the times they have had *you* and you have *not* had them. Action is called for.

Your motives for entertaining will vary from wingding to wingding. Some of your guests will be the saintly married couples who have fished you off the streets on national holidays and your birthday. Other times you'll bring home the office crowd. Some cook-ins will be straight charity . . . a friend is coming apart at the seams and has to be restitched.

138

You'll have girl friends and family over to gossip. Still other times you'll cook just to show off your apartment and your cuisine. The impressionable can range from a maiden aunt to the most devastating man in the world.

My theory about the guest list is that you invite people you feel *comfortable* inviting, as well as a few now and then you have no damn business inviting, but have your reasons!

I always died about ninety-five deaths at being turned down. On the other hand, my friend Marguerite *never* gets turned down. She has the knack of getting everybody from the chairman of the board of her company to a visiting troupe of ballet dancers over for sukiyaki. However, she has special psychological things going for her. She comes from a social family that boasted a governor and a mayor. Hoards of people were entertained where she was growing up, and she is as comfortable with a Tiffany tea service as with a skillet of eggs. Girls of this background simply don't *know* fear! Marguerite also makes a hefty salary and can buy all the water chestnuts she wants.

I think you can acquire enough poise and confidence to pluck guests from outer space if they appeal to you. A single woman *must* broaden her horizons. But I do think it's kind of silly to track celebrities or spoiled-male animals who can barely sift *through* their invitations. Why bother with those whom you bother?

Dinner à Deux

When do you have *him* over?

My thought is that reciprocity is not entirely in order with beaux. I think the correct ratio between times on the town and *dîner intime* in your apartment is about twenty to one! If you aren't engaged—that's a funny old-fashioned word, but you know what I mean—you don't really have to pay back dinner *ever*. Part of the price bachelors pay for staying single is to spend money taking girls out. No use making their bachelorhood *easy* by feeding them like little mother.

Some single girls stir up a dinner nearly every night of the week for a loved one. And I guess they love it. Cooking *is* part of wooing when you have a live one, and I can't count the dinners I cooked old David Brown.

But no matter how warm your relationship, it doesn't seem right to dine at your place *every* night. After you marry you're home a long time, cooking, cooking, cooking. Better go out while the going is good!

My friend Gretchen is death on cooking dinner for a man *ever*. She occasionally has one over to make fudge. I didn't believe that fudge story when I first heard it. Fudge sounds so *sweet* . . . you might push an incipient diabetic right over the edge! Besides, what man would be *interested?* Two men have confirmed to me they really have made fudge at Gretchen's, however (divinity, caramel and first-rate pa-nocha). And from the tone of their voices, I gather they'd rather make fudge at Gretchen's than dine at Le Pavillon. Some girls have *all* the salesmanship! Anyway, that's one female's approach to entertaining men.

As for cooking for married men, that's sheer insanity!

One reason you see them is to add glamour to your life.

If you are going to be hidden away in *your* apartment fussing with *his* formula, that's very Back Street indeed!

Once in a great while you may honor a married man with a dinner invitation, or let's put it this way: If he comes trooping over with two mallard ducks he shot especially for you and a bottle of Cordon Bleu, cook his dinner!

Guiding married men out in the open into the town's better restaurants is a more meritorious plan ordinarily.

Now . . . the better cook you are the more renowned you become as a hostess. You will collect a small coterie of devoted fans who will bay your praises to every rising moon. It's a nice sound!

Cooking gourmetishly is a particularly impressive skill for a career woman. Everybody expects fluffy dumplings from a wife and mother. (And are they ever in for some surprises!) *Your* head, they figure, is too stuffed with schemes for becoming the first woman President or stealing somebody's husband to be able to cope with recipes. It's fun to hand them a surprise! Put on an organdy apron, retire to the kitchen and come back with impeccable Eggs Benedict. Then listen to the purrs and praise . . . very soul-satisfying.

In the Beginning

Now, how does a single woman who doesn't get day-in, day-out practice learn to cook scrumptiously and entertain with confidence?

The magazine articles on entertaining certainly do not help much with your special problems. Where is the color spread on "Seductive Little Suppers"? Who tells you how to seat six married couples when there is no host? All the recipe pages do is make it pretty clear that if you aren't stuffing a twenty-pound bird with chestnut-and-bacon dressing you are weakening the moral fiber of America. It's enough to weaken *your* fiber and send you out to the kitchen for another peanut-butter-and-jelly sandwich.

The very word "entertaining" sounds kind of snooty and married—like the Turkish ambassador's wife having seventy for sit-down dinner, the actor and actress team ladling out marguerites at a pool party. Can they really call what *you* do—frozen pizza for three girl friends before a Dean Martin spectacular—entertaining?

Certainly! All you have to do to qualify as an entertainer is to cook something or pour something.

Let's talk about cooking.

I think many single girls get off to a slow start because for years they can't afford to feed guests, and nobody really expects them to. They seldom cook for themselves, beyond an informal snack. They get no workout. Then when they do begin to sneak up on cooking—possibly at age thirty—they are justifiably defensive and self-conscious. While other dames are comparing notes on Chicken Kiev and Artichoke Provençale, the slow starter is trying to boil a *four-minute* four-minute egg.

I'm certain some girls are frightened by their mothers, and the fear lasts into maturity if not forced out by a hungry brood of their own. Either Mother cooked like Henri Charpentier and wouldn't let anybody else near the stove, or Mother's taste buds were in her feet and she had no skills to pass *on*. I come from a long line of Southern cooks which never helped anybody off to a good start. The cornbread on my maternal side was so gummy that once when I left a glob of it between the pages of the *Delineator* (that was once a popular magazine, kids) as a place mark, the pages stuck together.

Mother's steaks resembled the hide of an armadillo. (I think they *fried* steaks in Little Rock in those days.) Never mind, Mother. I love you anyway and you have other talents!

Recipe books are hardly the ally they should be to a neophyte cook. Instead of taking a girl gently by the hand and making things *simple*, they have a cavalier way of calling for stock . . . or leftover chicken. Stock is *supposed* to be a broth, generally kept simmering, and replenished from time to time with scraps of meat and vegetables. I did very little simmering or replenishing in the *kitchen.* As for leftover chicken, tell me, pray, what single girl has any leftover meat of *any* kind? Leftover *gimlets* maybe . . .

The Escoffier cookbook, which a sadist gave me when I was learning to cook, set back my progress about two years, I'd say. The book is full of fascinating but mystifying instructions such as, "Over the garnish pour a quart of chicken consommé thickened by means of three tablespoons of tapioca, poached and strained through a cloth or fine sieve." I'm not much for tapioca hot *or* cold, but *poached!* . . .

The recipe for turtle soup is plain mayhem. It begins with the slaughter of the turtle. "Take a turtle weighing from 120 to 180 pounds[!], and let it be very fleshy and full of life. To slaughter it, lay it on its back on a table, with its head hanging over the side. By means of a double butcher's hook, one spike of which is thrust into the turtle's lower jaw, while the other suspends an adequately heavy weight, make the animal hold its head back, then, quickly as possible, sever the head from the body." It goes on for two more pages for the turtle-soup fancier with a strong stomach.

Escoffier to the contrary notwithstanding, I managed to become a pretty good cook after a very slow start—failing with the never-fail hollandaise a few times and all that. Gather around and I'll tell you how—using these three techniques.

Pussyfooting, Copycatting and Diversification

Pussyfooting means that on little cat feet you sneak up on one dish at a time. First you boil water, then you make Jello.

Next you make a mousse; and one day, sing choirs of angels, you have advanced on and overtaken . . . Beef Stroganoff!

To copycat is to borrow a friend's entire dinner menu and do what she did. Write down the names of what you ate on three-by-five index cards and send them to the hostess: Linda's Sweet and Sour Beef, Linda's Heavenly Little New Peas, Linda's Immoral Rum Cake. After you've praised everything to the limit, ask Linda please to give you the recipes in detail. Enclose a self-addressed stamped envelope. You could telephone, but it would take hours. From this kind of flattery a hostess can get writer's cramp.

Now you do what Linda did down to the last simmer, baste and boil. It's a good system because you have a rough idea of what something is supposed to taste like. (A beginner cook sometimes doesn't have any idea how far she's missed the boat until a well-meaning guest compliments her on her fish soup, when what she thought she made was coquilles Saint Jacques.)

This is a bachelor's dinner for two I once copycatted that is the *simplest*. Joe's menu: Barbecued chickens from the market cut in halves and reheated in an electric skillet (this bachelor didn't have a stove and didn't usually need one), a mixed salad of the crispest, crunchiest, sassiest greens tossed with bottled French dressing into which he had mashed a lot of fresh Roquefort, a Beaujolais wine served in chilled glasses, fresh cherries, grapes, plums, apricots, pears and peaches for dessert with a wedge of Camembert, instant espresso. It was exquisite. So was he—but a real bounder. I never felt guilty about stealing his menu.

Diversification means you don't cook the same thing twice until you've cooked everything at least *once!* I know that goes against the specialization theory where you become famous for your Boston Baked Beans. It's all right to have one dish you can't fail with, but I wouldn't play it safe very often. After all, you aren't going to cook fancy just for *you*. Practice on *company!*

I recall a memorable cheese-fondue evening at my house— a maiden voyage, to be sure. Fondue calls for grated Gruyère cheese heated in a crockery dish, with one glass of Neuchâtel wine added for each person, then everything bound together with a little flour and kirsch. What could be simpler? I didn't have kirsch and substituted vodka (they were both the same color), and since the recipe didn't say what *size* glass of Neuchâtel—peanut butter, Kraft cheese or beer stein—I just sloshed in most of a bottle of wine. What the hell! Get the guests drunk on food as *well* as liquor, and you're bound to have a good party.

I can only suppose something was chemically out of balance. The cheese coagulated nicely but just sort of *lay* there like Moby Dick in the middle of the wine. I added more flour and vodka to try to bind everything together, but the cheese only got more recalcitrant. I transferred the whole mess to a chafing dish, and ravenous guests jabbed their cubes of French bread onto a fork and dipped into the fondue mix in traditional fondue fashion. (If a girl loses her bread in the mix, everybody kisses. If a man loses his bread, you go chug-a-lug with the wine in your glass.) Of course getting the bread extricated from *this* mess was like trying to get a dinosaur out of the La Brea Tar Pits—hopeless! After we all kissed and chug-a-lugged until it was getting *silly*, we finally ate the fondue with our fingers . . . it was just like an Our Gang taffy pull.

This kind of fiasco doesn't happen nearly as often as you'd think. And one day after you've pussyfooted, copycatted and diversified sufficiently, you'll be a good cook. Then you can go right out and swap Chicken Kiev and Artichoke Provençale with the best of them.

Refining the Art

You must adore food, of course, and be able to taste the subtle nuances of flavor, to be a standout performer. You'll sharpen your taste buds as you go along. And you must pay loving attention to detail. I have never known a first-rate cook who didn't. Old hands often say, "Oh, I never measure anything," and they *don't*. But they go to *three* markets to get a really plump chicken, and they marinate lamb for shish kebab for three days.

Confidence you need to get your *magna cum cookery*. Once you exude this quality, you can serve cornflakes, and people will swear *your* cornflakes have that *je ne sait quoi!* Most people so love to be cooked for—by a *good* cook—when *you* cook they'll gladly eat Swiss chard and salmon aspic and things they'd never touch at home.

One popular hostess I know serves a course of bones at every formal dinner party. The guests just sit around and gnaw on these enormous bones, happy as clams. Can you imagine a beginner getting away with it!

Reading cookbooks like literature can help make you a good cook, once you get over your initial fright.

My favorite general recipe book is *The Joy of Cooking*, by Irma S. Rombauer. All the recipes seem to have a lightness and delicacy. Mrs. Rombauer gives very detailed instruction —none of that Reindeer Stew business—"Take one reindeer. Cook it. Transfer to a serving dish," etc.

Another cookbook I like is *Twelve Company Dinners*, by Margot Rieman. Starting with the marketing and finishing with lighting the candles, this clever woman guides you through twelve gourmet feasts Lucius Beebe couldn't snub. Of course we'll all be cooking the same company dinners!

I think Ruth West's *Stop Dieting! Start Losing!* (*The Famous Cottage Cheese Low-Calorie Cook Book*) is a must, dieting or not. It is a fifty-cent Bantam Book, easy reading and a fascinating account of how you can substitute low-calorie ingredients for high ones and still have great tastes.

Supply and Demand

You wouldn't . . . you couldn't . . . you *don't* . . . or *do* you . . . let a man drink up all your booze evening after evening without replenishing your stock (sounds like rather a drab life socially regardless of *who's* buying!). I just think there are better, cheaper and more reliable ways to get and hold a man than being his friendly neighborhood bar with all the drinks on the house.

Naturally you fix him a cocktail before you go out if he wants one (unless you're in a real pinch for money).

Naturally you serve liquor and in quantity at your dinner parties and other parties.

Naturally you don't grab the bottle away like a mother lion protecting her cub as he's pouring his third drink.

But you *can* gently discipline the sponger. Just be "out" of anything when he comes over . . . or down to the last ounce even if you have to siphon the gin off in a milk bottle and hide it in a cupboard. Some chaps are just careless and a mere hint will shame them into generosity. In severe freeloader cases, however, I don't think the frank approach is out of order. You could say something like, "Charlie, darling, for six months you have been drinking up my booze and I think it would be a nice idea, since you adore Old Forester, if you brought a bottle over here *with* you next time."

If you don't speak up and your liquor supply seems inexhaustible, old Charlie may assume one of your other beaux is a liquor distributor and *never* do his share.

Entertaining Him

When a lucky man does get an invitation to your apartment for dinner, a preplanned, not just a spur-of-the-moment one, I think his head should swim for days with happy memories. It should be one of the most exquisite little meals he has ever eaten, served in the most serene and beautiful atmosphere.

Here's your check list.

Spic-and-span the apartment. He *does* notice, if only subconsciously.

Have fresh flowers about or at least masses of green leaves in vases.

Look beautiful. Smell fragrant.

Wear something feminine and offbeat. This is no time for capri pants and a shirt. Often you *can* pick up pretty hostessy things on sale.

Chill the cocktail glasses.

Don't fill him up on stupefying hors d'oeuvres. An assortment of crisp raw vegetable sticks would be fine. If he hates vegetables, Rosa Rita frozen cocktail tacos are delicious. Heat them for twenty minutes. Big fresh mushrooms sautéed, filled with hamburger lightly cooked and placed under the broiler a few minutes are ambrosial.

Unless he's a drinker, don't postpone dinner indefinitely. He may be hungrier than you think. You want to *get* to dinner.

Have enough records on the record player to last through dessert.

Do serve wine if he likes it . . . one of the romantic clichés that got that way because of its potency.

Eat by candlelight.

Use *cloth* napkins, perferably beautiful big ones. It's not much trouble to launder two napkins.

Cook everything you can well ahead of time, so it will seem that you haven't fussed at all.

If you're not sure of his pet dishes, perhaps you'd better skip casseroles. A lot of men *still* equate them with leftovers. Try one of the known man-pleasers—double lamb chops, a small luscious fillet, any of the chicken dishes. If you'd prefer to show off a bit more, and have a sure hand, try one of the feasts you'll read about in a moment.

A dessert that makes the dinner seem absolutely Lucullan is a scoop of rich ice cream atop some kind of fresh fruit—raspberries, peaches, pineapple. Then give your guest his choice of liqueurs to pour on top—Grand Marnier, Cointreau, crème de menthe. You have to be a spendthrift to afford this assortment, but they last for ages. Hide them from your alcoholic friends.

Make lots of coffee, hot, strong and for *real*.

If he smokes, add a Gigi touch to dinner—offer him a fifty-cent cigar.

Leave the dishes in the sink.

Let's Picnic

Here is another delightful way to entertain a beau. Take him picnicking to the beach, the mountains, a public park, your own back yard, wherever and whenever you can find grounds. Go a little romantic with the menu—no hearty beef sandwiches does he get from *you*. Try this:

A thermosful of cold Vichyssoise (Campbell's frozen potato soup mixed with half and half) poured into china cups you have brought along. Top the soup with chives (or finely chopped green onion tops in wax paper). The entree will be cold roast chicken, one-half for each of you, or chicken fried greaselessly. Have lots of dainty cucumber sandwiches. (Chop cucumbers fine, mix with low-calorie mayonnaise, spread between crustless, thinly sliced buttered white bread. Cut each sandwich in quarters.) For dessert, the most diabolically fudgy cake you can obtain. Share a bottle of white wine—Inglenook Pinot Black is elegant. Spread out a red-checkered tablecloth. And why not wear a ruffled frock, as Emma Bovary might have done, instead of the redoubtable pedal pushers? You may be attacked, of course . . . a girl who can *cook* and *look* that way takes a chance.

Other Ways To Pay Back

Dinner parties are admittedly expensive and can only accommodate a few at a time. One popular way of handling multiple obligations is the cocktail party. Much has been said against it, and I for one am a detractor. Trying not to be left alone with a martini (after the hostess blows her whistle, and all guests reassemble in new locations) is, for me, too reminiscent of trying not to get stuck with a partner more than three dances in high school.

However, that's me, and you may *adore* big parties. Give one!

These are cocktail party rules from my friend Mark, who gave the best cocktail parties I have ever attended—and in a one-room apartment. He has since gotten rich, moved to a posh neighborhood, and his parties don't *compare* to the old stretch-the-dollar-to-the-limit affairs.

These are Mark's rules:

Give the party in a small space and pack the people in. Never be afraid you've asked too many. Play Rumanian gypsy music (interspersed with a little Perez Prado) to heighten the intimacy and drama. Serve gobs of weak martinis which you have made up beforehand and stored in the icebox. A constantly circulating martini pitcher creates a feeling of well-being and good fellowship in guests. Let any two friends bring *hors d'oeuvres*—deviled eggs, clam dip, guacamole or whatever they wish. Praise them lavishly. Never let anybody contribute liquor. Don't ask any but charming and attractive people. Lump the lugubrious and hostile together on another occasion and pack them all off to the movies! Invite plenty of single people.

Mark usually tossed in a couple of fifty-five-year-old lady fascinators who had lived in Europe. You never saw the men and women congeal on opposite sides of the room at *his* parties. When the hour grows late, gather up everybody and take them to a prechosen supper place. Let everybody go Dutch. This host favored Barney's Beanery—a ramshackle chili house with great atmosphere.

I think many of these rules are sound. However, you can go as posh as you please. Hire a bartender if you like.

Marguerite adds this rule. Invite *all* your beaux at once. (She has a lot of beaux and can say a thing like that.) It gives them a good shaking up to see the competition.

Ruth says forget that business about having fun at your own party. When a hostess enjoys herself *more*, the guests may be enjoying themselves *less*.

You must be twice as effervescent as you are in real life, even if you feel it's slightly phony and even if your eyes glaze over. Be out there with your troops all the time, smiling but in command.

Economy-minded party-givers say it's okay to use inexpensive bourbon and Scotch, but it must be potable! Your friendly liquor-store dealer will tell you the price you do not dare drop below.

Sunday Brunch

A party *I* have always had good luck with is Sunday brunch. It seems to sort of go with career girls and is a chic, inexpensive way to entertain. The hour is interesting. Invite guests for twelve noon. You can often round up people you might not have the nerve to ask for dinner.

If you'd like to be notorious in a nice way for your brunches, start with chloroform cocktails. These will unlimber a log and clobber more sensitive timber altogether. I remember one sweet girl who came over directly from church, had two chloroform cocktails because they tasted like coffee malteds and was still asleep (to put it euphemistically) under the coffee table at five in the afternoon.

Here's the recipe:

Make a pot of coffee. Then boil down six cups of it in a saucepan to one cup. In a big bowl or pitcher mix the coffee with a fifth of gin or vodka and one quart of rich vanilla ice cream. Serve in Pilsner beer glasses, Old Fashioned glasses or almost any kind. Top with nutmeg. At a brunch for eight people you should probably make up at least two batches of chloroform.

The rest of the menu (and you can go much more elegant than this) might include scrambled eggs with fresh sautéed mushroom blended in; lots of canned sausages piping hot; canned peach halves with grated orange peel, brown sugar, cinnamon and a maraschino cherry on top, baked half an hour; really *good* coffeecake from the bakery, heated; and pots of coffee.

Games are fun at brunch . . . charades, truth or consequence, blindman's buff. I've found everybody likes to perform . . . the shyer the person the more he likes being *on,* but you have to coax him. Make each guest do a little act—sing, soft-shoe, or just tell a joke. You could also let each guest pick a book from your library and read his favorite passage. Give a prize for the best reading.

A mildly naughty but great party game is to let guests guess the number of garments other guests are wearing. Whoever is "it" is looked over by the crowd. No feeling or pinching allowed. Each person says what he thinks is underneath the outer garment. Then "it" tells who was right. Or you can give each guest a pencil and paper and let him write down total number of clothes "it" is wearing. Count jewelry, shoes, etc. Give a prize for the most right answers. You must take the guest's word for what he's wearing. No undressing—it says here.

The Not-Quite-Sudden Guest

As sometimes happens, you didn't *know* the night before that you were going to have a guest for breakfast, but there he is . . . *ravenous!*

I assume you like him, or he wouldn't be there. In that case, *feed* him!

What is needed is a hearty little breakfast you can toss together quickly while he is taking a shower.

How about half-clam, half-tomato juice with a wedge of lemon squeezed and dropped in, Omelet Surprise (the surprise is how many things you can find to go in it), toast and coffee.

I'm sure you know how to make an omelet. Just put lots of beaten eggs in a skillet like for scrambled, only *don't*. Let the eggs set without stirring; and, when firm on the bottom side, put any of these things on top: chopped onion, chopped pimiento (from a little glass jar), small can of drained mushrooms, chopped yellow cheese or grated Parmesan, chopped green bell pepper. Or use canned tomatoes instead of *all* of these. Fold the omelet over and let it cook a few more minutes.

If you have no bread to make toast, perhaps you'll have a can of icebox biscuits or a boxed muffin mix. Most of the ingredients for this breakfast are things you could easily keep on hand.

The more poised you are, the more deft and unruffled at your chores, the more pleasant this could-be-awkward little repast will become.

If you have something on your mind to discuss—possibly a grievance—save it for a later hour and send him away thinking you are a dreamboat.

THREE FABULOUS LITTLE DINNERS
(and one semi-fabulous brunch)

Like all other cooks, especially ones who are not quite over the wonder of having finally mastered part of the art, I can't resist giving you some recipes to round out this chapter on food. Here are three dinners and a brunch that would be divine for *him* or *them*. Recipes for the first two dinners are for two, the third dinner and the brunch are for six. You can increase or decrease recipes to serve different numbers. A lovely girl named Noreen Sulmeyer helped compile these menus. She's a better cook than I am and I'm not through copycatting *yet!* We borrowed heavily from *Thoughts for Buffets* and *Thoughts for Food* (Houghton Mifflin Co.); *The Gourmet Cookbook* (*Gourmet*, New York); *The Something Special Cookbook*, by Ruth Mellinkoff (Ward Ritchie Press); *The Joy of Cooking*, by Rombauer (The Bobbs-Merrill Company).

Unfortunately these dinners are sparing neither of calories nor cost. They are strictly to show how talented you are and to make guests groan with pleasure!

DINNER # 1 (*for him*)

Crabmeat Puffs
Escalopes of Veal

Tomato Sauce Provençale
Château Potatoes

Broccoli Almondine
Green Salad

Dinner rolls

Coffee
Cheese & fruit

Chocolate Soufflé
with Vanilla Sauce

CRABMEAT PUFFS

6 slices white bread, crusts removed
3 1-ounce slices American cheese
1 cup crabmeat, fresh or frozen
2 eggs

1 cup milk
½ teaspoon salt
freshly ground pepper

Place three slices of bread across the bottom of a buttered shallow pan and cover each with a slice of cheese. Cover the cheese with crabmeat, and top with remaining slices of bread. Cut each sandwich into three strips. Beat the eggs with the milk, salt and pepper and pour over the sandwiches. Chill for two hours. Bake in 350° oven for 30 minutes or until puffy as a soufflé. Lift puffs out of baking dish with spatula, arrange on top of paper doilies on platter or tray. Serve immediately with cocktails.

ESCALOPES OF VEAL

6 veal slices ½ inch thick
⅓ cup butter
1 cup stock (can be made with
    bouillon cube and hot water)
¼ teaspoon garlic powder

½ teaspoon seasoned salt
2 tablespoons chopped fresh
    parsley
2 tablespoons chopped onion
salt and pepper, freshly ground

Pound veal with edge of saucer until very thin. Melt butter in a skillet and when hot, sauté escalopes for 3 minutes on each side until brown. Add stock, garlic powder, seasoned salt, parsley and onion and blend; sprinkle with salt and pepper. Cover and simmer 20 minutes. Serve with Tomato Sauce Provençale on top.

TOMATO SAUCE PROVENÇALE

8 large tomatoes
1 large onion, thinly sliced
¼ teaspoon thyme
1 bay leaf
1 clove garlic, minced

1 tablespoon flour
1 tablespoon butter
½ teaspoon salt
¼ teaspoon freshly ground pepper

Place tomatoes in a heavy skillet and crush. Add onion, thyme, bay leaf and garlic. Simmer 20 minutes or until tomatoes are tender. Strain through a food mill or ricer. Return to skillet. Blend flour and butter and stir into tomato puree. Season with salt and pepper and simmer 15 minutes.

BROCCOLI ALMONDINE

Try to buy fresh broccoli if you can; if not, frozen broccoli spears will do. Boil them until just tender but not overdone. Top with generous portions of butter and lemon juice. Just before serving, sprinkle with blanched almonds (white ones) which you have browned in a pan with a little oil in the oven about 20 minutes.

CHÂTEAU POTATOES

Cut raw potatoes into balls with melon scoop and let them soak in cold water until ready to cook. Drain well. Season with salt and pepper. Cook very slowly in heavy skillet in lots of butter until they are golden in color. They should be crusty on the outside and soft in the inside. Sprinkle with finely chopped parsley and serve at once.

GREEN SALAD

Splurge and buy several *different* kinds of lettuce, using only a few leaves from each for this salad. (You can eat the leftovers yourself.) Add thinly sliced cucumbers, scallions and water cress and chill. Serve with either garlic-oil-vinegar dressing or a concoction of sour cream, mayonnaise, garlic powder and *lots* of fresh dill.

CHOCOLATE SOUFFLÉ WITH VANILLA SAUCE

Melt 3 tablespoons butter in a saucepan and blend well with 2 tablespoons flour. Gradually add 1 cup milk, stirring constantly, and 2 squares baking chocolate. Stir until chocolate is melted and sauce thoroughly blended. Mix in ¼ teaspoon salt, ½ cup sugar and a 3-inch piece of vanilla bean. Add 4 lightly beaten egg yolks and beat well. Fold in 5 egg whites beaten stiff.

Butter a soufflé dish, sprinkle it with sugar, and pour in the batter. Set the dish in a pan of hot, not boiling, water. Bake in a hot oven (400° F.) and cook for 15 minutes. Reduce the heat to moderate (375° F.) and cook for 20 to 25 minutes longer. Serve with vanilla sauce.

(Soufflés are *not* easy and probably you should *not* practice on him. They're well worth the effort though.)

FOAMY VANILLA SAUCE

1 3¼ ounce package instant vanilla pudding mix	½ teaspoon vanilla
	1 cup cream, whipped
1 cup milk	dash of salt

Make instant pudding according to package directions, using only one cup of milk. Add vanilla and salt to beaten cream and fold into the custard just as it begins to thicken. *Voila!* Let guests spoon over their soufflé.

DINNER # 2 *(for him)*

Stuffed mushrooms
Lobster en Brochette
Artichokes with Polonaise Sauce   Caesar Salad
Tomato Stuffed with Rice   Dinner rolls
Coffee   Cheese and fruit   Chocolate Angel Pie

STUFFED MUSHROOMS

Select large fresh mushrooms, wash well and cut off the stems. Stuff with seasoned ground meat, brush with melted butter and broil under broiler until hot and brown. Serve hot with cocktails.

LOBSTER EN BROCHETTE WITH DEVIL SAUCE

3 large lobster tails (cook the tails, remove the meat and cut into 1-inch squares)	½ cup dry bread crumbs
	¼ cup melted butter
	4 metal skewers
12 large fresh mushrooms	lemon wedges

DEVIL SAUCE

⅔ cup catsup   3 tablespoons mustard
2 dashes Tabasco   1 tablespoon Worcestershire sauce

Mix ingredients together.

Alternate mushrooms and lobster on skewers. Brush well with melted butter. Then brush on the Devil Sauce. Roll the filled skewers on the crumbs. Place on greased broiler and broil for 5 minutes on each side. Serve very hot with lemon wedges.

ARTICHOKES WITH POLONAISE SAUCE

2 artichokes

Wash and soak artichokes for one hour in salted water. Drain. Trim off their spikes with scissors or sharp knife. Cook them in rapidly boiling salted water to which you have added a few tablespoons of vinegar. They should cook almost an hour.

POLONAISE SAUCE

¼ pound butter   1 tablespoon chopped parsley
1 tablespoon olive oil   ¼ clove garlic, minced
½ cup bread or cracker crumbs   4 tablespoons white wine
2 hard-cooked eggs, diced finely   2 tablespoons catsup
                     salt and pepper

Melt butter in a skillet. Add all other ingredients and cook about 5 minutes over a low heat. Pour sauce over cooked artichokes.

TOMATOES STUFFED WITH RICE

2 large beefsteak tomatoes   ¼ cup butter
2 cups cooked rice   ½ green pepper, finely chopped
½ onion, finely chopped   ¼ cup piñon nuts (or other nuts)

Do not peel tomatoes. Cut a slice off the stem end and remove all the pulp. Turn tomato upside down to drain. Sauté the onions and green pepper in the butter until tender. Add the nuts and cook one minute more. Add the rice and toss thoroughly. Remove from heat. Stuff the tomatoes with the rice mixture. Place in a baking pan and cover lightly with foil. Bake at 350° F. for 15 minutes. Remove foil and bake an additional 15 minutes. Serve hot.

CAESAR SALAD

Make croutons by cutting good-sized cubes of French bread and sautéing them in butter and minced garlic until golden brown. This should be done way in advance and refrigerated. Tear chilled romaine lettuce into medium-sized pieces and place in salad bowl. Combine ¼ cup good olive oil or soy oil, ¼ teaspoon salt, freshly ground pepper, ½ tablespoon Worcestershire sauce, ⅛ cup lemon juice, ⅛ teaspoon dry mustard and mix thoroughly. Pour over the greens. Break one coddled egg (boiled one minute) over greens and toss well. Sprinkle with ¼ cup grated Parmesan cheese (preferably fresh from your local Italian delicatessen) and croutons, toss again and serve immediately. Garnish with anchovies.

CHOCOLATE ANGEL PIE

Meringue Shell:

Beat 3 egg whites with a beater until foamy. Add ⅛ teaspoon cream of tartar and a pinch of salt and beat until they stand in soft peaks. Add gradually ¾ cup sifted sugar and beat until very stiff. Fold in ¾ cup finely chopped pecans and 1 teaspoon vanilla.

Turn the meringue into a buttered 9-inch pie plate and make a nestlike shell, building up the sides ½ inch above the edge of the plate. Bake in a slow oven (300° F.) for 50 to 55 minutes and cool the meringue after it is removed.

Filling:

Place 4 ounces sweet chocolate and 3 tablespoons strong black coffee in a saucepan over a low flame. Stir until the chocolate is melted and smooth. Cool and stir in 1 teaspoon vanilla. Whip 1 cup heavy cream, fold in the melted chocolate, and turn it into the meringue shell. Chill the pie for two hours.

DINNER # 3 (*for six*)

Stuffed Lobster Tails

Pepper Steak España

Rice Marguery   Hot rolls

Marinated Vegetables   Spiced Cherries

Cheese and fruit   Coffee   Chocolate Cookies

STUFFED LOBSTER TAILS

Try to purchase cooked lobster tails from a poultry or fish market and ask that nice gentleman behind the counter to scoop out the lobster meat and then put it back in the tail. Allow one lobster tail per eater. You can buy your lobster tails a day before your party but no earlier. Then the morning of your feast you can prepare this dish and have it ready in the refrigerator.

Scoop out the lobster meat into a bowl. To it add some finely diced celery, several hard-boiled eggs, chopped, and a small amount of finely diced pimiento. Then add Louis Sauce and mix. Scoop the contents back into the lobster tail, piling it high and garnish with a sprig of parsley or watercress. This can be served as a first course at the table but my preference is to serve it with cocktails in the living room, thus eliminating that dreadful chore of playing waiter at your own party and having to clear away between courses.

LOUIS SAUCE

1 cup mayonnaise	1 teaspoon Worcestershire sauce
¼ cup French dressing	salt and pepper
½ cup catsup or chili sauce	several drops of lemon juice

Combine and mix well.

PEPPER STEAK ESPAÑA

3 lbs. beef tenderloin, sliced thin	3-4 tomatoes, quartered
¼ cup butter or margarine	½ cup tomato paste
1 pound fresh mushrooms	1 teaspoon oregano
3 green peppers, cut in large strips	salt, garlic powder and freshly ground pepper to taste
1 bay leaf	¼ cup sherry wine

Brown meat in 2 tablespoons of butter; add seasonings and cook until tender. (This depends upon the kind of meat you buy. If it's fillet, 3 to 5 minutes on each side is plenty. For best results, ask the butcher. I do.) Have your green pepper, mushrooms and tomatoes waiting for you from an early-morning cutting; sauté for 5 minutes in the remaining butter and add to the meat along with the tomato paste. Heat thoroughly and let simmer until the green peppers are cooked the way you like them but no more than 10-15 minutes. Add sherry and serve at once.

RICE MARGUERY

½ cup butter	2 cups white rice
1 onion, chopped	2 8-ounce cans undiluted consommé
1 pound mushrooms, sliced	3 cups water

Melt butter in skillet. Sauté onions and mushrooms for 5 minutes. Set aside. Wash rice and drain well. Place rice in skillet in which mushrooms were sautéed. Brown and add consommé, then combine with water, adding the mushrooms and onions. Bring to a boil, cover and simmer about 25 minutes until the liquid is absorbed and rice is tender. Serve at once.

MARINATED VEGETABLE PLATTER

If you have a many-divisioned dish or a Lazy Susan, use as many different kinds of vegetables as you have compartments. Otherwise, set the vegetables in beds of lettuce on a large platter.

In your grocery store select small-size cans of vegetables such as artichoke hearts, celery, baby carrots, miniature onions, string beans, cauliflower and others. Drain the cans and marinate vegetables separately in French dressing for at least 4 hours in the refrigerator. Drain off the excess dressing and serve.

SPICED CHERRIES

(Spiced fruit goes beautifully with almost any entree. Here is a recipe for cherries. If you'd prefer not to "spice" yourself, your market will have cans of spiced fruit such as peaches, pears, crabapples, etc., which will do nicely.)

1 28-ounce can large Bing cherries, drained	⅔ cup vinegar cinnamon stick
1 cup drained juice	1 teaspoon whole cloves
1⅛ cups sugar	

Place fruit in a shallow pan. Combine remaining ingredients in a saucepan. Boil 5 minutes. Pour over cherries, then allow to cool. Refrigerate several hours at least. This is a good dish to make the night before for the overnight chilling is preferable.

NOTES ON ALL THREE DINNERS

Rolls can be homemade, bakery-bought or "brown 'n serve." Any of these will be delicious; just be sure they're hot.

I like to end all dinners with a big platter of fresh fruit (many

grapes) and assorted cheeses and have suggested it for these dinners. The more lavish the fruit tray the more gasps of pleasure
from guests already overwhelmed by your cooking. Pass little
glass plates and fruit knives if you have them.

Something chocolate goes well with nearly everybody, especially men. If you don't want to bother with a soufflé or chocolate
angel pie, something chocolate, gooey and deadly from the bakery
will serve. A platter of rich chocolate cookies—probably store-
bought—are suggested for dinner number 3. The idea of a double
dessert—one healthy, one immoral—makes every dinner seem
ultra lavish.

For a gay flourish, add a cinnamon stick to everyone's cup of
coffee.

HEARTY BRUNCH *(for six)*

Peaches and champagne

| Breakfast steak topped with exquisitely fried egg | Golden brown potatoes Watercress |

One basket of Swedish Breads
One basket of heated Danish Coffeecake
Sweet butter   Lots of coffee

CHAMPAGNED PEACH

Peel a fresh peach and place it in the bottom of a glass. A
Pilsner beer glass would be fine but any glass not too large will
do. Fill the glass with chilled champagne (a domestic variety is
all right—it's the spirit that counts!). Refill glasses several times—
the peach takes up quite a bit of room. Provide spoons to eat the
peach eventually.

BREAKFAST STEAK WITH FRIED EGG

Buy one small steak per person—they should not cost more than
a dollar apiece—and broil it quickly to be piping hot but not

overdone. On top of it lay gently an elegantly, perfectly fried egg. Eggs are fried this way by cooking them slowly-slowly in a covered skillet. Let guests add their own coarsely ground pepper.

P.S. Tenderize the meat if you think it needs it. A druggist friend of mine says it also tenderizes the lining of your *stomach* but let's don't worry about that *now!*

GOLDEN BROWN POTATOES

Peel and cut up five or six potatoes. Slice them thin. Fry them in gobs of butter or margarine until they are crispy and brown. Put big sprigs of watercress around the potatoes on their serving plate.

SWEDISH BREAD AND DANISH COFFEECAKE

Possibly there is no Scandinavian bakery in your town but just get the most wonderful, bakery-fresh (not grocery shelf) bread you can. Ideally you would serve limpa, pumpernickel and Swedish rye. Cut these in half pieces easy to handle. The heated coffeecake, served in a separate basket, should be cut in about the same size pieces as the bread.

Cut sweet (unsalted) butter in squares and place tiny smidge of parsley in center of each one or make butter balls with wooden paddles.

Serve gobs of piping hot coffee.

The peaches can be fixed ahead of time. Potatoes take about 25 minutes so start them first. Near the finish fry the eggs, broil the steaks, and heat the coffeecake.

All dinners and the brunch would be served buffet style from your dining-room table or bar or any flat surface. Then guests take their plates to an already set TV or card table or to the dining table if you haven't used it to serve from.

If you have no reason to cook an elaborate dinner or brunch like the ones outlined but would like to try your hand at *one* dish guaranteed to get you raves, this is it—Marilyn Hart's Herb Bread. It will glorify the simplest meal (even a TV dinner) and is so good guests will think you crumbled the yeast, raised the dough and did the whole assembly yourself. Why tell them you didn't?

HERB BREAD

1 loaf sliced sour dough French bread
2 cubes sweet, unsalted butter
1 teaspoon each: garlic salt, Beau Monde seasoning, celery powder
½ teaspoon each: summer savory, rosemary, thyme, basil, oregano, chevril
3 teaspoons of parsley
6 teaspoons sage

Soften the butter at room temperature. Add the spices. (If you don't have all these, you could leave out a couple.) You will now have greenish-looking butter. With a knife, spread it between the slices of bread. Really sop it on. Spread the remaining mixture on top. Now wrap the bread up in foil paper. (You can do this a day in advance.) Bake the bread half an hour in medium oven (350° F.). Time it to come from the oven right at dinner time, so it can be rushed to the table. The crust will be crispy, crunchy, the inside moist and fragrant. Nestle the bread in a cloth napkin inside a wicker basket or on a silver bread dish.

CHAPTER 9

THE SHAPE YOU'RE IN

W<small>HAT YOU FEED</small> him and them bears no resemblance
to what you should be feeding *you* when they aren't around—
to keep you sexy, vibrant and unmorose about being single.

I'm sure you've been talked to before by a health nut or
two about breakfast, protein and blood sugar, and you've
yawned right through the lectures! "Normal" eaters always
wonder why us health nuts can't just take our yogurt out under the banyan trees and leave *them* in peace and quiet with
their Danish.

But single girls *need* lecturing. You are the world's *dumb-
est* about nutrition!

And can you think of *anybody* who needs her glossy hair,
waxen skin, stalwart nails, shiny eyes, peachy cheeks, glassy
tongue (sick tongues are furry), bouncy step and racy blood
more than a single woman? What you eat has only just *everything* to do with them.

Animal, Vegetable or Mineral?

Your entire body . . . muscle, bone, brain tissue, blood vessels, red blood cells, hormones and enzymes . . . just about every squiggle of you . . . needs protein every day to renew itself and go on living.

The nutritionists say you also need minerals, vitamins, a little fat, some smidges of carbohydrates (natural ones like the sugars and starch in fresh fruits), and that's about *it*. No expert has ever got a good case going for corn chips or Monte Cristo sandwiches or any of the other tissue-paper, blotters, and fluff a single girl is apt to subsist on.

Very likely you eat *some* of the good stuff every day, but that won't shine your eyes. When you fill up even *part* of you on hamburger buns, root-beer floats, sauces béarnaise or vegetables with the life cooked out of them, you take up valuable space that's needed by the *builders*. And it takes a mess of builders to keep you running efficiently.

If you "starve" your body *long* enough for vital supplies and cram it full of gook, you can develop a severe vitamin, mineral or protein deficiency. Then being single really does seem a good reason to hop off the roof. (You'd feel just as lousy if you were married!)

I became a health nut one Saturday morning about four years ago. I'd been working at the Miss Universe Beauty Pageant in Long Beach, California, for two weeks, helping with the television show. My job was to get information from the contestants about their families, home towns and aspirations, so the emcee could pre-plan his questions for the show.

Have you ever been connected with beauty contestants of this caliber? There were fifty from the fifty states, thirty from foreign countries—all pretty high-powered dazzlers.

Back home in Los Angeles I had a small group of admirers

who thought *I* looked nice. In Long Beach I was the invisible woman.

I would get into the hotel elevator with the girls (I had to track them where I could find them), shorthand book and pencil in hand, pressing for news of dating at Keokuk High or water-skiing in Helsinki, only to be hurled against the bell captain's desk when the door opened and the autograph hunters went after the girls. (I never could figure what they wanted autographs for. Nobody had swum the English Channel or anything.) Anyway, I *had* to be invisible because people would walk right through me clawing to get at the girls!

Fourteen invisible days after it all began (Miss Japan won the crown), I was free to go home; and, driving up to Los Angeles, I passed Gladys Lindberg's health food store. It's hard to miss Gladys' if you're anywhere in the neighborhood. Wired with neon, it would look right at home on the Las Vegas Strip. Gladys doesn't think health foods have anything to hide their heads about.

Friends had suggested I see her years before when I complained of feeling lower than an earthworm. (Who *isn't* badgered by health nuts in her time!) I *did* telephone one day to see if she'd send over some vitamins, but she wanted to know what I'd had for breakfast. I didn't think it was any of her business and the conversation ended. This morning her store looked like Mecca and I would have told her Miss Guatemala's real bust measurement or *anything*. I parked and went in.

Since Gladys holds court sort of like Gandhi—too many people to see and too few hours to see them in—I explained to a cast of about thirty that I was suffering from an acute case of jealousy as well as symptoms of disappearance. Gladys had me stick out my tongue, which she said was purplish, heavily coated and had a deep groove down the center. Since these were the first words of a personal nature anybody had spoken to me in fourteen days, I started to cry all over her blood sugar manuals. She said what I was really suffering from was acute fatigue and probably a vitamin deficiency brought on by years of lousy eating habits.

I went home with the makings of Serenity Cocktail (recipe in a moment), several whole-wheat grains to cook with, the Varsity Pack (a Technicolored collection of vitamins and minerals Gladys feeds athletes) and pounds and pounds of soy pancake mix. Health nuts always placate you with something that *sounds* like what you used to eat that actually bears no resemblance to it. *Delicious*, though!

I won't bore you with my deficiencies and how they didn't grow after that. Just suffice it to say I used to spend half my life in doctors' offices, which is very expensive on a secretary's salary, and I don't anymore.

I later became a guinea pig for a biochemist in Pasadena who is studying the correlation between diet and mental illness. I'll call him George because that's his first name. He works with schizophrenics and paranoids mostly, but has let down the bars to a few run-of-the-mill neurotics like me! George has had fantastic results rehabilitating people who were hopelessly at odds with their families, jobs and society just by giving them large doses of whatever they were missing in their systems. I'm not at odds with society except that I can't stand baseball, but his super-vitamins plus Serenity Cocktail *do* give me the energy to hold a pressure job from nine to six every day, drive more than an hour in heavy traffic to get to it and back, work all day Saturday and most of Sunday writing this fascinating book, go for a five-mile walk every Sunday morning with David as well as amuse him at other times, manage a large house and gad about a bit.

Never mind about me. The possibilities of what good nutrition can do for *you* are equally impressive.

You have some very real and special problems. Being *one* in a world of twos is a bloody bore and lonely at times. Combine this vexation with the everyday problems life hands *everybody* and throw in a possibly half-starved body (even though it's ten pounds overweight), and no *wonder* you have the blues!

People like the doctor in Pasadena and Gladys Lindberg fervently believe that when your body is properly fed and gets into peak running order you can cope with problems quite efficiently. They don't get *to* you as much.

I'd be arrested for prescribing for you and certainly not everybody's body is undernourished, but, subject to your doctor's iron whim, I believe the following rules might change your life—and certainly won't end it.

The Build-Up

1. *Try to get at least 51 grams of protein into you every day.* More would be better but try for at least 17 grams a meal. Here are approximate protein values: you'll need a big helping of *one* of these at every meal.

FOOD	APPROXIMATE GRAMS OF PROTEIN
Lean meat, poultry, fish—1 oz.	6
Tuna fish—1 oz.	8
One egg	6½
Milk—1 oz.	1
Cottage cheese—1 oz.	5
Yellow cheese—1 oz.	6 to 7
Yogurt—8 oz. jar	11

Nutritionists say the protein in gelatin, beans and vegetables is an incomplete kind, missing in important amino acids (whatever they are, but we need them), so you can't count them in your 51 grams.

It's silly to say you can't afford protein! A cup of cottage cheese (40 grams of protein) is 25 cents. Add some fresh peaches, and that's dinner. A quarter pound of ground round steak (24 grams of protein) is also about 25 cents. Slice some tomatoes—*another* dinner. You can eat beautifully and healthfully from your icebox in impeccable single-girl fashion if you eat the right things!

2. *After protein, fill up with fresh fruit, raw or lightly cooked vegetables, a little oil every day, and that's about it.* Whole-grain breads are fine if you make them yourself or get them at the health-food store. Most breads are pretty starchy in spite of being labeled "Enriched." That means they only put back a *fraction* of the food value they took out in milling the flour. The natural carbohydrates in fruits and vegetables take care of *that* department, so don't go kidding yourself you need candy bars for a pick-up . . . *or* rolls *or* macaroni to round out your diet.

3. *Eat breakfast like a king, lunch like a prince, supper like a pauper (except on a date), not the other way around.*

4. Eat *breakfast, you idiot!* Coffee and a cigarette is no way to break a fast between a night's sleep and lunchtime. Get your crazy blood sugar up with protein, and it will stay up. A Danish jacks it only a little while, then *ker-plunk*—back to the cellar.

Maybe you can't face a raw egg so early in the day! Drop two eggs in the *shell* in boiling water and four minutes later fish them out . . . butter a piece of whole-wheat toast. Breakfast is ready and the eggs are now *cooked*.

You can also fix breakfast in a Waring blender. Throw in

skim milk, a raw egg, a fresh-chopped orange with skin barely peeled off, Sucaryl for sweetening, vanilla, powdered protein from a jar (you get it at the drugstore). Tastes like an orange milkshake. Put in instant coffee if you like. You can drink breakfast while you do your face.

5. *Don't ever go too long without eating.* That's when you start shoveling in junk.

6. *Keep things in your desk to nibble that are not your enemy:* raw carrots (don't peel or scrape—just wash them), a few peanuts or walnuts in the shell, celery stalks, an apple, an orange. To eat a whole orange with just the orange color peeled off is *brilliant.* If you can heat water in your office, Romanoff MBT instant soups are calorieless and luscious.

7. *Go for high-powered vitamins and minerals.* While I'm not qualified to diagnose you and maybe it's mental, I *think* they did worlds to chase *my* single-girl blues. With half the health stolen from foods by overprocessing, being picked green and ripened in warehouses, being cooked improperly (by other people, of course), could some vitamins and minerals *hurt* you?

They only work with other food, so don't take them in *place* of. And don't bother with cheapies. The dollar variety are so priced because the *expensive* vitamin components are left out.

8. *Drink a Serenity Cocktail.* If you have a pretty good idea you're beat inside and would like to fortify bones, blood and beautiful outlook, here's the recipe no purplish coated tongue could hold out against. Take a pint of Serenity to work every day in a thermos inside an ice-cream bag to keep it cold. Thirty-five grams of protein right *there!* Have half mid-morning, half mid-afternoon. A jar of yogurt or wedge of yellow cheese could be lunch. Of course, you'll have to find

something else to do during lunch hour. What about a juicy novel or a nap?

GLADYS LINDBERG'S SERENITY COCKTAIL

Put into blender ½ cup chunk pineapple, 2 tablespoons soybean oil, 1 teaspoon calcium lactate (from druggist or health-food store), 1 teaspoon vanilla, 1 cup milk (preferably raw certified). Start motor and add ½ cup powdered skim milk (not instant) and ½ tablespoon brewer's yeast or dried liver powder (from drug or health-food store). When well blended, add mixture to remainder of quart of milk. Banana, frozen orange juice, berries or other fruit may be used instead of pineapple. Gradually increase the yeast or liver powder from ½ tablespoon to 1 or 2 tablespoons.

9. *Fresh fruit is best*. Buy *fresh* fruits and *fresh* vegetables even when just cooking for yourself. Learn to habitually bypass the neatly packaged frozen and canned goods.

10. *Cook with a light touch*—to the point of having things almost underdone . . . meat, too. This was the devil of a rule for me to learn. Anyone raised on Southern cooking thinks meat slightly pink is *alive*. Use less water for vegetables than recipes call for; then drain it off in a glass and drink it yourself. That's where half the vitamins are!

11. *Make these substitutions in cooking:* Use stone ground whole wheat, soy, cottonseed or peanut flour instead of white. Usually you can't tell a scrap of difference in the taste. Try soy pancake mix if your health-food store has it. The pancakes are luscious. Use spinach, artichoke or whole-wheat noodles instead of starchy white ones. Use brown sugar instead of white. Use honey instead of either. Try Kellogg's "K" cereal in place of cornflakes. Make salad dressings and sauté foods

with soybean oil exclusively. Soybean oil has tremendous amounts of polyunsaturated fatty acids which every cell of your body cries for. Buy sweet (unsalted) butter. (If this has turned rancid, the fact can never be hidden by salt.) Whip two softened cubes with ¾ cup of soybean oil and store this in the refrigerator. That's the only butter you ever use. Cook with powdered skim milk from a box (just add water) instead of milk from a bottle. Make this substitution every time you can. Cook what you please for company—reputations are still made on the indigestibles—but no guest is ever going to detect these replacements.

12. *Read a couple of good books on nutrition.* This brief discussion doesn't begin to cover the subject. You could start with *Let's Eat Right To Keep Fit* by Adelle Davis (Harcourt, Brace). Mrs. Davis is the firebrand of food circles and infuriates doctors, but she's fascinating. *She'll* start you thinking nutritionally, all right. Bob Cummings has shared his stay-young secrets (mostly about food) in *Stay Young and Vital* (Prentice-Hall). Very readable. As you may know, Bob Cummings is a fantastic fifty or more. Some girls from my office saw him at the Brown Derby the other day and said he is indeed a man to make you all hippety-hop inside.

13. *Keep your lip zipped.* If you decide to go the health route, don't talk about it on dates. Think how cleverly Dracula concealed his vampirehood. Quietly order the least gooped-up entree on the menu, skip rolls and butter, leave the fried potatoes on your plate (you'll soon be revolted by anything greasy or fried anyway), eat your baked potato without tons of butter *or* sour cream, have melon instead of seven-layer Napoleon. Nobody is even going to suspect you for the health fiend you are.

14. *Yes, you can drink in moderation.* Drink a real cocktail when you wish . . . just like normal people! *But* . . . if

you even *think* you tend toward alcoholism—the for-*real* kind —read *Body, Mind and Sugar* by E. M. Abrahamson, M.D. and A. W. Pezet (Holt). Diet may even be of help for *that*.

15. *Don't be any nuttier than you have to.* Don't fret if you eat "impure" concoctions occasionally. If you're food-wise most of the time, you'll stay more than radiant.

It's kind of a serious step changing your eating habits violently, and one you may have to creep up on. The closer you are to forty, or the farther past it, the more I'd recommend you step up the creep to a canter. It may take a whole year before you really feel and see fantastic changes in your body, depending on how deprived you were. But boy, will you love them!

Sexy Foods

I have been pestering George, the biochemist in Pasadena, for a list of foods that would increase sexiness in a person. I thought it might be fun to keep these aphrodisiac items in a cupboard just for special occasions, or merely for a conversation piece. (Your problem is probably in keeping everybody's boiling point *down*.) Well, all I got from George was sneers. "You know very well," he said, "that the only thing in the world that will give a man or woman more of a sex drive is to build him up nutritionally. A strong healthy body has all the sex drive it can handle. Of course, an individual could lack sexual potency because of a diet deficiency. Just correct the deficiency and you'll get him back to peak performance."

On George's theory, a girl would have to keep a food inventory roughly comparable to that of the A & P to be sure of having the copper, sulphur, zinc, potassium or whatever to counteract the specific deficiency a guest might have. She'd also have to be a biochemist to find it.

There are no real aphrodisiacs in drugs *or* food. Oysters got their aphrodisiac reputation because they were fed to somebody starved for zinc. Oysters are *loaded* with zinc. Chicken croquettes might do just as much for someone *you* know.

Alcohol seems aphrodisiac because it puts sex hormones into the blood—pulls them out of other tissue—to give you a temporary surge of sexual energy. But if you continue drinking, this trick won't work. The tissue has already given its all.

Since there's no other instant route to animal magnetism, eat your protein, *will* you?

If the man you love should happen to have a heart problem, aside from you, and has been warned to keep his cholesterol low, Ancel and Margaret Keys' *Eat Well and Stay Well* (Doubleday) will tell you how to feed him. It has text as well as lightweight, light-hearted recipes.

The Skinnies Have It

Would you believe it, we health nuts are never fat! And never have to crash-diet. The foods that make you sexy, exuberant, full of the *joie de vivre* are also the ones that keep you slender.

You almost can't *get* too much protein. The excess you acquire over your daily requirements helps you burn up extra fat. But it must be *just* protein. Goop it up with gravy, Yorkshire pudding and sauce diablo, and you'll enlarge like Paddy's pig. You can eat tons of steamed broccoli or *any* vegetable without avoirdupois-ing. Hollandaise them and your ideal weight has *had* it.

Now if you are already mounds of pounds overweight, you must *Do Something*, or you can't hope to be blissfully single.

You have only to look at two of the most beautiful women in the world—Marilyn Monroe and Elizabeth Taylor—twenty pounds overweight (as they both occasionally are) and compare them to the goddesses they are when sleeked down to a size ten. Even *their* beauty can't survive runaway fat.

The few men who insist they like girls plump are usually the ones who prefer cleaning rifles or exchanging jokes in the locker room to flirtation. They aren't sure of their masculinity and appeal; so, of course, a chic, glamorous woman challenges them. They keep their wives encased in baby fat, so *they* won't be a challenge too.

The glandular dodge is out. Doctors find that behind nearly every fat person lies a history of compulsive, secretive eating. A dear friend of mine who was supposedly "glandular" was actually bolting a quart of chocolate ice cream every day *after* work and before dinner.

Even women fresh from childbirth have proved *they* can be slim again quick.

Where *can* you hide?

Take it off and you won't have to.

How To Diet

See a doctor. He can help with the emotional problems that drive you to wolf down the forbiddens and he can inspire you to make another serious reducing start. It doesn't matter how many times you've slid off a diet. One of these days you'll stick. If by some chance your inordinate craving for sweets *is* organic (I think it's called hyperinsulinism), a doctor will spot that too and put you on an anti-blood-sugar-starvation diet. Unfortunately, that means no candy, no sugar *ever*, so don't hope *that's* your problem!

I'd suggest you read cover-to-cover Ruth West's *Stop Dieting! Start Losing!* (Bantam). Like a lot of other food literature, it's written for *wives* to help their husbands reduce, but you're worth saving too! This book tells you how to stay on a kind of painless diet forever and deliciously.

If you'd like to crash away six pounds in two days, here is a diet men like. Invite one to join you. Follow this plan only two days; then back to sanity!

Breakfast	1 egg any style, no butter	One glass white wine
Lunch	2 eggs any style	Two glasses white wine
Dinner	1 steak	Finish the bottle of white wine

I'd suggest the weekend for the crash. Sufficient nutrition is here, but you get fuzzy.

Stop thinking of diet as a case of measles to be gotten through with. Except for the fortunate freaks whose bodies can't seem to turn calories into fat, *everybody* over age thirty has to change eating patterns to stay scrumptious. You can no more stoke the furnace with the trash you ate at twenty and stay yummy than you can go back to jacks and leapfrog as a way of life.

I weigh 109, and people are quite snooty when I try to join a diet discussion. "Go drink a milkshake," they say. "Eat some pretzels!" Fatties never give skinnies credit for any will power. They prefer to assume you're one of the freaks. Well, I diet every day of my life by willfully selecting health foods. Cookieholics, like alcoholics, are only arrested, never cured.

The health-nut kind of diet is a pretty easy one to live with, however. Once your body gets used to expecting and *getting* the good things, it stops craving sugar and junk as it used to. I swear it does! No longer do you sneak down to the lobby for a Milky Way at four o'clock.

If you *do* occasionally eat a forbidden goodie, which you almost certainly will at dinner parties (just *try* not to accept a freshly baked peach popover from a determined hostess), it will seem kind of alien to you . . . like a friend you used to have everything in common with but haven't anymore. And if you don't get chummy again, you can fly right back to safe, sane eating and be perfectly happy.

The Shape of Your Shape

Do you remember early in the book when we said you could be an exciting single woman and attract like a magnet without doing anything show-offy—that you tunnel from within?

Well, there is one tunnel from which you will emerge so attractive, so sexy, so young-looking that you wouldn't have to go through any other tunnels to get whistles, compliments and probably date invitations every day of your life.

Yet possibly a scant handful of women in any one city ever avail themselves of this sure-fire route to sexiness.

It's exercise, of course—the brisk, your-body-knows-something's-*happened*-to-it kind—one hour nearly every day of your life for *life!* No wonder even the valiant throw in the towel—such monotonous, brainless, unpleasant business.

Yet that kind of workout could make you smooth and sleek and glossy . . . your tummy flat enough to wear a bikini . . . your fanny cute and asking to be patted . . . your head carried like a swan. Yes . . . all that with *your* basic equipment. The "shape" definitely can do more than gorgeous clothes, a flashy convertible or an annuity to get you that "Come with me to Majorca on my yacht" look from a man.

There they are . . . the Incompatibles! The glittering rewards that accrue to girls with shapely shapes (even the make-them-yourself kind) and the total impossibility of stay-ing with push-ups.

Maybe this is the answer. Create a teensy, weensy little ex-ercise program you *can* live with—and then *live* with it. It's worked for me for ten years.

All exercisers say it's consistency that counts. A few rounds of tennis twice a year do *nothing*. The modified daily push can't make you look re-*poured*, as would an honest hour a day, but it definitely is enough to keep the jungle from en-croaching, if you know what I mean. You can never get really sloppy. As a matter of fact, the repetition can keep your hips quite patable.

The trick is to incorporate a five- to ten-minute exercise period with your regular getting-off-to-work chores.

Did you ever hear the original joke to which "Doesn't *everyone?*" is the punch line?

A woman goes to her doctor for a check-up. He can find nothing wrong. He says, "Will you please tell me exactly what you do every day from the time you wake up in the morning till you go to bed at night." "Certainly," she says. "I turn off the alarm, get out of bed, go to the bathroom, wash my face, throw up, brush my teeth, take a shower—"

"Just a minute," he says. "Will you repeat that?"

"Sure," she says, "I turn off the alarm, get up, go to the bathroom, wash my face, throw up, brush my teeth, take a shower—"

"Young woman," he says, "do you mean to tell me that every single morning of your life you throw up after you wash your face?"

"Sure," she says. "Doesn't *everybody?*"

That's how morning exercise has to be—so automatic you could do it in your sleep, and you *do* usually! If you can get yourself in the habit of squeezing in some sit-ups and rollovers between brushing your teeth and taking your shower and if you do it *long* enough, you may even forget what you're doing! Did Pavlov's dogs know they were salivating?

I do one fanny-chipper, two tummy-levelers (my tummy should cave in like a cereal bowl by now, but it still doesn't), a double-chin routine and some lifts with three-pound dumbbells. You really can do quite a lot in five or ten minutes. Longer than that and you may get that "let me *out* of here" feeling again. On the mornings when getting out of *bed* is too much of an effort, don't scootch around on the floor. As a matter of fact, you can goof off for a week or two; but, if the exercise habit has been inculcated in you long enough, you'll *scootch* again!

Do get dumbbells. A woman's upper arms give her age away faster than slip-ups about remembering Kay Francis in *One Way Passage* (not on television). Also, hoisting your dumbbells even in a stupor, makes you feel so *en rapport* with the rest of the world's athletes. If you don't know a store that carries them, order from Terry Hunt, 50 N. La Cienega, Beverly Hills, California. Three-pound dumbbells are three dollars, five-pounders are five dollars. Add postage. Your post office will tell you how much it costs to ship them.

The rest of the exercise-program-you-can-live-with calls for a three- to five-mile walk every week. Go at a good pace but don't bolt. This walking business is *fun*. Find a woodsy trail up a mountain if you can. I walk in Griffith Park and Will Rogers' State Park—both woodsy places in the heart of a big city. Wear tennis shoes and as little clothing as possible.

Take a girl friend with you. You can usually find one who is also looking for painless exercise. A gossipy walk almost *is*. Or bring along a boy friend. The walk only takes from one and a half to two hours and is something you can ask a man to do with you that isn't as serious as asking him to dinner or to

be your date for a party. You can also take a married couple
. . . you needn't have the same companion every week.

If there's nobody available, walk alone. One Labor Day
weekend I walked three days in a row by myself. It sounds
kind of pitiful, doesn't it, but who *saw* me but lizards? By
Tuesday I was tummyless, lean and feeling very smug about
the whole thing.

A mountain climb is the *greatest* way to work off a rage at
a man who has done something awful. Don't take him with
you, of course. When you get off the trail, you just haven't
the strength to hate until *much* later.

Walking won't re-pour you either, but it does jangle things
up nicely. Marvelous for your legs, your lungs, your fanny,
your circulation; and you can eat *more* without gaining.
Here's a luscious treat you could have when you get home:
fresh-squeezed orange juice mixed with half a bottle of ice-
cold No-Cal orange soda, topped with a small scoop of
vanilla ice milk. Who needs French pastry?

Try to walk every week without fail. Just get yourself out
to the trail somehow. When you see the sun glinting at you
through the trees, you'll be so glad you're there, hangover
and all.

You may already be taking far more strenuous exercise than
this, and that's great. I'm sure your figure shows it.

As we mentioned earlier, prowess at sports is another tunnel to a man.

If you just know a man or woman who *looks* great because
of exercise, that's an inspiration. The friend who showed me
the Griffith Park walk has the most gorgeous legs I've ever
seen, and he's fifty-two. If I could have legs like that at fifty-
two, I'd wear Bermuda shorts all winter. If you haven't an
athletic friend to inspire you, one who's stayed vigorous and

glamorous through exercise, just get a load of Cary Grant in any movie.

Now, I think, is the time to confess I'm just on the nervous edge of trying to increase my ten-minute exercise period for the thirtieth time in my life. There will probably be a thirty-first, thirty-second, etc.

This accursed book has fallen into my hands—*How To Keep Slender and Fit after Thirty* by Bonnie Prudden (Geis).

Now Miss Prudden is an exerciser from way back, with the figure to prove it. And her book describes about ninety-three hundred thousand things you *could* do if you had a rubber body and the stamina of King Kong.

My first inclination was to write her a letter and say how ridiculous it is to expect a woman to do a fraction that much. And maybe we're turtles, but turtles have feelings too—and don't like to be criticized for hating "bicycles."

Well, I didn't write her but kept reading, and a little farther on was a whole chapter on exercises you can do when you aren't doing anything *else*—waiting for an elevator or for the light to change, walking or driving . . . times like that. She's got a thing about stairs. Never just *go* upstairs. Go up two at a time, hop, skip or *jump* up. Come down backwards! I've been walking up the seven flights to my office just on the strength of this nonsense. And no coronary yet!

Farther on in the book is an absolutely fabulous chapter called "Sexercise" which tells you how to develop your pelvic muscles, so you'll be a better bed mate. She doesn't say this stuff is for single girls, but she doesn't say it isn't.

And she keeps reminding you, page after page, that women and men with beautiful bodies usually have more fun in bed because they're proud of themselves and the way they look in the buff.

One of her really fun projects is: after a shower put your

feet up on the washbasin, one at a time she says, to dry them off. This stretches *everything!* It's a good time to rub baby oil into your ankles and heels too . . . something you always mean to do.

She's got exercises for when you talk on the phone or just stand still. If you could sum up Miss Prudden's exercise philosophy, I think it would be: "Never leave anything lying around unused."

Well, after doing a bunch of the "painless" routines just two days—gluteals at the elevator or a pelvic walk if nobody was looking—I went to a party. And for the first time in my life I stood up straight all evening, tummy tucked in, chest out, shoulders back and felt perfectly comfy. Somebody even told me I had a lovely posture, and I've always had a *crummy* posture. It's a dangerous book!

As for passive exercises by machine, or muscle-tightening by electric impulse, it seems to me that's for *old* folks. It's just as big a headache as do-it-yourself, takes as long, and you can't have the fun of a playmate to do it with.

This shape business is important—inside and out—if you're not going to take singleness lying down—except when you want to.

CHAPTER 10

THE WARDROBE

Lodged in your pretty head somewhere is the image of how you'd like to appear to your public. You're a sophisticated gamine, a creamy and elegant princess. You're tweedy, sexy, Grecian, a bird of paradise or any of twenty other fascinating creatures. I'm sure the least specific image you have of yourself is that of an attractive, nicely dressed woman.

I don't think anyone should try to tamper with your image. You should dress in a manner that preserves and strengthens it—makes it feel cozy and secure!

But how about men? Shouldn't you dress to please *them?*

One of the best ways *not* to, in my opinion, is to let them get into the act. Why is it assumed just because a man is a man he knows what *you* should wear? Do you tell *him* what to look for in a car?—a subject on which he is undoubtedly more knowledgeable than you. Do you tell him how to *shave?* The *expert,* it seems to me, is the woman who has

186

spent years (*most* working women) shopping for and buying women's clothes, perusing fashion magazines and getting acquainted with her figure and what it looks nice in.

A man can have a knack for picking out gorgeous dresses but not necessarily for *you*.

There you are in the gold lamé sheath old Henry Higgins conned you into, your complexion looking like mud, your bank account in shreds and your bust line definitely not making the scene.

Admittedly *some* men do have a sense for clothes. I have known several who had far better taste than I and I tried to learn from them. I think the idea is to see through their eyes for a while, listen to their ideas, then try to inculcate them into your own clothes judgment. Otherwise a man gets to be a bit of a bore telling you when you *may* and when you may *not* wear your peach chiffon. Leave those chaps to the girls whose chiffon they're *paying* for.

Occasionally a man you truly adore has a clothes preference, and you must humor him, of course. My husband is a fiend for slinky black . . . wants it worn winter or summer, day or night. I remember one hot August afternoon when we were first dating, he said, "Get into something slinky black. We're going over to meet my friends Jackie and Ernest."

Naturally I wanted Jackie and Ernest to like me, so I got right into something slinky and black. Well, everybody was out by the pool in wet swim suits and faded denims, and there was I—Vampira at high noon.

When I get my slinky-black instructions *now*, unless it's *night*, I just pretend everything's at the cleaners or fell into the bathtub when I was trying to steam the wrinkles out.

Unless he's *the* man, it seems to me it's better not to pander to his idiosyncrasies anyhow. While you are running around in little dimity peasant blouses to please *him*, you are hopelessly alienating other men who prefer you in Indian saris!

Now we know pretty definitely that men love pink, and a girl in pink summer cotton is a delectable concoction indeed. Most men like girls in slinky black for that matter. These two are as standard as "White Christmas" and "God Bless America." Have them in your wardrobe if you truly like them, but a far more important rule for man-pleasing to my way of thinking is DRESS TO PLEASE YOURSELF. If you do it with exquisite taste, you'll be amazed how few men or anybody else will try to change your stripes for polka dots. (Can you imagine anybody trying to get Audrey Hepburn into more black satin or badgering Princess Grace to go more froufrou?!) And never mind what Grace and Audrey are spending—their taste came first.

The question is: Is your image really coming through?

If your clothes aren't saying "Wow!" it's probably the lack of taste. Not *money* . . . *taste!*

Good taste doesn't mean you have to dress sedately or even elegantly. Gina Lollobrigida has much more flamboyant taste than Grace Kelly, for example, and usually looks terrific too. (I'm sorry to use all these movie-star examples. *I* certainly don't know them, but at least we both know whom we're talking about.)

Let's take the sexy image. I maintain that when you add the element of good taste to it, even *this* look can be enhanced.

Suppose the shoulder-length hair were clipped evenly around the bottom with ends blunted to add body and bounce . . . isn't that sexier than the scraggly, split-ends, nine-different-lengths look? In the first place you'll seem to have *more* hair. Suppose the sexy black dress is beautifully short and even around its hemline too. Isn't that come-hitherer than the three-seasons-ago mid-calf length?

Suppose the neckline is a recent vintage—say a low, low

V front and back with little underneath instead of the much-
boned and stayed strapless style of five years back. Wouldn't
the uniform have more woo and wow? What if you left off all
junk jewelry and just let your ivory *skin* gleam at him? Very
likely all but a most deez, dems and doze guy who doesn't
notice what a girl is wearing anyway, except whether it zips,
would find this look a hundred times more alluring than that
of the floozie.

David and I were recently in Cyrano's, a coffeehouse on the
Sunset Strip frequented by what surely must be some of the
most beautiful young women in the world, median age
twenty-three. (It was David's birthday so I let him stay exactly one hour.) Most of these girls—young movie hopefuls,
models, starlets—outdazzle the Miss Universe contestants by
a million kilowatts. Several nights a week with their dates
they mill about Cyrano's, to be seen by agents and producers
and to talk shop.

Was there a tousled hairdo? A fat fanny? A limp T-shirt?
An ill-fitting garment in the whole place? Not that I could see.
Just total chic, even in the pants and sweater contingent.

My point is that whatever their income—and I'm sure many
were on a diet of Mounds Bars—they were doubling and
tripling their sex appeal, their chances of being discovered, by
looking as tasteful as a cappuccino royale.

Usually when people attack ycur clothes, they aren't at-
tacking your *image*. They are just saying, "Look, kid, it isn't
coming off!" In other words, you aren't applying enough taste.

Taste Buds

Why is there so much lousy taste among working girls who
should know better? (And we won't even bring *up* the sub-

ject of *home* bodies!) I think it's because they can't *see* themselves as others see them. Yet one word of criticism and the
guilty girl will crawl right into her hollow log, dragging in
with her the twelve petticoats that make her look like an
apple dumpling! Oh how we hiss and resist and tell ourselves
the detractors are just *jealous!*

What is this highly touted little item called good taste and
where do you get it? I think good taste is what's beautiful
. . . what looks most pleasing to most people. And you get it
by absorption!

Everybody can't have the same taste, of course, but it's
amazing how many people can agree on someone who *has* it.
Even the Las Vegas jeweled-sweater-and-wedgie crowd concede that San Francisco women have chic and Los Angeles
women don't.

Before writing this chapter, I polled the thirty girls in my
office to see who they thought had the best taste, so that I
could describe her to you. I knew who *I* thought did, but
there are lots of different "images" where I work.

Well, the secret ballot was cast overwhelmingly for my
girl, and here's what she looks like: Jeanne (that's her real
name) is thirty-six, single, not beautiful, a whopping big girl
but graceful. She has a small bust, small fanny and big sense
of humor. Her wardrobe runs the gamut from Harris tweeds
to Taibok silks so loud they look as though they could burst
into a chorus of "Babalu." She isn't conservative. At client
meetings she sometimes wears black dresses just this side of
cocktaily. Yet on office Saturdays the rest of us feel over-
dressed in jump-ins because Jeanne is tooling about in an
ancient sweat shirt, scruffy poplin jeans, and barefooted.

This was her yesterday's outfit: black cotton dirndl skirt,
little-nothing black and white polka-dot crepe blouse, bare
brown legs (with feet, of course), fragile black patent sandals

with fiery red toenails peeking out, a rhinestone clip at her waist. Bizarre? But the *Harper's* kind! (Of course, we work in an office where bare legs are permitted.)

She has a backless evening dress of blue and green checked silk that would make you want to give up your day job and find something to do nights, so you could wear evening dresses.

I've seen her make a hat out of dead leaves that had dropped off an indoors plant in her office and wear it to a cocktail party. She also has gray flannel and cashmere sweaters like all good career girls. Yes, I *know* she sounds revolting . . . like one of those oh-so-clever girls magazines are always making up to taunt you. Only this girl is *real* and isn't revolting at all. She spends money on clothes, but her taste came first. She too used to pinch pennies. About half her wardrobe she made herself. Some of her good suits are twelve years old.

I have gone into detail about Jeanne's clothes because they definitely help her get what she wants—recognition in the business world and men for her charm bracelet. She's been married, and I don't believe she's champing at the bit to do that again. She has a gang of beaux—the tennis-playing you-could-take-anywhere kind, which aren't so easy to collect. For all her chic and clothes sense, I've never seen a girl more at ease around a bunch of fellows.

Your taste may not necessarily be Jeanne's, and it needn't be. And we can't legislate good taste for you. But I would like to share a group of rules that I think can help you dress beautifully and please a man. They're mine, not Jeanne's, and my only qualification for passing them on is that I used to wear artificial flowers in my hair and tight sweaters and things like that. I think I've come a long way in the taste department since then. Naturally all the rules are budget-minded.

Acquiring Taste

1. Count the fashion magazines—*Vogue, Harper's Bazaar, Glamour*—as *friends!* Within their pages you will see the best photography, the best clothes, the best looks of our time, assembled with loving care by people whose profession and sole aim is to show you what's beautiful.

If the styles seem extreme, it's only because they are *new* and you aren't used to them yet. If *Vogue* presents a hair style a yard wide, they hope perhaps you'll be jolted into poufing your page boy out just a *trifle*. That's all they're after . . . not total, slavish follow-*me*.

It isn't so important to read what these books *say*, though their articles and stories are terrific. But look at the *girls*. Click them into your head to remember when you shop.

2. *Do* follow fashion!

Nobody is asking you to give up your beloved shirtwaist, but get it at the length skirts *are* this year. Wear it with a totally new shade of sweater . . . and lipstick.

If you will get yourself in the way of thinking that changing "looks" is not just capricious and expensive but a means to being a totally new and fascinating *creature* every so often, you'll feel happier. Fashion is your ally. Would it were that easy to get a new face!

The obsolescence factor is exaggerated by the grumps, I feel. Each new crop of styles usually looks fine for years, up to and including the much-maligned sack dress if you will go to the pains to remodel. I have thrown out only one dress in the last ten years because fashion said, "Out!" And it was never pretty to begin with.

3. Re-examine the dictum, "Wear only what's best for your figure forever and ever. Never mind what fashion is decreeing."

If you have potato-puff hips and a large stomach, it's true you'd better stick with your best style, which is undoubtedly a tent. But if you have a young body, there is practically no new fashion you can't embrace some version of, and that's the truth! Why miss out on this very female kind of fun?

The current easy fit with blouson top does *nothing* for my 23-inch waist. I'll gladly show off my waist four days a week, thank you, but on the fifth I'll look new and fashiony in the blouson.

Don't men *loathe* high fashion? Do you hear many complaints about Mrs. Kennedy, Mrs. Ferrer or the Monacan princess? Fashion addicts all. If your most pooh-pooh-to-it boy friend were to chat with any of the ten best-dressed women in the world, he would probably be so charmed by their *effect* he wouldn't realize he was face to face with *haute couture.*

The girls who offend are those who go high-fashion without taste, and those girls could set your teeth on edge in a Mother Hubbard.

Teen-age girls are nutty about boys, aren't they? Do you find *them* clinging defensively to last year's checked ballerina? They can't *wait* to get into what's new and sizzling *this* year . . . and please *men!*

4. Copycat a mentor with better taste than yours. I copycatted the West Coast editors of *Glamour* and *Vogue* for years. I didn't buy so much as a hatpin without asking myself if it was a hatpin they would buy. Was this spineless? I think it was the smartest move I ever made. When I was just pulling out of the artificial flower stage, these girls had stabilized beautiful taste. I don't know where they got it, but

they had it. Someone like this can inspire you and keep you on the track.

5. Don't just admire ... *study* beautifully gowned women. You're at an advantage as a single woman because you probably get to more restaurants and theatres. Figure out *why* a particular stunner knocks you out. Is it her hair? Her cyclamen matte jersey dress (everybody else is in black!)? Her pin —a huge white cameo? It's *everything!* Make notes.

For years I've studied the fabulous creatures who stroll Fifth Avenue and Park Avenue. They still make me feel like a country girl every time I visit New York no matter *how* I plan, but *one of these days I'm going to discover the secret!*

6. *Listen* when people tell you something is wrong. You may even listen to men! Most friends are extremely tactful, and your plastic spring-o-lator pumps must *really* be getting on their nerves if they bring the subject up. (Families are something else and sometimes seem to be trying to asphyxiate your image instead of improve it. When they criticize, check a second source.)

Friends told me for years I might just do something about my *hair* (even after the flowers went). My hair to me was casual, sexy, even glamorous. To them it was Australian Bushman! I finally saw it their way and have kept it tamed and combed for quite some time now.

Yesterday, at the beauty shop, I watched a young blonde getting ready to leave. Her dress had a purple skirt, lavender-checked top with big puff sleeves, white cummerbund, artificial flowers pinned on, etcetera, etcetera, but she might possibly have gotten away with it because she was young and her hair was beautiful and neat. Then before my eyes she took a heavy gold necklace with double-fringed medallions out of her purse and put *that* on. Then she reached in and pulled out two matching gold bracelets and put *them* on. I was swooning in my oilcloth wrapper! I *twitched* to go over and take the jewelry off her, but there are laws which govern ladies in beauty shops. Someday somebody *is* going to tell her about the jewelry. And I hope she listens.

7. Get acquainted with good clothes even if you can't afford them. It will teach you what to look for in cheaper ones. At least twice a year get all dressed up and beard the lionesses in their French Rooms and Designer Rooms. Ask to see what you are actually interested in at the time—black dress, pink coat, beige suit. You're on your own as to how you get out of there without buying. Visit these salons at sale time too. The confusion will be greater, and you can browse.

8. Study the best store windows. Gape, gaze and drink in.

9. Attend good fashion shows and gape and gaze some more. The major stores in your city usually have several a year. Check with a buyer to see when.

Buying

1. Don't buy *anything* . . . not so much as a garter belt . . . you don't *adore*. Everything in your wardrobe must be important in its way, *especially* if you're on a budget. Yes, this could very easily mean *fewer* clothes!

If a dress doesn't thrill you initially, the chances of its lifting your spirits in six months are practically nil.

How often do you *buy* a bulky white sweater . . . a pure silk shirt? Why not save up and make it *the* bulky sweater . . . *the* shirt?

2. Never buy anything because you *ought*. If you find a good black coat that will go with everything, is reasonably priced, conservative, can double as a raincoat, will be good five years from now but bores the daylights out of you, skip

it. Somewhere there is a black coat with most of these virtues that will make you feel like a princess. FIND THAT COAT!

Give each purchase the acid test. Ask yourself if it cost one dollar, five dollars or ten dollars more (depending on its classification), would you still want it? If the answer is no, price is influencing you too much; and you aren't mad enough for it.

Some of my girl friends bring back their two-dollar blouses and shoes from the sales with the comment, "For two dollars how could you go *wrong?*"

My notion is, "For two dollars how could you go *right?*"

3. Shop where you can return without embarrassment. Many women are in love with their decisiveness and claim never to have taken a purchase back in their lives. Bully for them! I'll bet their closets contain more boo boos than mine do.

If there's any doubt in the cold light of your bathroom mirror about a garment's glow power, back with it! Store mirrors can be liars!

4. "Embrace" the manufacturer whose clothes consistently do nice things for you. If you don't see labels, ask the sales-girl whose is what.

I discovered Anne Klein's Junior Sophisticates years ago when they were out of my price range, but I still managed to squeeze in a few every year. These chic, sleek junior dresses were always ego-lifting.

Trusting a manufacturer's taste doesn't mean *you* haven't got any. It's just another safety factor when you can't afford $$$$$ mistakes.

My favorite dresses now are by Walter Bass or come from Jax. Jax also has stores in New York, Chicago, San Francisco and Palm Beach. One Jax dress can speed up a flirtation by several weeks or more. How anyone can put so much good taste and sex appeal into one garment is astonishing!

5. Make a store *your* store. Pick one out—it may also be a trifle over your head price-wise—whose merchandise you trust and have fabulous luck with. Buy everything you can afford to there. Yes, you may attend sales!

6. Shop in large-volume, low-overhead stores, too—Ohrbach's, for example—but use caution. Lots of chaff among that wheat.

7. Don't pay too much or too little. If your salary is $350 a month, no $200 coat in the world could be worth the sacrifice in shoes and underwear. If you pay too *little,* you can't wow even a rubber plant.

One of my good friends recently bought a navy wool suit for $33. It is a knock-down of a knock-down, cute but classless. It will never do anything to help her image, which I'm sure is that of a beautifully dressed career woman. This girl makes a pile of dough. For something as basic as a navy blue suit, which could go on and on like a fur coat, I can't think what she's doing with this little number.

8. Pay most for clothes you wear most . . . your suits, your coats and classic cocktail dresses. I have worn a black Jax sheath ($89) every two weeks for about two and a half years. (Of course, I live with a slinky-black fiend; maybe you wouldn't use this kind of dress that much.) Anyway, it has figured out at about 68 cents a wearing plus upkeep, and that's pretty good.

9. Buy one complete outfit each fall-winter, spring-summer season—a *good* suit or dress, plus shoes, bag, coat and a hat if you wear one. You can never wind up with a closetful of fluff and nothing to look fabulous in. This year's two major outfits then become next year's second outfits, and you gradually build an excellent wardrobe.

10. Stick to one or two colors in shoes and bags while you're budgeting. This is a stuffy rule, I know, but girls can get so hopelessly loused up trying to have shoes and purses in all colors of the rainbow. Everything reeks cheap.

At this moment I own three pairs of plain black leather pumps that alternate all winter, some black beaded evening slippers, one pair of flats. In summer I switch around three pairs of black patent and one pair of bone pumps. Finish.

The cheaper the shoe, the simpler the cut should be. (I can't stand pippy-poo things on *any* shoes.)

My one good black leather purse goes to work *every single day* all winter. So could yours! (Or your brown or navy one.) For summer I alternate a bone and a patent bag. All right, maybe it wouldn't hurt to have a handsome straw basket and one lovely pair of striped-silk shoes; but, if that basket has seashells and flowers on it, you and I have had it.

And no white shoes with dark dresses. Okay?

11. Spend brain units instead of dollars for the once-in-a-lifetime, big-occasion dress. Even if it's the Embassy Ball and you are going with the President of Tanganyika, a wear-it-once dress sopping up a hundred clothes dollars is *madness!* Try to borrow a gown, or remake one, or create a creation out of thirty yards of cheesecloth! Who cares if it falls apart the minute you get home.

You could haunt sales for *this* item too. Try for the third mark-down on a mark-down.

12. Keep only a small basic glove inventory. Gloves can't make your taste reputation.

As for cheap jewelry, a few blue and green plastic bracelets (15 cents each) can be stunning. So can clumpy orange beads and shocking pink ones (a couple of bucks). But junk-jewelry fanciers are so weak-willed! Just one more bracelet and a few more beads, and first thing you know every Ubangi in town is in a jealous snit.

None of that little-bitty, teeny-tiny stuff like grandmothers give baby granddaughters either. You're a grown female. What jewelry you wear should be important.

13. Wear lots of your best shade. Cosmetics can make you look *better* whatever your *worst* color is, but there's nothing like *your* color to make a man get the I-want-you's. A wealthy redhead I know doesn't *own* anything but blue, and her *house* is *too*, from cellar to dome.

Make absolutely certain you aren't missing a glorious color out of prejudice. You might get an outside opinion on whether it's for you.

14. Don't buy the dotted swiss that takes an hour to iron unless you solemnly swear to *iron* it, and *often*—after you've washed it, of course. Slightly "had-it" summer cottons are the *worst*. And the most delish when fresh.

15. Love yourself enough to wear clean lingerie every day even if it isn't ironed. Some young ladies have absolutely gray-looking bras. Take a bath or shower every day while you're at it. Could it hurt?

After you've absorbed all these taste rules, add some vervy and reckless ones of your own. That's what makes it *your* taste—and what makes *you* exciting.

I Made It Myself

Learn to sew! (I already *know* how, of course, because I'm so smart and because my mother started teaching me when I was very young.)

Buy a bone-simple pattern like for a muu muu, some 49-cent cotton and let one of your sewing friends help you at first.

Don't tackle major items that need tailoring until you're an ace, which may be *never!* Do swing with your Singer for a splashy print silk Hopi coat, floor-length at-home skirt, five-yards-long evening stole.

I Made It FIT Myself

Far more important than *making* your clothes is making them *fit*.

The waist seam below the belt, the "narrow" skirt that's miles wide at the bottom are telltale signs of a chic-bleak dresser.

Doing your own alterations can save you a hundred thousand dollars if you're like me and can't buy a garment that doesn't need *something*. (Some manufacturer some day is going to make dresses for swayback girls.)

Maybe you'd like to have a sewing circle! About every six weeks several girls from my office and I round up all our clothes that need altering, and we gossip and sew for an evening. Isn't that jolly?

If you don't sew, or even if you do, you'll want a good alteration woman to tackle major adjustments. I wouldn't tell *anybody* mine because I don't want her finding out how much Saks charges to put up a hem. I hope you can find a Mrs. Linnes too.

Don't be afraid to alter spanking new garments if they can be made more *you*. Rip off the buttons. Cancel the bows! Make a new ribbon sash. My jewel has just taken the big pleats out of two inexpensive wool dresses and shirred them all about the waist, so they look more expensive, custom-made.

Take inventory of your clothes often to see what needs bringing up to date. Try everything on. Fantastic how you can turn your back only a minute, and the zip is gone! Maybe you'll crop the sleeves. Or erase the collar. Good stuff will alter again and again. Some of my Walter Bass and Jax dresses have had the hems up and down five times.

While you're at it, throw out that persimmon taffeta you haven't had on your back in three years! A closet jammed with half-decent and half-indecent stuff can make you feel you haven't got a thing to wear.

The Wearing

Try on the dress you will wear to the party, the important date. Look at yourself in the full-length mirror to see how the dress moves from all angles . . . both seated and standing. A certain style may look better if your weight is rested on one foot, the other foot slightly in front of it. A long tube of a gown may work better with your weight rested on the front foot, the other leg and foot straight back or slightly to the side.

Like a *fashion model?*

You're damn right!

Isn't that a little too *much* if you're just a nice, plain, civilian girl?

Let's review our lesson.

You're single. You'd like to be able to stop apologizing for the state. Better still, you'd like to get out of it. Well, maybe getting out isn't so easy just this minute, but you *can* stop apologizing!

One way to be successfully single and have a lot of friends and beaux around who admire you and tell you so is to look terrific . . . just a little *more* terrific than some of your complacent married girl friends or some of your fellow bachelor girls who only have the strength to complain but not the guts to *act*.

Okay. You'll have to go to a little more *trouble* than they do.

Psychoanalyzing this dress, and figuring out how to wear a dress to its and your advantage, are part of your arsenal.

No, you don't have to be self-conscious all evening long and to preen like a peacock. Quite the contrary. Do your homework well at home and go out and have a ball. Once you get the hang of showing off clothes, you'll do it without thinking. Jeanne, for example, never sits facing anyone head-on in a bare-top dress because her shoulders, as she puts it, are football. She confronts you at a bit of an angle. I would defy anyone to detect that her pose is calculated. It *isn't* anymore! It's second nature.

Isn't it awfully self-centered to spend so much time perfecting a wardrobe, to say nothing of checking off body angles in a mirror?

Psychiatrists say that to look your best and present a pleasing image is *true* self-love . . . that fatties and slobs are not in such hot emotional shape. They say that only when we love ourselves are we free to love anybody else. You want to be free to do *that*, don't you? Okay then—lights, camera, *action!*

CHAPTER 11

KISSES AND MAKE-UP

THAT FABULOUS FACE . . . can you achieve it by being very, very clever with make-up?

I don't think there's a prayer!

The even-featured, alabaster-skinned, meltingly, gaspingly beautiful beauty men go to pieces over can't be achieved with make-up, prayer, incantations or sending your face back to the factory!

You *can* have something *else* with make-up . . . an interesting face, an alive face, a sexy face.

Many people try to deprecate the joys of possessing great beauty. They say it's a curse, a cross, and what's *inside* is all that matters. Of course, what's inside matters, but a beautiful outside has a way of making the most rational, charming and intellectual man go all apart. It's hard to describe what a pretty girl does to him, except to say she's like catnip to a kitty. Men act *funny* around her . . . and agitated . . . like little boys falling out of trees to attract attention.

Maybe you consider this carrying-on downright unpleasant, and maybe it's been centered about *you*, but I think it would be fun to be gone nuts over without having made any personal effort!

Yet I would defend vehemently that you don't have to be beautiful to attract men . . . to keep them by your side a dozen years or longer. And once a man discovers the true fascinator you are, the question of your technical beauty just never comes up!

I'm not talking about girls who are near-beauties . . . the kind magazines dote on showing in "before and after" layouts. Old Plain Jane "before" only has a Grecian nose, chiseled mouth, even white teeth, firm clean chin. About the only thing wrong with Jane is freckles and dirty hair which they fix for the "after"! A man can spot that kind of beauty *too* and respond. I'm talking about women who are really more plain than pretty.

But to get into the position to sink *into* a man you must at least create the illusion of beauty by *acting* beautiful.

You don't have to lie your head off and say I am, I am, I *am* when you know damn well you *aren't*—a stunner. But you must love yourself enough to employ every device . . . voice, words, clothes, figure, make-up . . . to become one.

When you do, you can outdistance a beauty in beau-collecting. It happens all the time. And, of course, beautiful women often cancel their advantage by being hopelessly narcissistic. They also suffer incessant insecurity, wondering if a man loves them for anything but their looks.

Nearly every woman is part-beauty. She has one good feature even if it's just smooth elbows. You play up that feature. You draw a face on the elbow with little eyes and a mouth. (I'm *kidding!*)

And something happens to a woman who has used every

cosmetic trick to be more alluring. You think people start calling her "Old Paint"? Nonsense! Because she feels more beautiful on the inside by having made the maximum effort *outside*, she even begins to *look* better. Something of her lifted spirits shows on her skin, in her smile.

I know this sounds like that optimistic drivel you've heard many times before. But take Exhibit A: Karen, a very shy girl I mentioned earlier, dressed at the office the other day to go to an important party . . . authors, tycoons, people like that. She brought her clothes to work because there wasn't time to go home. During mid-afternoon she realized, after talking to friends, that she'd brought the wrong dress. It was cotton; and the party, though outdoors on a weekday evening, apparently was to be very grand.

There was nothing she could do about the dress; but at five o'clock she slipped out to the beauty shop next door and had them recomb her hair into a very fancy upsweep. (It was freshly shampooed, so they could.) Then she took a fifteen-minute nap. (Her boss was conveniently out of town, the darling.) After that she slowly, ritualistically, painstakingly put on her make-up, starting with false eyelashes and finishing with a good sousing of Ma Griffe. Karen said she padded back and forth from her office to the ladies' room (which had the only decent mirror) about twelve times. Then she put on her dress and went to the ball. Karen reported she'd never felt like that at a party before . . . sort of flawless and go-to-hell! And it netted her a wonderful evening.

What Are You Afraid Of?

Few women wrest from make-up half the magic it offers. They figure it's okay for *others*, but an exquisite job on *their* faces—pure wishful indulgence!

You probably wear lipstick, powder base and a little eye make-up every day. But have you ever considered drawing in completely new eyebrows, wearing false eyelashes, putting hollows in your cheeks with darker foundation, a cleft in your chin with brown eyebrow pencil or enlarging your mouth by a third? These are just a *few* sorcerer's tricks available.

Let's consider the reasons why you, a smart young woman, may not be taking full advantage of make-up.

OBJECTION 1: *You don't know how.*

Then *learn!* The beauty pages of magazines tell you continuously what to do to your face and feet and hair and hands and shoulders! If you missed last year's issues or this year's so far, start *now*. *Glamour, Mademoiselle,* and *Seventeen* go over the same instructions again and again, slightly regilded to make them current.

Vogue's Beauty Book ($1), which appears on the news-stands yearly around September 29th, is a treasure house of information. There have been five so far. This is one instance where it would pay to go back to the well. You might try to pick up back issues in a secondhand bookstore. All the articles are reprints from regular issues of *Vogue*.

Several full-length books deal with make-up, but they're a little stuffy; and besides, I can never make head or tail out of the instructions for shaping your hair to go with the angle of your chin.

The best way is to experiment. Put your make-up on different ways. Ask girls who know more about it than you do and do what they're doing. Try new foundations, new colors of everything. Since you wear make-up to work, that's a good time to be creative. Every morning, for two weeks, try doing your eyes a different shape—big and round, elongated like a ballerina's, shadowed, unshadowed. For the same two weeks, wear a different shade of lipstick every single day, especially the colors you've been snubbing. Draw on a different mouth. At first, you can't tell the difference between good and bad on your face, but your eye grows keener and then suddenly, one day before the two weeks are out, you *can*.

OBJECTION 2: *Cosmetics are too expensive.*

It's true you need a *variety* of cosmetics, especially at first to get you used to working with them. And *especially* later on when you'll refuse to give them up!

If you're a new adventurer (you could be forty!), start with cheap things at the dime store. At least you'll learn about colors.

It's also true that these skimpy little packets that cost from one to five dollars each don't look like much on the shelves, but remember . . . Queen Elizabeth I would probably have traded the British fleet for what's available to you at Walgreen's.

Several major companies make samplers of eye make-up shades and lip colors—as many as twelve to a package. This is an inexpensive way to plunge. Sometimes they make small trial sizes of other products.

Fortunately, make-ups last. Can you imagine ever getting to the bottom of a bottle of eye-liner?

OBJECTION 3: *You haven't time.*

Hal King, chief make-up artist at Max Factor's, says a woman can do a professional job in twelve minutes—foundation, rouge, powder, mascara, eye-liner, shadow, brows . . . the works. The trick is to know what you're doing—and *do* it.

The elegant beauty editor of an eight-million-circulation woman's magazine says she gets hundreds of letters from housewives who "haven't *time* to be beautiful."

"What do they suppose people like *me* do?" she asks. "I have a husband who eats breakfast just like other men, beds to make, errands to do, buses to catch and have help only for parties. I don't think anyone could be a great deal busier in the early morning, but somehow I get my make-up on."

I do my lipstick in the car driving to work—a respectable job, too, with a brush—*after* massaging my gums and *after* rubbing hand lotion into my hands and elbows—also en route. Yes, I drive but I have fifty-seven light signals each way, so there's ample opportunity. I just wish once I had my lipstick on *before* I got a ticket.

OBJECTION 4: *Men don't like make-up.*

Men just *think* they don't like make-up!

If you listened to *them*, your lashes would be flaxen, your lips waxen, your skin Albino No. 2. And then—bing!—they'd be off chasing the first beautifully made-up girl who came along. Don't you *honestly* think you know more than they do by now about how to look nice?

Men don't like too *much* make-up, but I'm not sure they're even competent to judge about *that*.

A cutie-pie friend of mine wears black mascara, black eye-liner, beefed-up eyebrows, pale peach lipstick, all precision-applied, and her adoring husband brags to friends that his wife doesn't wear make-up.

The plot is to use all the cosmetics that can possibly improve your looks but use them skillfully. No streaks, no stripes, no jigs, jags or coatings . . . everything flowing and blended.

I consider top-fashion models the most attractive and beautifully made-up women in the world—not just on assignments but in their daily lives. When they come to our office for television or photographic interviews, all the men in the place sort of hum and buzz. And I don't know a man who doesn't adore to be seen with them. Well, you wouldn't *believe* the amount of make-up that's gone into that look!

Make-up, like clothes, can change your personality on different days. You can be a baby-eyed angel or a devilish, smoke-eyed siren with the same irises. Never knowing *who* you'll be next may shake your beau up a bit. That's good for him! Why always be good old Sue or trusty old Dusty when you know very well most men like variety in women!

A man hates make-up on his clothes, of course, especially if another woman sends the clothes to the cleaner. Well, maybe you don't like the other woman!

Certainly you needn't apply fresh lipstick if you know you're going to be kissed. You may even secretly take some off while he's walking around to open the car door. (He *does* open the car door for you, doesn't he?) Here's a quick trick if you want your lipstick to stay on your lips and not come off onto his: apply one coat, then blot on tissue; powder over the lips, apply a second coat and blot again. The color is on to stay.

As for making up in public, you don't have to do a complete overhaul; but I see nothing wrong with touching up lipstick at the table. Combing and eye stuff is for the powder room.

OBJECTION 5: *Make-up isn't natural.*

Deep down inside perhaps you still think this is a bit wicked, which is understandable. We *are* descended from Puritans, and the fun-is-bad Victorian era only closed officially in 1901. Probably your idea of a real beauty coup would be to get away with no make-up at all!

Come on, now, is there really anything so attractive about *natural?*

The chap who strolls under my window at Hollywood and Vine with his soft flowing brown beard and wavy brown hair, sheathed in the latest gunny-sack dress and barefoot, is *natural*—but appealing only to barbers! If we all ever went really *au naturel* we'd scare each other to death.

The natural look is what we get *used* to. One generation it's bee-stung lips, the next it's the Bardot pout. It hasn't been *no lipstick at all* for millenniums, except for a brief abortive fad recently. The girl who sticks with the pale coloring God gave her, when everybody else is tawny and sun-bronzed, is the one who looks spooky.

Make-up as introduced by the ancients was never intended to deceive, just enchant. In Egypt, long before Cleopatra's time, girls painted their eyes black all the way around with kohl to give them a distinctive almond shape. In the waning days of the Roman Empire, women rouged their bosoms and knees. How about *that!*

If you'll stop thinking the ultimate good is to wear as *little* make-up as you can possibly get away with and employ all of it that can add lure to you, you'll be happier!

Of course, you want the color to be true . . . your brand new flaming red hair to look as though it had *always* flamed. And you want the foundation to look like your skin—only better!

OBJECTION 6: *You haven't the courage to face the results of looking glamorous every single day.*

You'd be saying to the world, "Look, I'm a beauty! Or at least I'm *acting* like a beauty!" And people who "act" any role with authority are apt to be taken at their own value. Think hard. Is it possible you're a little afraid to be *on*—in the limelight—every single day. If your make-up were always flawless, you'd be making an open bid for attention. You'd probably get it. Then you'd have to follow through with no telling *what* kind of adventures.

Yet maybe, just maybe, you could steel yourself to the disagreeableness of being looked at and admired, once it happened. Worth a try?

Where To Begin

Would you like some make-up secrets of the stars? I'm not about to give them to you. I don't *know* any!

I take that back. I know one blonde bombshell with twin initials who wears white eyeshadow all the way around her eyes, then outlines them a good eighth of an inch bigger with a black pencil. But you wouldn't like it. That doesn't even look natural to *me!*

Make-up secrets of famous women are really not all that special . . . or secret. If you read every last one of every last dazzler, they wouldn't be any different, nor as interesting, as the excellent "how to" beauty pages of *Glamour* or any of the other excellent women's magazines.

And anyway . . . the foundation that does wonders for Jean Simmons might leave *you* looking ectoplasmic.

Movie stars and models use the best foundation they can find, the best mascara, the best lipstick . . . the same stuff that's available to you and me. No cosmetic maker is hiding anything on the back shelves for them. If you've got the money, he's got the desire to sell you.

Whatever you read isn't going to do you one little itty bit of good anyway until you try it! Five magazine articles can tell you to sharpen your eyebrow pencil to a fine point and sketch in extra brows, and that won't sharpen *you* while you're still doing a crossword puzzle and sipping Cokes.

I can't begin to write down all the instructions for putting on make-up because that's a book by itself. Furthermore, I think I can be much more helpful to you by bullying you into acquiring some new cosmetics and insisting that you start the fun and games with them this minute.

I *am* going to jot down a few special tricks I've learned while working on a cosmetic account in an advertising agency for three years, as well as some basic truths you may have misplaced.

Lips

Since they're virtually colorless, you can do marvels at changing their size and shape with color. I *know* because I draw on a completely different mouth than my own every day of my life. Takes about thirteen stop lights.

Go fuller or smaller, or even up one side. Jeanne extends her upper lip line slightly out beyond its natural border, but doesn't do it to her lower lip. I don't know why, but it looks terrific.

What's the matter you aren't using a lipstick brush? Got the shakes? The holdouts? The stubborns? Do you think people keep telling you to use a brush because they don't like you?

It isn't that complicated, honest, and a brush is absolutely vital if you're to achieve the chiseled, beautifully modeled lips men like to commit to sculpture . . . or kisses. Remember "natural" means smooth, even, flowing lines . . . no fuzzy edges. You can't possibly do any reshaping without a brush.

If you already have the beautiful lip line of Ava Gardner, all the more reason to make it more lush with a brush. (My copywriting training crops out every once in a while.) Outline first, lips closed, then part your lips and go round and round them with the tube. Stroke on positive, generous color. Carry it just inside the lips too. Blotting takes away something (like half the shine!), so I don't. Check your teeth in ten minutes to see if *they've* been blotting.

I prefer a thin black brush like a watercolor brush. You can buy these in an art store. The long handle makes it easy to use. I keep three lip brushes—one for oranges, one for pinks, one for true reds—out on a bathroom shelf where they're easy to get to.

Have a wardrobe of lipsticks . . . from pale to passionate. Although some shades will look better on you than others, you can probably wear two dozen successfully!

Lipstick that exactly matches an item of clothing is pure chic . . . not just nearly matches but *really* matches . . . the cyclamen of your blouse, the pink of your headband. Hot orange (*orange,* not orangey) with an orange knit swim suit . . . the *most!*

Take every trace of stale lipstick off in the morning before you put on the day's new. (You took it off the night before, but make doubly sure.) Soap and water on a washcloth does it best.

Eyes

You need mascara, eyebrow pencil, fluid eyeliner, brush, shadow in several shades and a regular brushy eye brush . . . *all* of these for eye-citement! Your look will more than justify the investment because eyes, above all, respond to make-up.

Jeanne outlines her not too large eyes with jet black fluid eyeliner all across the upper lids around the outer eye halfway across the under lid . . . almost Egyptian fashion. Her eyes look twice as definite and important.

Alice uses liner from the center of the upper eyelid to the outer edge, ending it in wing-swept effect beyond the eye.

Some authorities say eye shadow mustn't show . . . it's just supposed to be a *shadow*. Piffle poofle to that! Why shouldn't eye shadow show when it's so pretty?

Marguerite wears eye shadow to match her dress every day, and *it* shows . . . enchantingly. One day her blue mist shadow exactly duplicates the shade of a blue silk blouse. Another day it's chartreuse to match a chartreuse frock. With a persimmon-red suit she strokes on black eyeshadow . . . one of the most glamorous hues ever hued for blondes. It makes Marguerite look like Lorelei in *Gentlemen Prefer Blondes* . . . insouciant and devastating.

Iridescent brown carried beyond the edges of huge brown eyes makes them huger.

Nearly everybody says to blend your eyeshadow all over your eyelid. Well, that happens to make my eyes disappear, so I wear a heavy, narrow ribbon of color right next to the lashes. Winifred blends her shadow not only over the lid but all the way up to the eyebrow.

Marguerite powders over shadow to keep it set all day. (Powder absorbs oil and prevents streaking.) "Setting" seems to dim my shadow, so I skip it. You must experiment to see what *you* think.

For a real glamour touch, dust sparkles from a small bottle—silver, gold or pink and blue—high on the lids. They shimmer and they stay.

Instead of the standard sharp pencil to thicken brows (a pencil sharpener is a great honer), try fluid eye-liner on a brush practically wiped dry. Just stroke, stroke, stroke in extra little brows.

Agnes uses black *and* brown eye pencil to get a very believable shading of brows; then she brushes to "subtle" the color.

Keep your brow brush where you can get *to* it. If it's in plain sight, you'll remember to brush your brows and lashes as often as you do your hair. I keep a brush in my purse and office desk drawer too.

Here's the recipe for really thick, sooty eyelashes: apply mascara; then separate lashes with your brow brush. Dust them with talc or face powder. Apply another coat of mascara, brush again, and another coat of powder. Brush again. Apply mascara one last time.

To have even thicker, sootier lashes get false ones!

The best cost about four and a half dollars, and those are the only kind to bother with. I think you'll love them if you'll just *try* them! They are so utterly flattering, so able to make you feel *femme fatale*.

Trim off a quarter inch or so from the original length and buy a tube of Johnson & Johnson's adhesive to put them on with. Give yourself plenty of time. Jeanne has cut hers in half and wears them only toward the outer eye. I like mine full-blown and Southern belle.

Why even pretend they're real lashes? Do you try to convince people your chiffon cocktail dress is real skin?

Rouge

If you think rouge went out with the Stutz Bearcat and tea-dancing, you'll be pleasantly shocked at how pretty and "blossomy" it makes you. Creme rouge is a snap to apply. Place in the middle of your cheeks if they're full . . . high up and far out on the cheekbone if your face is thin. You *can* rouge your earlobes—and make them blush.

Make-Up (Foundation)

Fluids, tubes, cakes, compacts, sticks—they're *all* good. Isn't it bewildering? I can't tell you which one is right for you. I don't see why your complexion should wear the same look every day. Why not have the lady-in-the-drawing-room matte finish on one occasion (from the new tube make-ups), a dewy schoolgirl glow the next (from fluids).

The two most glamorous make-ups I know are Anita d' Foged Day Dew—all creamy and blendy and blemish-hiding—and Max Factor's Pan-Cake. I started using Pan-Cake twenty-two years ago to hide acne scars, and I still don't think there's anything like it for changing mere skin into porcelain.

This trick I learned from Max Factor's make-up director, Hal King. When your make-up is complete, go over it—with powder to set it—puff, puff, puff. Then with a small damp silk sponge go over *that*—pat, pat, pat. This gives your face an *alive* fresh look.

No need to clobber your neck and shoulders with a coating. If you've picked the *right* shade make-up for your face, just blend it down barely under your chin.

There's no easy way to *find* your best shade. An experienced saleswoman should be able to help. After years of mistakes you finally can tell by looking whether it's too pink, too tan, too pale or just right for you. Usually it should be darker in the bottle than your skin is.

Want to reshape your face?

Use *darker* make-up than *you* to make an area smaller, pale and light to make it larger.

To minimize a big nose, run a streak of dark make-up right down its center. To make it shorter, concentrate the dark make-up at the tip end.

To make a protruding chin smaller, smooth dark make-up over it.

To make a "weak" chin stronger, use a *light* shade.

To give a round face contours, apply dark make-up in hollows of cheeks.

To set eyes farther apart, apply a light shade between them.

Powder or use your regular fluid make-up over all the re-contouring.

When *don't* you wear make-up?

My husband told me of a girl he used to go with who never let him see her in the morning without her "face" on. (He didn't say just how early in the morning this *was!*) I think that girl was missing a bet.

It's great fun to be *super* natural at times. Alone with him in your apartment is the best occasion to play Lady Eve. Leave off your lipstick and let your freckles show. He knows you as a glamour girl. Let him see you as a kitten.

Fingernails

Gorgeous nails can make you look rich and pampered. Ever notice how wealthy women's toes and fingernails are nearly always freshly lacquered . . . not gone over with ninety coats of new polish?

A good manicure should last a week, however.

Start with Sally Hansen's "Hard as Nails" (59 cents at the drugstore). Hardly *anything* manages to break off under it. Use three coats of polish. Between coats, you can lie down in bed and read. Let them get *really* dry. Now a top coat. Here's a manicure you can *peel* off in six days, if that's your weakness.

All polish seems to deteriorate in the bottle, so don't try to keep too many shades.

If you have scruffy nails, the Knox Gelatin people have some impressive research to show their product, downed daily, makes your nails hale and hearty. Use one package in fruit juice, water, milk, cocoa or whatever you drink. (P.S. Us health nuts have strong nails anyway.)

Hands

I once asked a beautician how to make hair grow, and she said, "You won't do it, but I'll tell you. Pull on it every night about an hour while you're watching television or reading. Just take a hunk at a time and pull." I resented her saying I wouldn't do it, and she was so right!

You won't do this either, but I'll tell you how to have nice hands. Goop them with cream at bedtime and wear soft white little cotton gloves (35 cents at the drugstore) all night. Your hands come out like kitty fur and velvet next morning.

Massage your hands with lotion—feet too, okay?—every possible chance. It's a good idea to keep cheap lotion in your bath, bedroom, kitchen, car and desk. Very Lady Macbeth, all that rubbing, but it definitely softens.

Hair

It's every girl's mortal enemy, I guess. Yet it can be so two-faced and friendly on certain occasions!

These are the few pippy-poo things I have learned about coping with hair.

You know the old wive's tale that washing hair often isn't good for it? I'm the old wife who is still perpetuating it! Shampooing oily hair every forty-eight hours just makes it oilier at the scalp, while it may stay quite dry on the ends and break off. Soap-and-watering makes dry hair drier.

Once a week, Marguerite (dry scalp), Veronica (no problems), and I (oily scalp) have a nice woman come to the office and comb, brush and massage our heads forty minutes apiece at lunchtime. She uses seven brushes, seven combs and a lot of energy on each of us. This distributes the oil properly and gives the scalp a real workout.

Could you find someone to do this for you on a regular basis? Mrs. Chase charges two-fifty at our office, a dollar fifty in her home.

Loretta Young, who has beautiful long flowing tresses, uses a similar method and rarely shampoos.

Marguerite, Veronica and I brush our hair every night and shampoo about every two weeks. Then a shampoo really *means* something . . . hair gets squeaky clean and shiny bright. I use a dry shampoo between regular ones. Cornmeal is fine. Just toss it in and brush it out. This coats fine hair ever so lightly and seems to make more of it.

Hair sprays, though marvelous, should be eschewed if you shampoo seldom.

Chopping off the tiniest row of hair all around blunts the ends and makes it seem thicker. Every two or three weeks you should have grown enough to do it.

If you would look sexy, wear more hair. Not shoulder-length necessarily, but not that Joan of Arc little-pointy-snips business either. She was a *soldier!*

If your features are not classically beautiful, go glamorous with hair. It can get you the compliments Grecian profiles get other girls. Grow it long and pile it high. If it won't grow, or isn't especially good hair, buy a switch to use as a braid or chignon. Inexpensive nylon ones are quite lifelike. Real hair ones are terrific.

I remember sitting behind actress Agnes Moorehead at the Biltmore Theatre one night. She had miles and miles of carrot-red hair piled high on her head. Miss Moorehead *is* beautiful but not a youngster. 'Neath the hair she wore a pale pink satin floor-length evening coat and gown. Just wow!

I can't imagine going to the beauty shop for a conservative hair style. You can do that yourself. My Alice knows she's free to wire me for sound and to add laurel leaves if the mood strikes her.

I don't think anybody is even asking any more, "Does she or doesn't she?" They just want to know where can *they* get that color? Even the dyes are simple to do at home.

Excess Hair on Legs and Arms (Brunette Department)

If you have so much of it that hot-wax treatments would take four Sundays, then bleach. Use two-thirds bleaching peroxide, one-third household ammonia and some soap flakes. Stir. Slather this on thick over arms and thighs, sit in the sun to dry if you can; otherwise just do housework. Repeat several times. The whole treatment may take an hour, but you can do other things during it. The hair will become platinum blond and far less obtrusive. Shave the hair on lower legs and under arms, of course.

The Big Change

Here are four expensive and think-twice-about-it investments that can conceivably push you over the edge into real beauty —or return you to it.

CONTACT LENSES

Are you *sure* you can't wear them? Check with someone who has successfully overcome the tedious running-in period. You may be inspired. (It *would* be nice to gaze into your soul not under glass.) A *Harper's Bazaar* writer tells of using hypnotism to curb her involuntary prejudice against contacts.

BUY A WIG

A young friend of mine has been appearing in one for several weeks now, and she looks prettier and "more natural" than I've ever seen her. The wig is lighter than her hair, and she's lightened her make-up to match.

I ordered one this week in champagne blond (I'm mouse brunette), and I can't *wait!*

A good wig of real hair costs $75 plus postage. (They've come way down in price this last year.) The wigs are in ten colors, all head sizes, and are beautifully coifed. You can match your own hair or go more glamorous. If you'd like more information or would like to order, this is where: Gilbert's House of Charm, 1105 Glendon Avenue, West Los Angeles, California. Send a photo and snip of your hair if you want it matched.

THE NOSE

Plastic surgery is admittedly expensive, not covered by Blue Cross, horribly uncomfortable for a few days—but oh my foes and oh my friends—the results! The lovely cataclysmic results are the kind you can't get any other way.

Your nearest and dearest ones may discourage you from alterations. They love you as you are, bless them. But the change is for *you.*

I had my nose revised last spring and couldn't be more delighted. It's very much like my old one but smaller. Close friends I haven't seen for a while don't even realize anything's new. They just tell me I look pretty, or rested, or something. Yes, plastic surgery is very, very "natural!"

Other kinds—breasts made smaller, chins increased or decreased, heavy eyelids tautened, faces lifted—these I am not at all familiar with. People I've heard of who "bought them" seem to be smiles and praises for the results. However, I assume you'll consult with a first-rate doctor if you're interested in plastic work of *any* kind. I'm just a cheerleader.

A "FACE-SAVING" MACHINE

This small electrotherapy machine exercises facial muscles (which you can't begin to get at yourself) so that they hold up your skin again; it also increases circulation and erases small lines. The treatment is relaxing. Afterwards, you use a mask if you want to, and your face does indeed come out sort of "newborn." The procedure is troublesome. And you must do it often. But an aging skin (which everybody's is, isn't it?) is a potent beauty problem and not readily susceptible to milder attack.

The best electronic "face" machine I found (which I

bought) is made by Venner Kelsen, 121 North Almont Drive, Beverly Hills, California. The not inconsiderable cost, at the time I bought it, was a good two hundred and fifty bucks.

Venner also makes a variety of high-powered treatment items: black mud-pie mask, a stinging shocking-pink circulation cream, hormone oil that almost seems to undo damage right before your eyes and some good salves for acne. Write her if you're interested in any of this sorcery.

I must reiterate that all my personal recommendations are only that. They work for *me*. And I *pay* for the products, so please don't think I get any kind of rake-off on these recommendations. I'm just trying to tell you what I would tell a friend. And it would be pretty silly (wouldn't it?) for a friend to beat around the bush when it comes to prices, trade names, and where to get things.

Now I think you should rest your face and all of the other basic equipment involved in self-improvement for a while. The time has come at last to talk about men again—and how to get involved with them without really trying.

CHAPTER 12

THE AFFAIR:
FROM BEGINNING TO END

THE *Reader's Digest* once published an article about an unmarried woman who had Given In, suffered unspeakable guilt and humiliation, decided she could no longer face the degradation of the relationship and had moved to another city to Start Over. The *Digest* left little doubt that she'd done the only thing a single woman under such circumstances *could* do.

Most magazines, other than *Playboy*, seem to go along with the *Reader's Digest*.

A recent issue of the *Ladies Home Journal* summed up its stand in the last paragraph of an article entitled "Is the Double Standard out of Date?" by stating that a single woman confronted by a man who "insists" can do one of two things. "She can marry him, or she can say 'No.'"

I don't know about girls in Pleasantville and Philadelphia where these magazines are published, but I do know that in Los Angeles, where I live, there is something else a girl can say and frequently does when a man "insists." And that is "yes." As for moving to another city to Start Over, if all the unmarried girls having affairs in my city alone felt called upon to do *that*, there would be the biggest population scramble since Exodus.

Nice, single girls *do* have affairs, and they do not necessarily die of them! They suffer sometimes, occasionally a great deal. However, quite a few "nice" single girls have affairs and do not suffer at all!

As for the girls who do as the *Reader's Digest* and *Ladies Home Journal* would have them do—or not do—one young woman who remained chaste for many years stated it this way:

"I have yet to encounter a happy virgin. Quite the contrary, I feel she eventually finds social, religious and maternal approval quite inadequate compensation for not ever really belonging to anyone, and her state of purity becomes almost an embarrassing cross to bear. She harbors a feeling that life is passing her by; and, as she grows older, her position with men and with herself becomes increasingly defensive. In other words, it is my belief, she is no longer a virgin by freedom of choice but is instead hopelessly trapped by her own inhibitions, drastically reducing her chance for happiness and/or marriage. An affair represents a whole *new* set of problems, of course, but to my way of thinking they're *healthier*. The point is, either way you suffer, but I think remaining chaste is worse because you have *no* pleasure to offset the pain. Having an affair can be agony, but it can also be ecstasy and *is* . . . more often than we masochists are willing to admit!"

In defense of the mature affair, it must surely be stated that it is the sexiest of all alliances. Teen-age experimentation is shallow and lacking in plot. Married love can be sunny and sweet and satisfying, but an affair between a single woman and her lover can be unadulterated, cliff-hanging sex.

An affair between a *married* woman and her lover may be that way too, but the danger of being found out and the guilt if you aren't would spoil most of the fun, I should think.

Why Does She Do It?

A single woman has an affair for these reasons:

1. *The Urge.* Her body wants to. For weird and wonderful reasons that she will never really understand, some lucky special man "has it" for her.

2. *Super Warmth.* She adores and respects a man and wants to have the closest relationship with him possible, even though her body may not hunger for him.

A psychiatrist friend of mine says that a girl who has a physical relationship with a man for any but these two reasons is prostituting herself. I'm afraid some mighty nice girls fall into his shady-lady category because they also participate for the following reasons:

3. *The Urge To Merge.* A woman hopes to sink into a man so completely he will never be able to unsink her. He'll have to marry her!

4. *Fringe Glamour.* She is going with a man over her head —glamorous, rich or famous. She enjoys the glitter life; and, though she is not kept, she knows she could not possibly be the constant companion of such a prize if she didn't sleep with him.

5. *Security.* A certain kind of woman only feels "safe" when she extracts the supreme compliment a man can pay. Though

she may not actually enjoy the act of sex, she insists on it with almost every man she dates and is uneasy when it is not on the schedule. This isn't the clinical description but I would call her a nymphomaniac.

6. *Approval.* She isn't sure of her beauty, brains or background but knows her love-making is first-rate. She uses this talent to please and be popular.

Who With?

Crass and callous though it may make her seem, a desirable woman is usually more favorably disposed toward a man who is solvent and successful than someone without status. She prefers a tycoon to a truck driver no matter how sexy the latter looks peering down at her from the cab of his chrome chariot.

She doesn't rule out young or not so young strugglers, but if possible she wants somebody she can introduce to her friends with enthusiasm, not show off with shudders.

Most single women find no dearth of men to go to bed with.

A New York manufacturer of cosmetics is supposed to have brought down the house at a luncheon by saying that when a woman puts on her make-up she is thinking just one thing: "Tonight, boy, I'm going to get laid!"

Did you ever hear anything so silly? Getting Dial spelled backward is *not* her problem. Finding someone with whom it might be worth while *is*.

When?

A girl may "surrender" any time between two hours after she's met a "possible" to two years of going steady. There is no countdown prescribed by single-girl etiquette, though my guess would be that most affairs that are going to happen start after a few dates.

A girl can usually sense even on a first date whether or not a man is somebody she could become involved with. *No* matter how much she attributes "giving in" to persuasion on his part, something will have "clicked on" in her brain the day or night of the denouement that permits the affair to begin. In my opinion, no girl is technically seduced.

I agree with Dr. Kinsey that months or even years may elapse between affairs for most single women, not because of prudery but because of lack of a suitable him.

How Long Does It Last?

An affair can last from one night to forever. I know one rare couple, not married to each other, who are still happily at it after twenty years.

Trouble, My Friends

Certain types of women handle affairs well. Some are divorcees who want nothing more in this world than not to be married again. Some are women over forty who have stopped fussing and fretting about who owes what to whom and accept male companionship on terms most generous to a man.

Still others, though neither recently divorced nor mature in years, have the emotional make-up which permits them to enjoy an affair, unwracked by guilt, anxiety or unrealistic hopes.

One of my best friends is such a girl. "I think it's because I blossomed late," she says. "At thirty-one I have the glamour and looks and popularity I never dreamed of at nineteen, when I was considered absolutely huge for a teen-ager. I adore the whirl I'm having and haven't any wish whatever to stop it, though I've had two proposals this year. I love children and will have them a little later than most women —just as I've had everything else."

My friend is probably exceptional in her ability to take sex with equanimity. There is no question that an affair adds to the emotional problems of many women; however, the ones who suffer most are probably the ones who have the most emotional problems to begin with.

Since the married state in our culture is considered the most, if not the *only*, acceptable one for a woman, there is some basis for assuming that many women who fail to find themselves a suitable first husband by at least their thirtieth birthday are somewhat emotionally crippled to begin with. In her youth when there was plenty of marriage material around, the neurotic girl lost out simply because the race to the altar is to the healthy and strong.

This doesn't mean she wasn't and isn't attractive, intelligent, and possibly more alluring than her friends who married painlessly at twenty-two, but her neuroticism will not *let* her accept the adult responsibility of marriage or staying married. At least that's a pretty well accepted psychiatric theory. She finds no man good enough for her. She must stay home to care for her parents. Or she loves only "impossible" men whom she thinks she meets by accident but whom she virtually "stalks."

Embarked on an affair, the neurotic quickly runs aground on the emotional reefs. Her ego is probably so weak that the merest slight from her love—the missed phone call, too much attention to another girl at a party—is magnified beyond all proportion. Without being able to help herself, she makes demands that seem reasonable to her but are oppressive to her lover.

She wants him to make her feel proud, secure, confident, beautiful, intelligent and rich. She is the biggest insister-on-getting-married of them all. Never mind that her beloved is utterly neurotic himself (for many unmarried and divorced men her own age are "that way" too), a sadist, a pauper, a drinker, a Don Juan and as stable as four-year-old peanut butter. She blanks out every consideration but her blinding need for the society-approved, mother-sanctioned relationship of marriage.

And if her "intended" reacts to the marriage shackles by cowering against the wall, that seems to make him all the more desirable! Actually, if he were chasing, she'd probably be running. She has little confidence in anybody who finds *her* irresistible.

The point to all this is that many single girls having an affair should not be so hard on themselves, or the man, when it is altogether possible that there is something wrong with both of them that not having an affair wouldn't remedy . . . and getting married wouldn't either!

Conduct and Ground Rules

Now that we've established some of the facts of affairs, at least as I see them, let's see if we can set down a few ground rules.

How Often Do You See Each Other?

If it's a "working affair" (not the ragged end of an old one or a liaison so casual as not to qualify as an affair at all), I should think you would see each other several times a week. If you are relegated to mere Tuesdays and Fridays, wondering what the hell he is doing Wednesdays and Thursdays, etcetera, you are missing out on some of your justly deserved fringe benefits—the wining and dining and buzzing around.

A friend of my husband's says his idea of a perfect arrangement would be to make love to a girl, after which she would be quietly lowered through the floor and a table would descend from the ceiling on which would be seated three of his male cronies, a pack of cards and a bottle of Jack Daniels. That's *his* idea of the ideal arrangement . . . and it makes me quite nervous!

Where?

Just anywhere is fine as long as it is within the law.

One problem married people have is the eternal sameness of their surroundings. You, just by alternating between your apartment and his apartment, can keep things lively.

Your apartment is probably the best bet most of the time. There, you seem more like the seductress than the seduced. Also, when the affair ends, you can be sure he'll have one hell of a time getting you *and* your apartment out of his head.

Should a Man Think You Are a Virgin?

I can't imagine why, if you aren't. Is *he?*

Is there anything particularly attractive about a thirty-four-year-old virgin?

Of course it's all right to pretend virtue when you turn down an "insister"—if you can get away with it. And you probably can! A man would prefer to believe almost anything except that you don't find *him* appealing!

Once in bed, it's kind of silly to fake inexperience. Most men agree that inhibitionless and even aggressive enjoyment from a woman is an asset so far as their own enjoyment is concerned. If he is the kind of man who is only interested in deflowering virtue, he should stick to unraveling chrysanthemums!

The only man who might "suffer" from your experience is the man who is no great shakes in bed himself. If you have no one to compare him with, he might get an "A"!

As for never literally going to bed to preserve your technical purity—i.e., you make love without being together in a cool, comfy bed—let's say you can get just as pregnant and have missed a great deal of fun.

As for not going quite *that* far and merely teasing your young man to the jumping-off point while you turn your own feelings on and off like a gas jet, you can get your responses so out of whack you'll never get them straight again.

Do You Date Other Men While Having an Affair?

My answer to this question would be that it depends on the intensity of the affair—and I consider any affair rather intense—and what stage it's in. In the first blush of great love you may think it disloyal even to smile at the news delivery boy, whereas later you'll be rounding up everybody from old grammar school flames to poker partners of your father to go out with on a spite fling.

The trouble is that, even when you are both utterly loyal, royal true blue, things get sticky. If you are not going to marry him, it's insane not to keep date channels open. Of course if *you* go out, you must accept the fact that *he'll* go out. He may *anyway*. Grit your teeth and don't let him do anything silly—like getting booked for New Year's Eve.

Even if the affair is much too intense for extracurricular dating, at least keep in touch with your friends. Letters, phone calls, invitations to the country swirling around you, are *desirable*, no matter how much he grumbles about never having your undivided attention. A little healthy anxiety is *good* for him! Besides, when that awful time comes—the end of the affair—you'll need every old friend you can muster, and you'll be in real trouble if you've snapped them off like butter beans.

Can You Sleep with Two Men at Once?

Gracious, what a greedy girl!

I'm sure many girls do.

I was chatting this week with a friend about thirty years old who makes $18,000 a year as a fashion photographer. I mention her income only to establish her status and talent in the professional world. She said, "I understand you are writing a book about sex and single women. I'd be happy to tell you a few of my experiences." She then went on to keep me on the ropes for twenty minutes with tales of assignations in the front seat of convertibles with twenty-year-old college boys, on yachts with dashing old men, and with assorted other types in boarded-up summer cottages and unfamiliar bedrooms while a party was raging downstairs. She is currently enjoying an affair of long duration with a famous young actor, and had just embarked on a new one the night before with a blind date who'd made up a fourth at bridge.

There is no doubting her veracity. She is a merciless teller of truth.

I don't *think* she's typical, though I must admit her story shook me into wondering if she is more typical than I know.

I believe there are more girls like my average "prototype" girl who simply wouldn't know how to handle a multiple-affair setup. Instead of gaining emotional security with numbers, she'd likely wind up a gibbering idiot, so she eschews them.

An affair can overlap, of course, but it's more likely that one will be finished before another begins.

Suppose You Like Girls

You've already worked out a way of life for yourself to which I could contribute no helpful advice. I'm sure your problems are many. I don't know about your pleasures. At any rate, it's *your* business and I think it's a shame you have to be so surreptitious about your choice of a way of life.

You're Frigid

If after some experience you are still unable to enjoy making love, and this bothers you, psychiatric consultation may be in order.

He Has Problems

Him you don't need. One of the things a single woman *can* have is a good sex life, and the disturbed boy is doing you out of it. A married woman has every reason to help a semi-potent mate get back to normal, but *you* have no more incentive than a short-term tenant has in rebuilding his apartment.

Not all of your beaux need to be he-males . . . just the one you sleep with.

The Married Man

As a woman grows older and the eligibles become fewer, it becomes increasingly tempting to take a married lover; but it is best to know what you're in for.

A friend who had a long-term affair with a married man had this to say: "It's a real education in human suffering and makes all past and future relationships less painful by comparison! Having an affair with a man you *know* belongs to another woman, a man who is with *her* on important days, is simply too degrading. If a man is single, you're at least on somewhat equal footing!"

Another friend with whom I discussed the subject said, "We know married men do get divorces and marry their girl friends, but it happens so seldom as to be hardly worth mentioning; and I think it takes a special breed of woman to see it through.

"We also know that sometimes they get divorces and *don't* marry their girl friends. The hand that held theirs during the crisis years now seems a little careworn."

I think those are sage remarks.

Yet married men do keep buzzing into your life like mosquitoes on a June night, don't they? To a single woman it sometimes seems as though they are the *only* thing buzzing!

I would like to suggest that for the next three minutes you be a big girl and consider with tolerance and compassion what a married man wants and why he wants it. (You expect *him* to listen respectfully when *you* talk of wanting to be married. Then you must give him equal time!)

A married man may quite desperately need love on a sexual level and reassurance of his male prowess.

That old bunch of tripe, you say! Babies, rump roasts, wall-to-wall monogrammed towels, that's all that *really* matters! Not to him! He's *had* all that. And his needs may be as tearing and searing as *your* needs, just different.

Though it may look as though a man has a loving wife, that may be only for show. She may only have tolerated him in bed for many years, and now that the children are all spawned she is quite, quite finished with him in that department. On the rare occasions when they do sleep together, she is like the woman the following joke was told about: A man and his wife are having a violent argument. Finally after an hour of haranguing he says to her, "Oh, for heaven's sake, Constance, let's forget all this arguing and go to bed." "Over my dead body," she says. "Of course," he replies, "why should we do it any different *now?*"

The last thing this kind of woman wants is a divorce. She is used to the convenience of having a man around the house and has long since forgotten how to support herself. She just wants to be left in quiet and peace in her bed. It is my firm old-fashioned belief that a man who is well and enthusiastically loved at home, even if a certain amount of showmanship is required on his wife's part, can be kept safely and happily at her side with only minor excursions into the unknown. The man who comes to you needs reassurance.

The fact that a man wishes to corroborate his maleness away from home may *not* be his wife's fault. The two may be devoted to one another but have been married so many years that neither is really able to excite the other.

I should be careful to qualify everything I say on this subject and will add that being married many years doesn't positively presuppose sexual boredom, but in many cases it *does.*

Many husbands and wives have an "understanding" that he may frisk about a bit without recriminations. I remember being shocked and offended at twenty-two when an older man I was dating (thirty-six!) told me a married-woman friend of ours had called him that morning and said, "Gerry, could you possibly find Lew a girl for tonight? He's really long overdue." And these people had what might be called a very happy marriage!

Other wives know their husbands stray but they *don't* know . . . if you know what I mean. They never ask pointed questions because they don't really want any definite answers. I would call it "tacit permission" on the wife's part because though she would be hurt to know absolutely of her husband's peccadillos, she wouldn't divorce him.

Other men cheat like hell whether their wives like it or not. A sex-goddess spouse couldn't satisfy them. Let's say they can't help themselves . . . or if they could, it would be at such a severe penalty of pleasure and prestige to themselves that they couldn't take it. Many rabid chasers are, of course, quite satisfactorily (if not happily) married to wives they adore, and divorce never enters their minds.

Unlike the really sexually deprived unhappily married man who falls for a single girl and falls *hard,* the reasonably contented husband with "straying privileges" is pretty rough on a single woman. He is usually no more faithful to a girl friend than to a wife.

You don't *like* his being this way and neither do I. (We were *educated* not to like it and not to accept it.) But to be trite and cliché, this is the nature of the beast. Man is *not* monogamous no matter how much religion and social writ tell him he is. You don't like your adorable Persian kitty dragging a maimed, half-alive pigeon into your living room but that's the nature of Persian kitties. Do you renounce all cats?

Naturally, you are prey to *all* erring husbands with or without a straying excuse simply because you are *there* . . . cool, sweet, pretty and unencumbered!

If given half a chance, the man frustrated by lukewarm affection at home will fall madly in love with you. And he will want you to love him as he has never been loved by his wife . . . want you to be his adored one, his passionate one.

Heaven knows a married man on an all-out I Love You

campaign can be one of God's most persuasive creatures. There's a warmth and earnestness about him. He holds nothing back. A single man is afraid to go that far for fear of being hauled off to the license bureau. A married man has built-in brakes.

He says what you want to hear—not that you are an enchanting diversion of the moment but that he is miserable at home, that he would *like* to marry you, that he would saw off his foot to have met you first!

He forgets that there's very little in a mere torrid love relationship for you—that you can get physical ardor from a dozen men. But you are probably just as unobjective in your thinking when you convince yourself that a divorce and subsequent marriage to you would solve his problems. Do you have any idea how much a divorce *costs?*

In spite of the fact that the area around married men seems loaded with mines, I believe they *have* a definite place in the life of a single woman—as friends and confidants, occasionally as dates and once in a great while as lovers (if they live thousands of miles from you and promise only to visit once or twice a year!).

Presents, Please

"I can't give you anything but love," is real depression-era stuff. There must be *something* else he can give—a book of poetry, one perfect rose, if he's a struggler; a vicuña coat, if a tycoon. Don't expect a Thunderbird from anyone just because you have bestowed *your* most priceless gift.

The more you can think of the relationship as a mutually rewarding one and the less you picture yourself as a poor, pathetic little Match Girl, the happier you'll be.

The situation of the kept girl is not under discussion—we

are talking of "love affairs"—but let's not be stuffy. Who's to say how long any of us would decline an offer of emeralds, chinchillas, and a portfolio of A.T. & T? Fortunately, or unfortunately, the problem never comes up! Any lesser offer . . . well, that would be like trying to buy a Picasso on postcard money.

As for combining a love affair with financial gain (being helped out with the rent or afforded a mink-trimmed bathroom), that's awfully tricky too. I'm inclined to agree with my pure-minded psychiatrist friend who says, "Sex is too precious and valuable a commodity to be sold or traded. It can only be successfully shared."

A lady's love *should* pay for all trips, most restaurant tabs, and the liquor. That's simply good affair etiquette.

In a married-man relationship there are subtle differences. There *is* no equal footing. If it is a liaison of some duration, if he is comfortably well off and you are a struggling ballet dancer, I think fairly handsome presents are in order. Presents can't make up for everything or even *anything*, but they can help ease the pain of inequity that exists in an affair between an unmarried woman and a married man.

Married men can be very defensive about presents. *"Pay* for her love," he scoffs. "Glenda wouldn't want anything like that. She loves me for *myself.*"

There is no easy way to handle this reckoning. The oblique way is undoubtedly best, for even the *hint* that something more might be expected of him than his extravagant enjoyment of your beautiful body will cause a sensitive married man great pain.

A friend of mine said to her married lover, "Darling, I'm thinking of getting a used Volkswagen to drive to work. I hate to move much closer to my office because it would be inconvenient for you to see me. Besides, I must be honest and admit it would be wonderful to have a car to go to the beach in or take to the tennis courts on weekends when you can't see me. I have three hundred dollars in cash now; and, if you would lend me seven hundred, I could get a very good used Volkswagen at Motor City. I could pay you back thirty dollars a month."

This speech happens to have a lot going for it. It is flattering. She wants the car so that she can continue to live near him. She is letting him off the hook for times when he can't see her. She has made some effort herself toward the luxury. And she has decided on the amount he can handle—not an outrageous figure. Her token offer to pay back (which, of course, will never be accepted) helps him rationalize to his ego that she's a nice loving girl not after his money. He's going to have a hard time squirming out of her request because how can he reason that any girl—especially *his* girl—would be better off riding the bus?

Not all married men are rich, of course, but they too should be doing lots of extra giving in *some* area—even if it's just helping a girl paint her back porch. The state of her bank account really has nothing to do with it.

Affair Aids

When an affair *is* in trouble, there is probably no other pain comparable to it. The remedies and bromides that seem to rout other sorrows—debts, job setbacks, family squabbles, inferiority complexes—have no effect whatever on trouble with a man!

Even a reasonably serene woman can find herself wracked with wall-to-wall insecurity. She fights herself all day and half the night not to call her lover to ask if he still loves her and if everything is still all right. The worst of it is that she knows when she calls, and he dutifully says he *does* and it *is*, it won't do a bit of good!

The news that there's another woman, when *you're* the other woman, can plunge a thousand samurai swords into your viscera.

What *do* you do when you can't give him up? (You tried that *last* week!)

Go for help—all you can get—at these first-aid stations:

GIRL FRIENDS

They are marvelously kind because they've been along this route themselves, and they are tireless listeners. Their viewpoint is anything but objective, of course, because it's all for *you*. (A man, incredible as it seems, has his side of the story too.)

Lean hard on your girl friends and go over and over the story as long as it gives you any solace to talk about it.

A RELIABLE MAN

He's even better than a girl friend in many ways—more constructive, shrewd and realistic. He won't feel so sorry for you and feed your self-pity. He can usually size up the situation pretty squarely and even explain what is going on in your lover's pulpy brain, because he too is a man. He will also point out why you *don't* want this guy for keeps even when you think you do. And all the time you're weeping on another man, in the back of your head you know that at least *this* man is a darling.

A girl I know has wept all over one of the smartest attorneys (married) in Beverly Hills for years. He obviously is in love with her himself, but he has often kept her from getting too maudlin or ridiculous over someone he knows isn't worthy of her.

HIM

Kick and scream at *him* if you've had all you can bear. Obviously this is not during the first few months of your relationship but after it has dragged on and on. A temper tantrum may not get you married, but acting the loving little stoic won't either. Honest anger can clear the air.

I know a "loving little stoic" who finally threw a bucket of ice cubes and icy water at her lover during a seemingly mild argument. He thought she'd flipped her lid. She had been pretending to herself she wasn't angry because he was spoiled and unfaithful, but inside she was seething with rage. Out it came—later than it should have.

YOUR COUCH

Cry and kick and scream alone if you'd rather he didn't see you. Have a tantrum if you can. Throw beanbags against your fireplace. Shred an old towel. It's *okay* to be mad. Your ego has taken a terrible beating, and a physical outburst of violence may relieve the pressure.

THE BIG COUCH

This is the greatest if your emotional trouble is of long duration. It probably is no accident that you become involved with one heel after another. A few visits to a psychiatrist may help you get perspective, and perhaps you do not need the full treatment.

CHURCH

Friends tell me their ministers are kind and compassionate, but don't go if you aren't ready to be told to stop the affair. What else can the clergy say? Sleeping with anybody you aren't married to is against the precepts of all conventional religions.

Church itself is a wonderful place for solace and quieting the spirit, and you can go *between* Sundays, too.

The Ultimatum

Hardly any bachelor wants to get married. Even the most adorable, non-phobic one has to be gently but firmly prodded into matrimony.

If the truth be known, many of your married girl friends whom you thought were the pursued darlings used everything from vapors to bloodletting to get their man. It's nothing to be ashamed of.

There's no question that it's often a matter of timing. Some men can be bloodlet by an expert (it being understood this is usually in the form of delicious little home-cooked meals including his favorite dishes, as well as being walked hand-in-hand past furniture stores) and resist to the death. At some other period in his life this same man may succumb to a far less persuasive bloodletter.

A man ought to be able to make up his mind about you as wife material within six months of your meeting. Give him the benefit of the doubt and say a year. After that it must be conceded you are facing a hardened veteran.

There are many moves you can make to stir him up a bit, but they will probably not get you wed.

When you declare you are devoting too much time to him, he will magnanimously offer to let you go out with other men. What is he risking? How can you possibly have a decent fling when your heart is still in his coat pocket? And no matter how many admirers you recruit for your "I'll show *him*" performance, how impressed can he be when you are still sleeping in his pajama tops?

Continuing to see him but withholding sex is not getting him to the altar either. And I give you two weeks!

Not answering your telephone several nights in a row may give you a small thrill of revenge but will it really change the basic *him* into a devoted, dependable, marrying guy?

If you are determined to marry him, you will probably have to take a stand. And the stand can only be effective if you *mean* it . . . if you are determined to leave him and stay left if the answer is "no." Threats are totally useless.

Sometimes it takes a long time to get to the stage where you'd honestly rather live without him than accept friendship on his terms one more hour. And sometimes it takes several ultimatums before you can stay gone for good. Don't hate yourself! One day, one of your ultimatums will stick and/or *he* will.

It's Over

Affording an impossible man is very much like living beyond your means any other way—paying too much rent, taking too many taxis, wolfing too many eight-dollar, three-martini lunches. And after you have overspent emotionally for a long time, you may decide that your extravagance just isn't affording you enough happiness units to justify its cost.

Very often his reluctance to marry may seem the principal issue, but marriage is not the real problem at all. Possibly you are both neurotic, or not enough alike, or too much alike, or a hundred other affair-destroying conditions exist.

No matter how difficult the man, a single woman often dreads letting go of a long-time beau for fear she'll never find a replacement.

Such anxiety may be justified in a married woman contemplating divorce, because husbands and daddy-replacements are admittedly hard to find. But a lover . . . particularly one who is grinding you up in little pieces . . . you can *always* replace. You wouldn't *believe* how easily!

And maybe it doesn't sound very reassuring, but you can care just as deeply, just as everlastingly again . . . and live to be just as unhappy about *him!*

The Recovery

Suppose the anguish has finally outweighed any joy received, and the affair is finally ended.

The end of a serious affair is in many ways like a death, and I believe a decent mourning period should be accorded it . . . a period in which to be utterly, flat-down-on-your-back miserable.

Friends who would hustle you out to play volley ball or to see what new instant men you can scrounge up at the local pub probably do you an injustice. If you anesthetize yourself with activity and fail to suffer properly at the time, you may have to go *back* and suffer at a later date.

I would suggest you don't even try to fight misery for at least a week. Have girl friends over or go and see them each night if you don't want to be alone, but don't force cheerfulness.

I remember when Karen parted from the love of her life after four years of togetherness—just three weeks before Christmas. No one knows why these farewells fall right smack in the middle of Christmas, but they often do.

Karen was responsible for most of the Christmas shopping for her boss. She bravely plunged in although she was no more in command of her senses than a zombie.

During that time she carefully wrapped a present for their major client and put it in a filing drawer for safekeeping—an expensive, ancient little book from Rosenbach & Company in Philadelphia, containing rare maps of oil territory in frontier America. Several weeks into January, when her boss still hadn't received a thank-you note, he muttered disconsolately to Karen about the ingratitude of clients. By this time Karen was enough out of zombiehood to remember the little book she had filed away. She made a full confession and rushed the book to the client.

Her company lost the account anyway during the year. Karen wonders to this day if she and her company wouldn't both have been better off if she had taken to her bed for a couple of weeks to mourn the end of her affair, and left the Christmas shopping to a live, functioning human being!

The mourning period, which can last several weeks, is obviously no time to accomplish major tasks, but you *can* get things done around the house—sewing, scrubbing, furniture polishing and curtain washing—the more exhausting, the better.

Then finally a day dawns when you can contemplate without rancor the blue jersey dress you bought to wear to the New Year's Day game with *him*. Since it's too late for football, and especially under *his* auspices, you decide just to wear the dress to the office. You do—and look kind of great.

From that day on your strength and interest in life begin to return. And the sap returns to your veins.

Even so, for a little while, every man you meet will be an oaf, an imbecile or have dandruff on his lapels. In the early recovery stages you're in no condition to know what to do with a crown prince offering a kingdom anyhow.

But one day, somebody good *does* appear, and by now you have a strange new asset going for you . . . derring-do!

Since it's possible you are still partially numb and in love with your departed beau, you figure what's there to lose—so you are a little bolder, a little more razzle-dazzle than you'd normally *dream* of being. It may be just what you—and the situation—need.

Karen sank into a wonderful man that way—a ruggedly handsome builder contractor with whom she had a blind date for cocktails. Karen suspects he wasn't sure he'd like her well enough to take her to dinner. Figuring that he was probably hopelessly out of reach, and knowing that she was immune to new love *or* rebuff, Karen decided over a third daiquiri to play Scheherazade and weave him a wonderful tale. She said she had met him many years before at a party (which she knew he'd attended because her friends who arranged the date told her about it) and at that time had fallen head over heels in love with him.

He couldn't remember Karen, naturally, because he'd never laid eyes on her before, but he was fascinated. He clung to every word as Karen revealed that he was everything she had ever wanted in a man—strong, responsible, brilliant, funny and lovable. She said, "Of course I think I'm over it now, and that's why I can see you." He said, "Of *course* you are," and took her right on to dinner to see if he could demolish her again.

They are still dating. Karen said that if she hadn't been sick in love with somebody else at the time she would have been her usual diffident self—and never have seen this exciting man again.

Two Detroit girls I know, both in the doldrums one Sunday afternoon, started calling up men and asking them to *tea*, never expecting any takers because they called improbables they barely knew. They had no refusals, as it happened, and turned several improbables into lasting friends.

You can fail in your brazenry. It's no disgrace. But you can win. I was astonished again and again in my single years at how much flattery, reassurance and kindness men can absorb. You only get into trouble when you try to trade your interest in men for a quick marriage proposal. If you will use it to make new friends, you can rise like a phoenix from the ashes of an old affair to a brand-new one with a better destiny.

CHAPTER 13

THE RICH, FULL LIFE

I NEVER MET a completely happy single woman . . . or a completely happy married one!

A single woman admittedly has a special set of problems, but I think her worst one is not the lack of someone to belong to officially but the pippy-poo, day-to-day annoyances that plague her. For example, she has purchased a secondhand TV set from a private owner, and the 400-pound bargain is waiting in the trunk of her car to be brought upstairs and hooked up. She hasn't a date until next weekend—and anyway she outweighs him by ten pounds!

Or she has called a taxi to take her to the airport for a 6 A.M. departure. The taxi is now thirty minutes late, and she must be on that plane to keep an important business appointment in another city. A married woman could simply wake up a husband. That's what I did once in such a predicament. I woke up a husband next door (*and* his wife, unfortunately, or I might have had more luck) and asked if he would mind driving me to a central part of town where I could find a cab. He was anything but thrilled with the idea, considering his wife's admonitions which I could hear from the bedroom, and I can't say I really blamed her. Mercifully, my taxi arrived while he was probably wondering how to say no.

These are the frustrating little experiences that vex and humiliate a single woman from time to time; however, they are not so frequent as to make life unendurable. I've jotted down a few suggestions for coping with them.

And for a finale I can't resist adding a few last thoughts on how I think a single woman can have a happier life.

Be Brazen When Helpless

If there's anything you can't lift, lug, tote, tug or tow alone, you'll just have to get help; and it will mean imposing on your friends as well as total strangers. You'll have to speak *up*, too. Nobody's going to know you need a before-work ride to the doctor for a basal metabolism if you don't say so.

You'll find ways to repay. You'll help move them to *their* new apartment when the time comes, or bake a cake or send a valentine. You can even offer money tactfully, though you'll probably be refused.

Even wives have to be brazen sometimes. I know one married to a mechanical incompetent; for weeks she has been hunting for somebody able to get the hard-top off her convertible.

Get Adopted

Every smart single woman I know gets adopted by a good butcher, an expert mechanic and an influential and/or rich couple.

In the case of the couple they often appreciate your *needing* and belonging to them as much as you appreciate their sponsorship.

As for the butcher and mechanic, I think it's best just to throw yourself at their mercy. If you are relentlessly wide-eyed and trusting, it would be like taking advantage of an orphan to give you under-aged beef or a faulty brake job.

Don't Compare Yourself to Married Couples

Your apartment, though charming, is not meant to compete with leading architects' houses photographed in *Better Homes and Gardens*. Your entertaining, often hostless, can't be like a couple's. Your guests, though highly amusing, could be considered a little off-beat in Married-landia. Your investment program can't begin to compare with a top executive's. But whose college education are *you* planning?

Married couples go places in neat little twos, fours, and sixes—which seems so orderly. Naturally they do! There are *two* of each, so they multiply for social outings in twos like themselves. But *you* are not one of Noah's aardvarks, and it is all right to move in threes and fives occasionally. Hearing Dixieland with a good friend and her beau is not the worst kind of evening when all you'd planned was to go to bed early. Having dinner with *two* delightful men can be sensational. Unmarried people's parties are often livelier because of the non-pairings.

The married usually go places on Saturday night, which seems so normal and American! Saturday is the *logical* night for parents to hire a baby sitter, do the whole bit and sleep late the next morning. What if your next big date is on a Tuesday? The food, the wine, the music and the chatter are just as sweet and the atmosphere is better for being less crowded.

Don't Fold Up over What You Read—or Don't Read

Many publications deal with the problems of single women in the same vein as their articles on fall-out. I read a newspaper editorial last night which stated among other philosophies: "The bachelor is only half-man or half-woman. They are to be pitied." Now really!

Still other publications—*most* others for that matter—ignore the existence of single women entirely! For example, an otherwise excellent book entitled *Emotional Problems of Living,* by Oliver S. English and G. H. J. Pearson (Norton), lists in the index under S:

> Sheep, neurosis in
> Shock therapy
> Siblings
>   adolescent rivalry
>   traumatic effects of birth of
> Sioux culture
> Social worker

Where would a single woman look to find something about *her,* I wonder. (Don't worry—I looked. There's nothing under U for Unmarried or under B for Bachelor girl, either.)

You see enough picture stories in national publications about couples and families to make you feel like the sole occupant of a life raft. To further depress you, the couples and families are always blueberry-pie normal, as industrious as gophers, and as much at home in the world as an egg in custard.

We know the married state *is* the normal one in our culture, and anybody who deviates from "normal" has a price to pay in nonacceptance and nonglorification. There is no one universal "normal" time, however, for participating in the normal state of marriage. Furthermore, part of what you are, at the moment, missing in marriage may be well *worth* missing!

Ernest Havemann, writing on love and marriage in the September 29, 1961, issue of *Life*, says:

Married love is not a constant round of candy, flowers and birthday presents. It is more likely to be a long series of sacrifices in which the fishing trip gives way to a down payment on a washer and the new party dress gives way to an appendectomy, and where even the weekly night out at the movies may have to give way to new shoes for the kids. It is not a guarantee of living happily ever after, for every marriage involves struggle, boredom, illness, financial problems and worry over the children.

The bridal wreath withers, the wedding dress is folded away. The bride's biscuits—as in the comic strips and the B movies, which are often a better mirror of life than the fairy tales, and the Lana Turner epics—turn out to be inedible. The groom, seen in a bathrobe, turns out to have legs like pipestems. The love nest in the suburbs has a leaky roof, crabgrass, a mortgage that burns up every second paycheck and mice which the bride has to catch and dispose of single-handed because the husband has an annoying way of being on a business trip during every crisis.

The groom, alas, is not quite so brilliant as promised. His job prospects fade. He never earns that million dollars. He loses his hair and his teeth. His wife loses her figure. The babies are not the dimpled darlings of the ads, but imperious tyrants who have to be bottled, burped, bathed and changed—and later agonized over when they start getting into fights in elementary school and staying out too late in high school. There are moments when the husband is fed up to the teeth and would like to run off to Australia. There are moments when the wife wishes she had entered a nunnery.

Are you *really* a great deal worse off than a wife?

Don't Run with the Mouse Packs

A solitary walk will get you more male companionship—and not necessarily with mashers—than visiting any bar and grill in town with eight other girls. Who'd have the nerve to beard such a group? A man seeing you with that many other girls *could* conclude you prefer girls anyhow.

Stay home with them if you like—girl socials are more fun than people give them credit for being—but don't broadcast to the world you've given up all hope of romance by swarming publicly with females.

While we're at it, why be sucked into outings with *anybody* who drags you down just because she's single too? You owe her nothing. You're probably better company all by yourself.

Be Patient with the Pressure Groups

The fond aunts, cousins, parents, neighbors, friends and bosses who dig at you like chiggers because you aren't married and aren't *getting* must be handled with fortitude and cunning.

Your best answer to them (if you can swing it) is to act as though they must all be off their rockers . . . *you* give up your precious *independence!* Then get off the subject fast before you wind up confessing how concerned you *yourself* are. This kind of discussion with *this* kind of partisan can have you looking for the razor blades.

If they insist on a more probing analysis of your singleness, look them straight in the eye and say, "But I'm much too *young* to marry," or, "I've never really been in love with any-body but King Farouk, and since he's gone and got so fat . . ." This should back them off to the bar for another Scotch and water, and you can make your getaway.

You're the Only One There Who Isn't Married

Many married hostesses (who are not working women them-selves) would be more comfortable with a Martian at the dinner table than a single female over twenty-five. They figure the only way to solve the whole embarrassing mess (a friend of their husband's brought you) is to bring you into *their* world and confine the conversation entirely to the chil-dren's summer camps, parties you haven't been to and what to put in the rock garden.

About once a year I used to come down with an illness I could diagnose as patio fever—total malaise brought on by having admired one too many split-level houses, basements converted into rumpus rooms or freshly landscaped patios.

In an all-married gathering, I always found the best course of action was just to shut up and smile. Nobody will under-stand or care a bloody thing about what *you* do anyway. Of course, if you absolutely insist on entering the conversation, you can open with, "I understand this is one of the few neighborhoods in the city where property values have gone down consistently since 1956." That will put you in the action.

The worst mistake I ever made at a party was getting into a game of liar's poker (you play it with the serial numbers on dollar bills) with all the husbands. I was not only getting hate-waves because our rather large splinter group was hav-ing such a good time but because I was winning all the money. Really unforgivable!

You do run the risk of collecting husbands at parties. Be prepared!

Don't Suffer So Much Getting the "Big" Date

You think the only person who will *do* for the classy bash, the wedding reception, the company banquet, is a roving prince. And the only person you can muster is a drag, a drone or a droop.

I found every time I moved heaven and earth to come up with Cary Grant (never, of course, succeeding) that it never really made that much *difference*. People are too preoccupied with whom *they* brought or weren't able to bring.

If it's the kind of party where you *must* bring a date, don't fight the system! Just bring anybody. Even escorts who are older, younger, dumber or seedier than you *deserve* sometimes look and sound quite nice in their party clothes. Also, couples *can* get separated from each other for quite a bit of the evening!

Trust in Retribution

When a beau, a boss or other person does you dirt persistently and efficiently, bide your time. Get away as soon as you can, of course, though this may take a while in the case of a job situation or death-grip love affair.

Don't even *consider* sticking pins in wax effigies. Without lifting a finger, you will probably live to see them lose all their hair, be named in a paternity suit by a fifteen-year-old schoolgirl whose legal counsel is your city's Jerry Geisler, be broken to junior account coordinator sharing an office with three other fellows.

One friend of mine has found the law of retribution so inexorable that she feels guilty about a major airline crash, as well as a head-on collision between two cars near Las Vegas last year. Her mortal enemies were involved in both.

There's nothing spooky about retribution. Pill-people louse themselves up with *others* just as they did with you. And then the Fates come marching in!

Put Your Guilt Away

Would it surprise you to know that your most wicked and base thoughts—secret fantasies—even leanings to homosexuality, are not unusual, and should not alarm you? You may share your desire to make love to an African lion with the vicar's wife—or even the vicar! Far from making you a depraved monster, your thinking is probably not even original. This is the consensus of psychiatrists. *Doing something* about these thoughts and not merely thinking them is what makes you cuckoo!

Perhaps you will reconsider the idea that sex without marriage is dirty. This is not a plea to get you into bed—your moral code is *your* business—but if you are already involved, you might remember that sex was here a long time before marriage. You inherited your proclivity for it. It isn't some random piece of mischief you dreamed up because you're a bad, wicked girl.

The psychiatrist I mentioned before frequently shows sexually guilt-ridden patients pictures from an entomology book. All the patients can figure out at first look is that they are seeing some kind of bug. "And do you know what the bugs are doing?" the doctor asks. No, they don't know. Well, the bugs, according to the text, are Mediterranean fruit flies engaged in the act of mating. "Okay, so what?" asks the patient. And the doctor explains that, by the patient's own concept of sex, he is looking at some *very dirty pictures, indeed!*

The point is, you may be much harder on yourself than you are on other creatures of nature who are less deserving of your tolerance. When you accept yourself, with all your foibles, you will be able to accept other people too. And you and they will be happier to be near you. (Big order, but you can fill it.)

Borrow Children

There is no reason not to have children in your world. Friends will happily relinquish two, four or more at a time to your care.

Shawn took two eight-year old boys to a Walt Disney movie last week and on to an ice-cream parlor for banana splits. They think Shawn is beautiful, smells terrific and is a swell Saturday-afternoon date.

I used to borrow Megan Buchanan, a six-year-old enchantress, for part of a weekend. Her parents would come for dinner on Saturday and leave Meg at my apartment until Sunday noon. She was the greatest for cleaning out closets. (*She* started it. I'm no child exploiter!) Any fifteen-year-old rabbit-fur slippers or old champagne bottles you weren't using, Megan was thrilled to take home in a brown paper bag.

Agnes and Betsy both teach kids' Sunday school classes. Laura does scout work.

Live a Little

There are a lot of half-alive people running around in the world, any number of whom are single women.

Possibly you learned as a child that to get on with Mommy

and Daddy you'd better keep your voice down, your anger contained, tears controlled, curiosity stifled, not get stung by wasps or dig any holes to China in the back yard. Gradually but surely your imagination was stifled, the fear of doing anything adventurous instilled.

If you're partially dead, it takes a little doing to begin to venture again. You may have to "discipline" yourself to care where a fire engine is going. I read that the great French writer Colette used to take flowers and leaves apart to figure out how they were made. Maybe *that* would be a place to begin. Or just try to change a washer on the faucet yourself!

Everyone has a favorite octogenarian who still has the zest for living. My pet is the eighty-one-year-old widow who sold us our house. People variously call her pushy, nosy, meddlesome and insincere. She is possibly all of these things, but I think she's out of this world. The last time I visited her, two teen-age grandnieces were her house guests for the weekend. They alternately giggled, squealed, drank Coca Cola floats and sun-bathed in their bikinis; and she was enjoying every minute of their visit. (I'd have been in the fit stage. Raucous teen-agers absolutely drive me nuts.) Shortly after that visit Mrs. M. took off for London for six months. The year before that she was in the Orient.

Paradoxically, living dangerously lengthens and strengthens your life.

R. S. V. P. Means Respond!

Many a popular girl's reputation was built on her *enthusiasm.*

Praise the switchboard girl who tracks you through the office to deliver your personal phone calls. Don't figure that's her job and let it go at that. It isn't. Don't just accept for dinner. An invitation from the Wine and Food Society for the same evening couldn't keep you away. There are so *many* ways to respond. When somebody hands you a paper or letter they've written for approval, start liking it from the first paragraph. Don't let them sweat out the whole thing before you give them a lukewarm grunt.

If you'd like to be loved, then *love* . . . appreciate and applaud and say "You did right," and, "I was proud of you," at the least provocation.

Mind Your Phone Manners

The first thing *you* say—or at least the second or third—after someone you've telephoned says "Hello," is, "Are you busy?" This goes whether it's a housewife or a tycoon and whether you're planning to chat two minutes or all morning. Everybody's been trapped by a friend who has nothing to do but gossip and you've got nothing to do but work.

Baby Your Friends

Be the hostess who gives a guest a big heaping tuna salad because he actually prefers it to the lavish and immoral lasagna you are serving everybody else. (Also pastas make him break out in hives.)

Let a guest who is absolutely beat flake out for a quick nap while the rest of your guests are sipping cocktails.

Give girl guests scuffs if their footsies are aching.

Let guests who are getting up at dawn to go camping leave by ten-thirty, if that's their pleasure.

Ask who'd prefer Sanka to coffee. (The sleepless nights you coffee fiends put us caffein-abstainers through! Never *mind* it's all in our minds!)

Give the nonalcohol drinker something special . . . like

orange juice squeezed by your own loving hands. Many hosts and hostesses seem to do their best to *punish* these people.

Let your apartment be a place where people can be *themselves* . . . comfy, cozy and uninhibited . . . up to a reasonable point.

Faraway Places

I hope you're saving for a European jaunt. It can be single-girl heaven if you go alone or with not more than one other girl, and if you collect lots of names to look up when you get there.

Is there a really good reason you couldn't live in another country for a while? Girls who've tried it are more interesting the rest of their lives, and some say they aren't sure they'd really been living up to then. There's *such* a long time to settle down by the hearthside.

A friend of mine just lined up a job in Australia which will pay her almost as much as she makes now, and living costs will be far lower. She only has to stay one year by contract, and they pay her round-trip boat fare. Since she'll already be halfway around the world, she's coming home around the other half. And yet the scaredy-cats are trying to talk her out of it!

Not Getting Any Younger

Men *adore* young women, it's true, it's true! . . . their honeyed skins, muscle secured firmly to the bone . . . even their innocence.

Every article written about aging gracefully reiterates that the only way to compete with younger women is *not* to compete with them. I agree. Your seventeenth year or twenty-seventh year are over and done with, but you have some *new* things going for you which the children haven't—your total chic, poise, professional standing, warmth, true friendliness born of compassion, charm and experience. Don't underestimate these qualities—they are surprisingly attractive to men. Nevertheless, as long as youth is made a cult of in our country I don't think you can afford *not* to try to *look* as young as you can.

What is so tsk-tsk-tsk about it? If your figure is still junior and petite at fifty, why should you wear any but the good, sophisticated junior clothes you have always worn? If you were a delectable blonde at twenty, why should you not have beautiful blond hair now?

Some writers on the subject of aging are very deprecating indeed. For example, a recent article in the Los Angeles *Times* stated:

The man of forty or fifty, with his thinning hair, his glasses, his paunch, his tendency to tire easily and to fall asleep in the shank of an evening should not be fearing that he isn't young any more. By George, he ought to be accepting the fact and going on from there.

If he sets out to prove he is still a young buck, what can he expect but some dismal confirmation of the fact that he is middle-aged after all—and everybody knows it?

One man of forty-five, who had been taking his secretary to lunch with a rather fanciful notion of where the relationship might lead, confided, "Everything was going fine until I asked her if she would call me by my first name, and she said, 'Oh, I couldn't do that—but I'd be glad to call you Uncle.'"

My reaction to this is that the man with the secretary has been spared a boring relationship with an idiot (*uncle*?!!) and the man with the paunch shouldn't be, by George, accepting *anything*, but should be out pricing rowing machines.

By that writer's standards, Cary Grant, William Holden, Photographer Paul Hesse (sixty-six and fabulous), Perry Como, Frank Sinatra, Bob Cummings, Fred Astaire (sixty-three and devastating) as well as many less famous men who make us drool, are all making fools of themselves by their efforts to stay young and sexy-looking.

While it is easier for a man to bring off this attractiveness late in life (the lined craggy look which becomes a man's features in later years is *not* so entrancing on a woman), women with effort can do it too. Look at Ingrid Bergman, Loretta Young, Susan Hayward, Marilyn Monroe, Marlene Dietrich, Zsa Zsa Gabor, Doris Day, Lauren Bacall, Rhonda Fleming, Lana Turner—none of them under thirty-five and some—which?—are now in their fifties!

Since bodies are easier than faces to keep taut and lovely (although the face machine I mentioned in Chapter 11 can do a lot of good), you should be making the maximum effort with *them*. After all, your body is what you make love with!

I believe the fetish for youth that makes people keep their bodies in good shape is *good*. A lean, exercised body is a healthy body and you will keep breath in it all the longer.

It, along with other attributes, can keep you attractive to men indefinitely . . . maybe not to hordes of men, and perhaps they no longer swivel around on bar stools just to gaze at you, but enough men to keep you busy. Maurice Goudeket fell madly in love with and married Colette when she was sixty-two, which brings me to still another point. Colette had genius on her side. As you grow older, it helps to have other things going for you—a little money (which should be no problem if you have worked for many years), a little travel, the ability to cook well and entertain.

Use the Time

The single years are very precious years because that's when you have the time and personal freedom for adventure.

Of course, maddeningly, the least appealing time to do *anything* is when you already aren't doing something.

If you can forget the stultifying concept that there are appropriate years for certain endeavors (like getting married) and appropriate days for being gay and merry (like Saturday nights) and use these times without embarrassment or self-pity to do something creative and constructive (what an assignment!), I believe half your single-girl battle is over.

I'm sure you do many constructive things in eventless periods already, like washing walls and having friends over for meat loaf, but I was thinking of something a little more ambitious. Laura decided to read when things were dull. She tackled Clifton Fadiman's recommended list of books and was still going strong a year later when she met a fascinating Englishman, followed him to London and married him. She acknowledges that year alone as the most intellectually rewarding of her life and thinks it *may* have helped her bag Hilary, a reader himself. Betty took up oil painting, without ever having drawn a line in her life, and it has transformed her previously dull weekends into a Gauguin-like fiesta.

A single woman's life is *not* particularly orderly. You have to catch as catch can . . . the riotous living when it's offered, the quiet when there's nothing else.

In a World War II book, *The Battle Is the Payoff* (Harcourt, Brace), war correspondent Ralph Ingersoll said that the early rugged training of the G.I.—the toughening of muscle, sleeping out in the rain, walking ten miles under a thirty-pound pack—although drudgery, was often the difference between life and death for a foot soldier when he got into battle. Five fewer obstacle courses run might have kept him from making the foxhole when he jumped for it.

I believe the same principle applies to single women. The unglittery, unglamorous, sound-pitiful-when-you-tell-anybody-about-them things you do when you're alone can be the difference between an interesting job assignment or a love affair with a fabulous man and getting absolutely passed over by both. (I'm convinced a fluent knowledge of French can make you more enchanting to a Frenchman.)

One night several years ago nearly all the girls in my office were invited to a shower. Except me. Ordinarily a shower is something to bless your stars for *not* being invited to, but have you ever been the *only* one who wasn't? I think I had offended the hostess by saying I wouldn't care to go bar-hopping with her some Saturday night, and she took it to mean I didn't like the company of women ever. Anyway, as everybody filed out of the office with presents under their arms, I felt like the blackballed freshman of the year. Partly for revenge (which isn't a bad motive for getting things done!), partly from the lonely fidgets, and possibly because one of my best girl friends had won the contest the previous year and envy had nearly unhinged me, I stayed at my typewriter and started to fill out the questionnaire for *Glamour* Magazine's "Ten Girls with Taste" contest.

It took about three hours.

Three month's later the magazine telephoned to say I was one of the twenty finalists (out of 40,000 entrants) and to ask me to come to New York. Eventually I was one of the ten winners. The contest changed my life. It strengthened my boss' conviction that I could write, and he let me try advertising copy almost immediately, bringing about the blissful end of a secretarial career. I spent three great weeks in

Honolulu in a glamorous wardrobe from Joseph Magnin. It was all quite princessy for a while, but it started with loneliness, a Remington with a new ribbon and lots of hours to kill.

Of course, I am a Goody-Two-Shoes as well as a coward! I'm scared most of the time that whatever it *is* out there is going to catch me . . . or, as an advertising man once wrote of his daily commuter-train thoughts, "Perhaps this is the day they'll *find me out* . . . how untalented, how inadequate I really am." I personally work like a beast, so "they" won't find out and "it" won't catch up!

You may not need to work so compulsively.

I know that everybody is always tugging at you to shuck off your slob suit, to be as dynamic as Ethel Merman, as well-adjusted as Lassie, to learn Portuguese, cook with seaweed, embrace Yoga, know Shakespeare. At the very least you must sandpaper your calloused heels and organize your closets.

If you worked hard enough to achieve one-tenth of these things, you'd have calluses on *everything*.

It's my opinion that people writing "onward and upward" books (like this one) get carried away because as long as they're giving advice they don't have to *do* anything. You ought to see *my* closets!

There are acres of days when you don't *feel* like doing a bloody thing but sitting stolidly on your fanny. That's okay. You can also start lots of things you don't finish. That's okay too. Tennessee Williams has a wonderful line in *Camino Real:* "Make voyages. Attempt them. That's all there is." (See, he *can* be constructive.)

You can fall on your face with some of the projects you *do* finish. (Having that scavenger hunt for grownups wasn't such a hot idea, as it turned out.)

But if you are worried about being single, or, more importantly, uneasy about being *you* all your life (as I was and still am), intermittent forays into dressing, cooking, looking, flirting, and flattering better can help you rout the trembles.

One last thought: When you *do* start on new projects, don't tell anyone. Once you've talked and bragged about your I'm-doing-me-over plans, you won't *do* them!

Finally

You may marry or you may not. In today's world that is no longer the big question for women. Those who glom on to men so that they can collapse with relief, spend the rest of their days shining up their status symbol and figure they never have to reach, stretch, learn, grow, face dragons or make a living again are the ones to be pitied. They, in my opinion, are the unfulfilled ones.

You, my friend, if you work at it, can be envied the rich, full life possible for the single woman today. It's a good show . . . enjoy it from wherever you are, whether it's two in the balcony or one on the aisle—don't miss *any* of it.

THE END